OUTPOSTS OF THE FORGOTTEN

OUTPOSTS OF THE FORGOTTEN

Socially Terminal People in Slum Hotels and Single Room Occupancy Tenements

HARVEY A. SIEGAL

Transaction Books
New Brunswick, New Jersey

Library of Congress Catalog Number: 76-1777
ISBN: 0-87855-141-7 (cloth)
Printed in the United States of America.

Library of Congress Cataloging in Publication Data

Siegal, Harvey A
  Outposts of the forgotten.

  Bibliography: p.
  Includes index.
  1. New York (City—Poor—Case studies.
2. New York (City)—Lodging-houses. 3. Alienation
(Social psychology)—Case studies. I. Title.
HV4046.N6S53   362.5   76-1777
ISBN 0-87855-141-7

to

MARY BETH

who somehow knows how
to put it all together

Contents

Preface
   Edward Sagarin   ix
Acknowledgments   xv
Introduction   xvii
1. The Scene and Its Setting   1
2. The Conceptual Context of the S.R.O. World   33
3. A Descriptive Portrait of the S.R.O. World   57
4. The Caretakers: Helpers and Exploiters of the
   S.R.O. World   77
5. The Social Life of an S.R.O.   129
6. Summary and Conclusions: The S.R.O. World and
   Beyond   185
Bibliography   199
Index   207

Preface

Nostalgia is almost by definition a joyous experience. For many of us, the past is romanticized, its blemishes overlooked or underplayed, and perhaps we see it in a different light because we were younger, probably healthier, and had the world before us. We were certain that, if we did not conquer we would at least improve it, although it did not cry out so much for improvement as did the world that we will leave our own children and grandchildren. So it is when I recall that once the letters S.R.O. meant, for New Yorkers particularly as we lived in the theatrical capital of the world, but for Americans elsewhere as well, that a theatrical or cinematic performance had standing room only. And stand we did, sometimes paying as much as fifty-five cents for the privilege, but without fear that our pockets would be picked. Disappointed as we were not to be able to obtain seats in which we could relax while we admired, we were nonetheless elated to be part of an era of such cultural vibrancy.

Now, in an irony if not a coincidence, S.R.O. has come to have new meaning: the initials stand for single room occupancy, a type of housing that existed in previous generations but that has proliferated, and for which residents in some instances, social service agencies in others, are paying exorbitant prices to exploitative landlords, protected by a combination of indifference if not hostility to these residents by others in the world around them, by corruption, bureaucratic entanglements, and the powerlessness of the poor and the wretched.

It is a world today, particularly in the urban areas, that has more than did previous decades of the lonely, the wretched, and the desperate: the flotsam and jetsam who are society's rejects and discards. For some, we move them off to small enclaves, out on an island where they will not be eyesores to the good people, or off to a small town hundreds of miles from what little family relationships they had had, where they might just as well be exiled to a Devil's Island, so formidable are the distances and so expensive a visit. Others are huddled into ghettoes, hospitals and asylums (what an irony, to use the word "asylum," with its connotation of a haven of freedom, for a place where one is locked up), stigmatized, and largely forgotten and finally, with an ability to look without seeing, to listen without hearing, we allow some of these persons to live in our midst, on our busiest streets, only next door to or down the block from a world of normal and respectables, yet we manage to ignore their presence. These include the denizens of single room occupancy hotels, and as Harvey Siegal has so magnificently captured in his title, these are the outposts of the forgotten. Yet not quite, for so long as one young sociologist, one young man motivated by a thirst for knowledge and by a suspicion that he would encounter people in desperate need of understanding, compassion, and advocacy, they are not forgotten. Hopefully, in the very title of his work and in the pages that follow, Siegal may have produced a self-defeating prophesy.

There are many ways of presenting a vision of life, and each has values that recommend it. The novelist, on the rare occasion that a novelist would look at the people who are Siegal's S.R.O.'ers (for the muckraking novelist seems to have lost favor in American and world letters, his day is over, and few of his works have survived him)—such a writer creates fictional characters and situations to delineate a world whose reality is inescapable. The journalist calls attention to social evils and reaches large numbers of readers, but interest flags and lags, and within a few days something new is holding the attention of the newspaper world. The psychologist will give us case histories, again on the rare occasions that he would even turn attention to such persons; they would have to be accused of serious crime, and bizarre crime at that, before becoming a case history for a psychologist, and as for psychological study of what living under such conditions does to an individual, we can imagine the worst, but of science we have nothing. So that while the social workers go about their tasks, difficult, frustrating, sometimes becoming as demoralized as the clients themselves—although always with the mental reservation that they will return to a better or at least a more comfortable world when the working day has ended—it remains for the sociologist to look at what is indisputably a far from pretty part of our urban scene.

This was a challenging risk, an important one, but in many ways unattractive, hardly beckoning to one who had grown up among the niceties of an upwardly mobile but nonetheless lower-middle-class urban life, and who had just emerged from the ivy but not ivory towers of Yale University. It would have been somewhat more pleasant, but at the same time barely worth the effort of a brilliant mind that was already fulfilling its early promise, to send out questionnaires, or even go personally and get them answered, all the right boxes filled in, each question worded in a careful manner according to all of the methodological rules, and then have the answers coded, the data computerized, and the information spread out on hundreds of tables, with the statistical significance of countless correlations—and all the rest of the meaningless claptrap and quantitative humbug that fills our journals and passes for social science.

Harvey Siegal was not the first to have chosen the difficult path of living with the people he was studying, working in various capacities for and with them, participating in as full a sense of the word, while observing, as it is possible to participate when one knows that there will be an end to the research and that he will abandon a world which holds these others as tightly as if it were a prison. It is a magnificent tradition in sociology that he followed, a tradition that has given us glimpses of the world of hobos, petty criminals, organization bureaucrats, slum dwellers, poor corner boys, and skid row alcoholics, among others. Yet, of all of these and numerous others that could be added, it is doubtful if any sociologist has ventured forth and successfully penetrated into a wold from which he was removed by greater social distance than did Harvey Siegal when he entered S.R.O. tenements and slum hotels.

What emerges here is a document of extraordinary value. He lived with these people, he looked, and he saw with eyes that delved profoundly into their world. He describes in the cold prose of sociology that world as he saw it, seldom, almost never, permitting

the reader to know his, that is Siegal's, own feelings, painting a
picture sometimes in prose so bereft of emotion that one wishes to
shout out to him from the pages, demanding whether he cannot feel
shame and indignation, repulsion and anger. But what he accom-
plishes, in this remarkable manner, is to arouse the reader while
never displaying his own sentiments. It is in the sociological
tradition that describes the world as is, refrains from taking sides,
issuing polemic, permitting selective distortion, and then ignites the
fires of sentiment in all those who are exposed to this view of
humanity, or of a portion of it. There is no lack of compassion in
this work, no lack of feelings for the sufferings of the people, but it is
all the stronger because it is interwoven into, one might almost say
concealed behind, the descriptions of their lives.

If there is one question that the reader faces soon after being
introduced to the people in this work and to the places that they
inhabit, it is how they survive under such dehumanizing and
wretched conditions. It is here that Siegal offers the insights of a
sociological analysis, finding within the apparently isolated lives
many complex networks, a great deal of mutual support, even rising
to the point where there are communities, mini-communites that
lack a great deal of the feeling of intimacy and shared concerns that
have been fast disappearing in communities that thrive under far
more favorable conditions (fast disappearing, assuming that they
did once exist). But communities nonetheless, no matter how
peculiar their forms may appear to those who are as far removed
from these people as if they were a tribe that spoke another
language and lived on another continent. Siegal saw, described, and
delineated the social network that not only binds these people to
one another, and even more to their lives and places of abode, but
binds them and these places to the society around them: to a welfare
system, a social work profession, police, landlords, inspectors, and
others.

To see and describe these relationships, the functions that the
different parts have in the system, is not to excuse, and it is not to
deny the possibility that there could be alternate ways of survival
that would help individuals rise above social degradation. It is by
understanding how the system, rotten and repulsive as it is (and one
can only admire Siegal for his restraint in his own choice of
adjectives), itself services, and fits into the economic, political, and
residential world around it, that one can gain enough knowledge to
be able to institute movements for effective change. All this, and
much more, is caught in a single passage by Siegal, one in which he

is describing physicians who "define their current patients and practice in pejorative terms." Siegal continues: "Like the S.R.O.'ers themselves, the world has passed them by, and both are trapped in a slowly stagnating eddy of the social structure."

For many, the stink of this stagnation will become more vivid, more real, and be a catalyst for meaningful action toward change, as a result of reading this book. If it does this for one reader, it will have been a success; that it will do so for many, I am extremely confident.

Edward Sagarin
City College of New York

Acknowledgments

The actual field work on *Outposts of the Forgotten* began in the summer-fall of 1970. The years preceding I spent at Yale University completing the requirements for a degree in sociology. It is much more difficult, however, to determine when the research was completed, and I officially left the field. Following the bulk of the work on *Outposts,* I did a number of similar ethnographic studies in other cities which were then incorporated into the larger research project. Because the work spans such a long period and involves so many things that have happened to me, a full acknowledgment of all the assistance I received is impossible; yet, I do feel the need to express my gratitude to those who offered freely of themselves.

The interest and concern with ethnographic research began at the City College of New York during my graduate days. There I worked with Drs. Charles Winick, Robert Martinson, Arnold Birenbaum, and Edward Sagarin. Each of these men has a keen appreciation of the complexity of social organization and was able to assist me in the execution of a year-long ethnographic study of ghetto alcoholics. At Yale, my interest was encouraged by Drs. August Hollingshead, Kai Erickson, Stanton Wheeler, and Jerome Myers. The idea of studying community units such as tenements and hotels came into focus under the direction of these sociologists. Each was available during the research and the lengthy period following the field work to help me make sense of an often incomprehensible and sometimes even malevolent world. Dr. Carl Chambers, then of the University of Miami School of Medicine, encouraged and supported the writing of the document which was to become *Outposts of the Forgotten.*

The largest vote of gratitude goes to those people whom I came to know, like and dislike, care for and love, during the field work. Here there are so many in so many different places that it would not be possible to begin to acknowledge them all. But, again, I do feel the need to include some people. Mr. Jack Scribner, who was then a New York City social service caseworker, had developed a beautiful rapport with denizens of the *Outposts of the Forgotten.* Jack shared this with me and, more importantly for the research, was able to bring me into the S.R.O. world. Others such as, Mendell, Momma, the Twins, Commando, Skeets, Ibn Khuldun, Barbara, Linn, D.J., the White Princess, and so many, many more are and will forever be a part of me.

Lastly, I wish to acknowledge the assistance of those who helped in the preparation of the manuscript. Sandy Mack worked hard and patiently in typing and retyping the final draft. Dr. Robert D. Reece of the School of Medicine at Wright State University provided the support and environment needed to transform a doctoral dissertation into a book. Mary Beth Pringle was, at once, demanding and sympathetic in her editing of *Outposts.*

Introduction

Each culture and every society has been troubled by members who either do not live up to societal expectations or cease being socially productive or even self-sufficient. The study of such persons has constituted a mainstay of the social science endeavor with studies of them falling in the realm of deviant behavior, social problems, or social disorganization; regardless of the designation, however, it is clear that these people do constitute a specific problem that a society must cope with. Ways of coping, of course, have differed from society to society and time to time. Our anthropologists have pointed out that in some cases the response is drastically simple: when a person is no longer productive (or can no longer meet societal expectations) he is eliminated, or expected to remove himself so as to no longer be a burden. In more complex societies we have seen a more structured approach to the treatment of socially nonproductive or troublesome people; typically, institutions and mechanisms have been established to assure both the containment (if called for) and sustenance of these people; formally, at least, this has been the stated policy of all the developed nations.

In the United States, in keeping with our orientation toward most social problems, the response has most frequently reflected a laissez faire philosophy. Perhaps the simplest ecological response to this problem population has been in the nation's urban slums. Slums, of course, are not new; crowded, dilapidated housing, a minimum or dearth of muncipal services, and social statistics reflecting family disorganization, juvenile delinquency and adult criminality, infant mortality, tuberculosis and all of the other maladies and social pathologies have traditionally characterized the image of the slums. Yet, at the risk of romanticizing or sentimentalizing a difficult or even brutal situation, many in the slums and ghettos have still retained a healthy measure of the American Dream. Sociologists have suggested that through the creation of dual opportunity structures, minority group members have been able to advance themselves economically and socially, thereby gaining (at least nominal) entrance into the mainstream of American life. Although they are often angry and frustrated, this expectation of upward mobility unquestionably plays a significant part in their lives; deprived of the chance for reasonable and meaningful employment and opportunity, they keep coming back again and again, at first asking for and then demanding what America has to offer.

Pervading both the life of the slum and the ghetto is a feeling of hope, and the hope, in not a small part, comes from the presence of children. Slum hallways and streets teem with children (children represent a hope for tomorrow) the certainty of some future. It is the presence of children that sustains the necessity of at least some future orientation. Given our cultural values, the presence of children demands that at least a minimum of medical, educational and other supportive social services be provided. Of course, questions about the adequacy or quality of the services can not even be considered; I still, however, acknowledge that some are evident.

What about those areas that can be characterized by the absence of children, how are they different? As in other parts of social life, expectations are of primary importance. Hope, or its converse formed in frustration, manifesting itself as outrage, is a major theme of slum or ghetto living. Yet there are those regions containing parts and segments of the population that have relinquished the expectation of even the meagerest improvement in the future, and instead concentrate wholly on getting through the day. Perhaps the most well known of these has been skid row, which has provided a homebase for the homeless population of the nation.

Skid row is a place; it is where the bums live. Skid row is a peculiarly American phenomenon. Again, it is not a "slum;" slums are characterized by streets teeming with children and a way of life in some respects reminiscent of a folk society or peasant village. Skid row is that dilapidated area found in most major American cities where the homeless can and do live. It is that loose conglomeration of flop-houses, fleabag hotels, cheap bars, rummage shops, seedy restaurants, pawn shops, and "vampire" blood banks, as well as gospel and rescue missions, all of which satisfy the needs and wants of the down-and-outer, the bum, the drifter, and the alcoholic. Skid row, as a distinct phenomenon, came into being roughly at the close of the Civil War. Up until that time the vagrant, the drifter or dysfunctional individual secured lodging where he could find it: in the slums, by building his own shanty from discarded material, some living even in the open. The term "homeless man" probably derived from the period before the vagrant community became spacially fixed in a boundaried area of the city which could be ecologically defined by the presence of a complex of specialized institutions. These early areas were known by a variety of locally descriptive names such as the Bowery, the Loop, the Duce, Two Bit Street—each unique to the locale or city. The name "skid road"—then popularly corrupted into "skid row"—derived from a street in Seattle, Washington, down which logs were "skidded" to the saw mill. The street was inhabited by lumberjacks who lived in a loose community of flop-houses, cheap saloons and brothels, all of these regularly associated with the homeless man.

The skid rows prospered at the turn of the century because the expanding economy demanded an almost endless supply of mobile men to build railroads, clear forests, dam rivers, and construct roads. Then the Great Depression made transience almost a way of life. However, with the recovery of 1936 and the onset of the war efforts in the late 1930s men began being reabsorbed into the economy at an almost astronomical rate. The social character of the nation's skid rows was drastically altered—the young, the vigorous, the psychologically intact departed and the human residue that remained were to establish the character of skid row as "the place where the bums live." Today, of course, we recognize skid row as being old, shabby, and run down. There appears to be minimal control and maximum toleration of exotic, peculiar, and even destructive ways of life; excessive drinking, nonproductivity, and all forms of bizzare behavior are well tolerated, even accepted. Social groups and other forms of social relations are readily characterized by their impermanence and the orientation of most skid rowers is towards an, at best, troublesome or painful present. Skid row has become a place of broken dreams and forgotten men; a place where people come and go and make, at most, only a minimal impact on their fellows or the world around them.

Like so many of our other social problems, we have wished that the homeless man and skid row would simply vanish; or, second best, that if we would delegate our police enough freedom, the homeless man and his troublesome presence would be confined to a limited area and impinge only minimally upon our consciousness and sensibility. In many ways the skid rower or homeless man is illustrative of our treatment of those who have become socially nonproductive, or who are adjudged as being *socially terminal*.

It is clear that the United States, in the near or even distant future, will continue to be troubled by members who cease being productive yet are not so troublesome or feeble that they require institutional internment. Up to the present, however, our treatment of such persons has paralleled the experiences of the skid rower; the same laissez faire ethic is in operation, demanding their containment, yet prohibiting any direct public funded assistance, support, or supervision other than police surveillance.

One such alternative has been housing this large population in the slum hotel or single room occupancy (S.R.O.) tenements located in urban areas. Like skid row, these S.R.O. hotels might be likened to sluggish, slowly stagnating backwaters, socially isolated from the mainstream of American society. The S.R.O.'s have been likened by some to the twentieth century equivalent of the nineteenth century poor house. Their denizens are either without family or estranged from those kith and kin that they do have. For the most part these are people who have either exhausted all of their economic and/or material resources or find that they lack the ability to effectively utilize what they do have. A substantial proportion of the population has a fixed income, provided either by disbursement from the Social Security (or similar federal) Administration or public assistance such as welfare. Alcohol abuse and alcoholism is common throughout the S.R.O. world; and, not unexpectedly, the S.R.O.'s provide housing for drug addicts and other deviants. The population is not a healthy one, with the majority reporting either general poor health or serious psychiatric problems, or both. Not unexpectedly, the population has a significant over-representation of the elderly and nonwhites.

Like skid row, the S.R.O. world is one that is essentially devoid of children. Interestingly, the period of time in which a large number of children could be found in New York City's "welfare hotels" marked the only period of sustained public interest and outrage at the conditions found in the city's S.R.O.'s. Again, similar to skid row, the S.R.O.'s provide a viable, intact way of life for socially terminal people. This book will provide the findings of an eighteen-month-long participant-style study of the social life of the S.R.O. world. Although the initial work was done in New York City, subsequent observations made in cities across the nation suggest that the patterns first observed were not dissimilar to those found in other urban areas. Instead, both the problems and population are similar and the range of adaptions evolved appear to be remarkably alike.

The research sought to understand how people, drastically lacking in material resources, could construct a social world capable of satisfying their many, varied, and often exotic needs. The study focused on the evolution of collective patterns and adaptions capable of sustaining life in an actively hostile environment. In a larger sense the book will be a sociological look at how society treats its social casualties and how they, in turn, are able to forge an intact, satisfying life out of the stuff of this deprivation and neglect.

The plan of *Outposts of the Forgotten* calls for examining the S.R.O. world on a number of different levels. Each of these can be considered discretely, but taken together they provide a progressively more intimate portrait of this social world as we move from journalistic accounts to the perspective of social worker, policeman, hotel manager and then finally into the day-to-day social life of an S.R.O. itself. In order to begin it is helpful to consider some of the history of the S.R.O.'s and place them in some kind of socio-geographical context.

OUTPOSTS OF THE FORGOTTEN

Chapter 1

The Scene and Its Setting

Perhaps the most oustanding characteristic of humanity's continuing experiment with large-scale collective living is the almost incredible social heterogeneity it seems to encourage. New York City, as one would readily find in the nation's larger urban areas, contains within its boundaries numbers of well-defined ethnic or social enclaves, clusters of similar businesses, and areas so densely occupied that they appear to be endlessly submerged under a stream of humanity. The difference, the flavor of each of these is so striking as to be apparent to even the most casual observer. There are areas in Manhattan which are in themselves microcosms of what twentieth century America is, or could be. The Upper West Side of Manhattan, the setting of the study's research, is one of these.

The Upper West Side begins at Columbus Circle, 59th Street, and stretches north to 110th Street where, past Columbia University, it is quietly transformed into Harlem. On the east it is bounded on its entire length by Central Park, and on the west by the West Side Highway, and about midway, by Riverside Park. Six avenues run its entire length, and the residential side streets are periodically broken by wide, east-west running streets that span the width of the island, river to river.

Each avenue has its own character: one is lined by stately multistory apartment houses, each crowned by a penthouse with its own garden. Another, the one in direct proximity to Central Park, can be characterized by its exclusive residential hotels, in front of which long lines of chauffer-driven limousines can be seen each morning. Broadway, perhaps the most famous street in the world, is at its center. It is a very wide street, divided by central islands on which city-stunted trees struggle to survive. Set on these island are benches occupied by people day and night, regardless of the season. The street is never without sounds, smells, sights and vibrations characteristic of the modern metropolis. Crowded with businesses—legitimate, questionable, or illegal—and people. The street is never empty; something is always happening. A violent fight or crime, a serious automobile accident, or even a fire causes only momentary upset to the human traffic—in almost no time the usual frenetic activity pattern reestablishes itself, the evidence is erased, and there remains no way of knowing that anything might have happened. The avenues east of Broadway are lined with six-story tenements that have stores and small restaurants (called "tax payers") at street level. These avenues are crowded with children and people sitting on folding chairs and boxes when the weather is pleasant; a medley of foreign tongues, dominated by Spanish, is often heard on these streets. The "area" (as it is simply known to most of its residents) also contains the Lincoln Center for the Performing Arts (characterized by its ultra-modern buildings), at least four major museums, complexes of modernistic, high-rise, high-income apartment houses, stretches of condemned, partially razed buildings (reminiscent of post-war Europe), and probably the greatest social heterogeneity of the entire city.

Pervading everything, the excitement and activity, is a feeling of change—something is always being built, some houses are being razed and others renovated—almost as though the character of the area is undergoing daily alteration. The people themselves demonstrate dress and styles reflecting both yesterday and today as well as foreshadowing a not-yet-arrived future. The ramifications that this has had on the area are profound. Since the 1930s there has been a constant change in the population occupying the area.[1]

The first residents of the Upper West Side were white Anglo-Saxon Protestants, who built and occupied the elegant brownstone buildings running contiguously on the cross streets. It was not long, however, before the Jews, Germans and Irish, successful in business, began arriving from further downtown. To accommodate families from these groups, some of the large "grey-stones," multi-story apartment buildings, were constructed, along with six-story tenements, for their less successful countrymen. "Greystone" buildings were generally quite large, each unit containing seven or more rooms. The advent of the newly-arrived immigrant groups initiated the exodus of the original WASP population from the area. As they left, their elegant brownstones were sold and altered to accommodate a larger number of people per unit. Late in the 1930s, however, the first real suburban push was felt. As their families grew, many left the area for the greenery, safety, and spaciousness of the suburbs.

Early in the 1940s, with the entrance of the United States into World War II, a tremendous housing demand was created by both servicemen and civilian defense-industries workers who flocked to the metropolitan area to fill the manpower vacuum created by the armed services draft. Landlords in the area responded by further subdividing existing housing. The "brownstones" were divided from three-story, two and three-family units into two "studio apartments" on each of the first and second floors, a basement "studio" and four or five "furnished rooms" (with neither cooking facilities nor a private bath for each room provided) on the third floor. The apartments in the "greystones" were divided into six or seven single room occupancies (S.R.O.'s). Each of these S.R.O. units retained the original kitchen and bathroom facility so that a single stove, refrigerator, sink, toilet and bath now serviced a minimum of seven seperate individuals. In the early days of S.R.O. housing, often an entire family would utilize a single S.R.O. apartment (i.e., one room) necessitating family members sleeping in shifts. Many of the area's hotels responded to the increased demand for dormitorylike housing in the same way; suites were divided and former elegance and service were eschewed in the interest of greater quantity.

The termination of the war, and the demobilization of the military and defense industries engendered yet another shift in the population of the S.R.O. tenements, hotels, and brownstone-roominghouses. The last phase begins with the end of the war, has its roots in the early 1950s, and endures to the present. In part, their population was to include the human residue of the Jewish, German and Irish ethnics who made the area their home until the war. Many of those who did not make the move out of the area, who were either too weak, too old, infirm or frightened to leave, found that the only housing available was in these buildings. Others, recently arrived from the South, without job or financial resources were placed by the Department of Welfare in such housing because it was inexpensive. Those just finished serving a prison sentence or recently released from a state mental hospital found that this was the only type of housing available to them. And still others, who wished to live alone and unnoticed, found that living in these hotels and tenements was very much suited to their needs.

What all of these persons seemed to have in common was their marginality—they were as peripheral to the mainstream of the life of the city and the nation as those effectively isolated in the ghettos or skid rows. Yet there is an essential difference: the ghetto, because of its social isolation, contains within itself an almost complete way of life. Deprived of many of the institutional services and supports available to the middle and upper classes, the people of the ghetto necessarily evolved their own patterns. Moreover, in a money-oriented world, ghetto dwellers learned how to make their way without money. However, the people living in the hotels and roominghouses of the Upper West Side found themselves confronted by an entirely different situation. They were a marginal, predominantly lower class group residing in very dense enclaves, nestled cheek-by-jowl with people of a much higher social class. They were poor people, seemingly isolated from the usual complex of indigenous institutions which sustain them. It is this dimension of isolation that will be considered in examining the life-style and constructing the ethnography of this population.

The situation and setting of other urban or metropolitan areas would not be significantly different. Areas in which S.R.O. type housing would be found tend to be older and have experienced far-reaching shifts in the ethnic and social composition of their people. Little or no housing begins as a S.R.O. facility but becomes such as need is established and the change becomes profitable. The important factor in the consideration of any S.R.O. housing is the curiously contradictory position it occupies in the ecology of an area. On the one hand it is wholly embedded in an area; the housing tends to be some of the oldest in the neighborhood. On the other hand, the transience or peculiarities of its residents forces it into a strikingly marginal position.

While the welfare hotel and S.R.O. tenement might be seen as a relatively new phenomenon, the people who live in furnished rooms, hotels, and boardinghouses have attracted a modicum of sociological interest. Studies documenting the life-styles of such unattached populations stimulated much interest in several of the Chicago sociologists.

In the *Gold Coast and the Slum*,[2] one of the first community studies, Harvey Zorbaugh details the life-ways of persons he saw trapped in "The World of Furnished Rooms." [3]

> The rooming-house is a place of anonymous relationships. One knows no one, and is known by no one. One comes and goes as one wishes, does very much as one pleases, and as long as one disturbs no one no questions are asked. ... Such complete anonymity could be found nowhere in the city save in the rooming houses. ... The peculiar social relationships of the world of furnished rooms are reflected in the behavior of the people who live in this world ... they seem to reveal the same isolation, loneliness and tendency to personal disorganization ....The conditions of life in the world of furnished rooms are the direct antithesis of all we are accustomed to think of as normal in society ... the rooming-house world is a world of political indifference, of laxity of conventional standards, of personal and social disorganization.... *The rooming house world is in no sense a social world, a set of group relationships through which the person's wishes are realized....* His social contacts are more or less completely cut off.... His wishes are thwarted; he finds in the rooming house neither security, response nor recognition.... Under the strain of isolation, with no group associations or public opinion to hold one, living in complete anonymity, old standards disintegrate and life is reduced to a more nearly individual basis.... Behavior is impulsive rather than social. It is a world of atomized individuals, of spiritual nomads.[4] [emphasis added]

Using a modified case history method, Zorbaugh sketches in personal accounts of the world of furnished rooms. His writing gives one the impression that the people trapped there have reached or are approaching the absolute nadir of human existence. Disorganization on the personal and social level is apparent and people live entirely isolated lives devoid of anything but the briefest, most peripheral social interaction.

Zorbaugh's description does not significantly differ from the impression of other sociological writers. All highlight the social disorganization and atomization plaguing this section of the urban population.[5] Other sociologists, rather than focusing on a rooming-house full of isolated persons, have chosen to study the social life of either residential or transient hotels.

> In the metropolitan hotel the guest is only a number. His mark of identification is a key. His status, in so far as he has any, is almost entirely a matter of outward appearance and "front". ... The modern hotel dweller is characteristically detached in his interests from the place in which he sleeps. Although physically near the other guests he is socially distant. He meets his neighbors, perhaps, but does not know them. He may become ill or die without producing a ripple on the surface of the common life. He loses his identity as if a numbered patient in a hospital or a criminal in a prison. ... Hotel dwellers have to a large extent, broken attachments not only to things and places, but to other people. They are free it is true, but they are often restless and unhappy.[6]

Norman S. Hayner, the author of this passage, emphasizes the themes of impersonality, "blaséness," and personal and social disorganization found in hotel life. Throughout the book he implied that such a life-style can only have deleterious effects on the people embracing it.

Previous research about the world of homeless or single people bespoke the deep commitment to traditional, agrarian values possessed by many of the scholars of that time. By emphasizing these values, they found themselves confronting a social world that could be seen only as destructive and disorganized. Focusing solely on disorganization blinded them to the incredible richness of social life necessarily created by people involved in their day-to-day interaction. Sociology was finally to begin to raise itself off this Procrustean bed when William F. Whyte published his now classic *Street Corner Society*.[7] In it he demonstrated that even the most seemingly "disorganized" slum was teeming with both well-defined social rules and informal associational groups. In order to study these the sociologists need only to liberate themselves from traditional values and the restrictive theoretical orientations deriving from them.

From this perspective it is worthwhile to reconsider the life-style experienced by those persons who have either chosen or have been coerced into the world of cheap hotels and furnished rooms. The interest necessarily has a dual focus. By employing a more sociologically sophisticated theoretical framework and methodology, it is possible to now observe, describe and analyze the life-ways and behavioral patterns of those persons who formerly were dismissed as "atomistic" and "disorganized." In these terms a reexamination of such a social world is legitimate in its own right. Secondarily, the ethnographic research done on poor or lower class peoples, although it may have focused on a single group, implicitly considered the larger ecological setting in which the group found itself, i.e., the people were still studied as part of the ghetto.[8] The slum or welfare hotel and S.R.O. tenement present an entirely different situation. It literally is *an outpost of the poor* located in a comfortable middle- and upper-class area which is actively hostile to its presence. Because they lack the same sort of institutional supports found within the heart of a ghetto or skid row, the study of the life-ways of these underclass people becomes even more interesting in terms of sociological inquiry.

New York City's Welfare Hotel Crisis: A Case Study in the Manufacture of a Social Problem

While the slum hotel or S.R.O. tenement offers a unique opportunity to observe underclass life in an isolated setting, in a larger sense the very nature of the phenomenon provides insight into some of our basic social processes. Again, of course, the New York City situation is unique, owing largely to the size of the S.R.O. population in the city. In terms of an arising community consciousness and the exemplifications of certain values (such as the concern for the well-being of children) an examination of the welfare hotel crisis of the late 1960s and early 1970s has much to offer. Using secondary sources, for the most part, the following discussion will be a sociological history of the manufacture of a social problem.

In the recent years New York City's welfare hotels attained nationwide notoriety. Of course, like any other social problem, the crisis did not spring up fully formed overnight. While slum or depressed housing conditions (such as are to be found in areas like skid row or the Bowery in New York City) are the episodic targets of reformers, the problems generated by a slum hotel or a deteriorated roominghouse nestled in the midst of a comfortable middle class area first attracted public notice in 1964. The scene was the Greenwich Hotel, located in the heart of the prospering Greenwich Village West, which emerged from being the seat of the city's, if not the nation's, bohemia. The Greenwich was different from hotels located on the Upper West Side since its interior structure was most similar to a skid row flophouse. It did not have rooms per se but instead was divided into small open-topped cubicles, some fifteen hundred of them on six floors. After some study a philanthropic group issued a report generally deploring manifestations of massive overcrowding, poor sanitation, and extremely unhygienic and psychologically depressing conditions found in the hotel. Presumably, some of the improvements suggested were completed, and it was several years before the Greenwich found its way into newsprint again.

Three years later, the problem of the welfare hotels was brought to public notice again. Mitchel Ginsburg, then commissioner of welfare (which later, after a massive reorganization became the "Department of Social Services"), was quoted as saying:

> A substantial proportion of the 150 million dollars a year that the city spends to house its welfare recipients is necessarily expended on housing unfit for human habitation. Some of the worst conditions are endured by about 40,000 people (most on welfare) living in rooming houses and hotels.

As a meliorative, Ginsburg suggested that the city take over these hotels, and transform them into "communities" capable of providing the type of humane living conditions to which every human being has a right.

On the Upper West Side, more affluent residents were beginning to note the type of social problems that the welfare hotels generated in their neighborhood. The presence of even one moderate sized hotel on a street was held responsible for initiating a cycle which ultimately would force "respectable" people from existing housing. The vacated housing would be further renovated so that rents-per-unit would drop, ultimately attracting a less desirable element. Once the process was underway other units would be abandoned by landlords who claimed they could neither realize a return on their investment nor even maintain the property. The blight would then spread, infecting block after block. There was almost unanimous agreement that the area would be a safer, more pleasant place to live without these hotels.

Late in 1967 some of these residents began organizing behind political clubs and civic organizations with the intent of shutting the welfare hotels operating in the area.[10] The interest and cooperation of a large number of governmental agencies was solicited. The Police Department, under the special direction of then Commissioner Leary, created a special squad of detectives and uniformed policemen to deal with the problem of street crime in the area, bringing into play both a decoy system and several new and sophisticated pieces of equipment. The departments of fire, health, and buildings all pledged and contributed manpower to this clean-up effort. Reporters from the major newspapers were invited by the leadership of the concerned groups to accompany them on their rounds of the hotels in the area. Mayor Lindsay praised the interest that these citizens were taking in improving their neighborhood and promised his unqualified cooperation. One of the mayor's personal aides was delegated to serve a liaison function between City Hall and the local neighborhood and plans were formulated to consider a long-range solution.

In a neighborhood adjacent to the one in which the repressive clean-up campaign was initiated, another civic group, the Planetarium Council, composed of affluent and influential New Yorkers, was becoming concerned about problems stemming from a large hotel situation in close proximity to their homes. A major complaint involved inebriated hotel residents who, on their way to Central Park, passed the apartment buildings of these concerned New Yorkers and were alleged to insult any tenants standing outside. The Planetarium Council requested that a representative of the mayor's office be dispatched to the hotel. This representative, after an inspection of the premises, recommended that the hotel be closed. However, closing the hotel would involve, among other things, the immediate relocation of several hundred people. This would prove to be such a formidable task, representatives of the Department of Relocation attested, that the idea of simply shutting the hotel was discarded. The Planetarium Council, however, was still left with the problem of how to coexist with this hotel and its rather bothersome tenants. Ultimately, they turned to a number of private social service and municipal agencies for help. After some consultation, a approach that utilized a team of professionals who would deal with psychological and social problems of the tenants on an ongoing basis was considered. It was argued that if crisis situations in the hotel itself could be averted, fewer problems would spill out into the surrounding community. A team of Department of Social Service (DOSS) case workers and a supervisor opened an office in the hotel itself. Frequent case meetings and conferences were planned involving DOSS personnel and professional representatives of the participating social work agencies. It was hoped that these meetings would establish the basis for therapeutic activities or provide assistance with difficult cases. The support of the hotel's managers was enlisted and they agreed to donate space for a tenants' meeting room as well as office space for the professionals. Ultimately the project was judged successful because the relation- ·ship between the hotel and the surrounding community improved, the vacancy rate decreased, and some tenants reported that the hotel was a "better place to live in now." [11]

Further uptown, in the Columbia University-Morningside Heights area another project aimed at the S.R.O. problem was initiated. While the program promulgated by the Planetarium Council in- volved a multiplicity of social service agencies in its project, all the work in the other project was conducted by the St. Luke's Hospital Department of Community Psychiatry. The St. Luke's project had a triple focus: (1) the identification and referral of cases to available health and social service facilities; (2) social group work aimed at transforming the hotel into a type of therapeutic community or more wholesome environment; and (3) research aimed at studying the people and life-styles found within the S.R.O. The social work/ treatment functions were to be the most important, however. Teams of social workers, social work students, and other professionals made their entrance into three target buildings. The program was experimental and would automatically terminate at the end of the year. By then, the social workers expected to have succeeded in creating groups and structures necessary to insure the desired level of functioning among the hotels' population. It was hoped that a level of organization capable of bridging the gap between the hotels and the existent but underutilized medical and psychiatric services would be established. The St. Luke's project was eventually termi- nated leaving the usual residue of a social service project: a continuing field office, several thousand pages of mimeographed reports, a book, a doctoral dissertation, and a mixed record of success and failure.

Early in 1969, the first rumblings of a welfare hotel crisis in the city were heard. The New York Times reported that for a welfare family temporarily housed in a midtown hotel the city of New York was paying $47.00 a day for rent plus a daily restaurant allowance of $21. The rent disbursed to the hotel alone had already accumulated to a sum in excess of $2,200.[12]

By mid-July of 1970, the press was giving more coverage to the S.R.O. problem. Almost weekly stories, generally carried on the back pages, claimed that the city was paying exorbitant rents for "temporary" housing for welfare families. Then, in July 1970, the

New York Times carried the first on-the-scene report of what life in a slum hotel was really like. The hotel was the Greenwich Hotel, which had long been a trouble spot for the "Village" community. In this article, carried on the first page of the City Section, Francis X. Clines, the reporter, coined the term "welfare hotel" as an "establishment accepting and thriving, for a large part of its business, on the relief cases that other places in the city turn away." [13] Shortly thereafter, "welfare hotel" was to become a household word.

The article quoted one tenant as saying that sleeping in the park was preferable to spending a night in the Greenwich. "That's just a bad place ... the word on Rikers [the municipal short-stay penal facility] is that checking into the Greenwich is the quickest way back to jail." [14] Complete with picture, the article was the first glimpse that most New Yorkers had into the S.R.O. world. It portrayed the horrors and constant terror that many of the S.R.O. people felt themselves exposed to. One old resident related: "Someone walked in here last Saturday while I lay in bed, reach across and take the bit of change I had right from my pants. . . . This joint is absolutely rotten from top to bottom." The victim was a retired clergyman who had worked on the Bowery saving souls for more than thirty years. He finished by saying, along with a sweeping gesture of his hand, "I'm through with people." [15]

Neighborhood residents and merchants were even more unhappy about the hotel and some of its guests. One businessman cited an incident in which he had to discontinue a play in his theatre because water coming from the hotel above was drenching his players and audience. Others complained that their customers were accosted on the streets by belligerent panhandlers or verbally abused by many of the winos loitering in the vicinity of the hotel; still other complaints alleged that refuse thrown from windows proved a real danger to street traffic. All claimed that the hotel had materially harmed their volume of business. One businessman, the owner of a famous village cabaret, summed it up by saying, "Society just sweeps some people under the rug. .. and that hotel is the rug." [16]

As summer turned into fall and reports of "hotel abuses" began to accumulate, not only were the unattached, old, and infirm mentioned, but word was first heard about families and children exposed to the deleterious effects of hotel living. The ax fell, however, right before Thanksgiving of 1970, when a staff reporter from the *New York Times*, Murray Schumach, published a front page article entitled: "WELFARE CASES IN HOTELS CALLED A

MODERN HORROR." The story stated that the city was paying an average of more than $600 a month in rent for each of the approximately one thousand families in some forty hotels.[17] Individual room rents in some of the hotels were over $1,200 a month—and this did not include additional allocations of $300 a month or more where the hotel rooms lacked cooking facilities. Deputy Commissioner Robert F. Carroll (DOSS) was quoted as saying, "It is an absolutely abominable way to try to raise a family," and "The city will pay more than $7.5 million to hotels this year in welfare rents." The hazards and difficulties of hotel living were outlined, highlighting the overcrowding and grotesque sanitary conditions which were held responsible for the poor state of health that many of the hotels' occupants were found to be in. The increase in street crime resulting from the lure of the hotels for drug addicts, the general threat the hotels posed to communities by wrecking schools, threatening businesses and theatres, and promoting racial tensions and hostilities were emphasized as the inevitable effects of having a welfare hotel located in a community.[18]

Despite the problems and costs, the number of families placed in hotels kept soaring. The figure had risen more than 300 per cent in the year ending in August 1971 and was steadily increasing. Moreover, whereas such families used to stay in hotels for only a week or so, the average stay was now four and one-half months, and many families had been in hotels for one or two years. The hotels themselves seemed to thrive on welfare business, some having between 50 per cent and 90 per cent of their tenants on welfare.[19]

Description of living conditions found in many of the hotels were reminiscent of novels by Dickens or Gorky. A Health Department nurse stated simply of hotel children: "I think they are doomed." She reported seeing children jammed five and six in a room, sleeping on filthy, wet mattresses dropped on the floor, and on broken sofas. Dingy rooms and dank, dark hotel corridors served as their playground, shared with roaches and mice. Ceilings were peeling, and walls and floors had holes as large as two feet deep and four feet wide. Many would have agreed with a community resident who felt that "these people in the hotels would be better off in tents in Central Park." [20]

The repercussions of Schumach's exposé were felt almost immediately. Within hours Mayor Lindsay called his top-level advisors into a special meeting to determine how best to deal with the Welfare Hotel Crisis. A front page article appearing in the *New York Times* on the following day (24 November 1970) quoted the mayor as saying that he "will now personally take charge and end all abuses in hotels." [21] Lindsay placed the blame for the welfare hotel crisis on the Washington and Albany bureaucracies, which, he felt, with their obsolete policies, made it impossible for the city to deal with the problem "creatively." The mayor promised weekly inspections by the departments of health, housing, and fire. Additionally, special teams of the DOSS workers would be promptly dispatched to the major welfare hotels (that is, the ones with the greatest number of children) to effectively expedite the relocation efforts.

During the remainder of November 1970 and for much of December, the welfare hotel problem, at least as was reported in the news media, became quiescent. Certainly no one expected a spontaneous remission of the problem, but most were confident, however, that the procedures instituted by the mayor would eventually relocate the families and defuse a potentially explosive political situation.

In January 1971, the occurrence of three unrelated events was to catapult New York City's welfare hotel problem into an issue of national importance. Mayor Lindsay was in Washington, D.C., lobbying to increase the amount of money allocated to the city for welfare use, and to modify the existing federal regulations, which would allow greater latitude in spending the money. Essentially, the tone of Lindsay's visit was that the city was on the verge of bankruptcy—somewhat over 50 per cent of the current municipal budget was allocated for welfare—and that more federal money was needed even to maintain a status quo with which no one was pleased. The mayor was both deploring the fiscal condition of the city and reassuring everyone about the wisdom and efficiency of his budget.

At that very moment, Mrs. Cleola Hainsworth, a DOSS client, and her five children were allotted accommodations in a hotel because her caseworker was prevented by departmental regulations from approving a rent of approximately $120 a month in her friend's Brooklyn apartment. The only difference between this transaction and hundreds of others involving "emergency" use of a hotel was that the hotel chosen was the world-famous Waldorf Astoria. The mayor learned of what had transpired at roughly the same time the newspapers published the front-page story. Besides vacating Mrs. Hainsworth from the Waldorf, he ordered the immediate suspension of the DOSS caseworker in charge of the Hainsworth case, the housing consultant with whom the caseworker had conferred, and the supervisor of the DeKalb Social Service Center. Several hours later, a very embarrassed Mayor Lindsay was to return to a city thoroughly enraged and holding him responsible for the entire welfare hotel crisis.[22]

By the next week, the newspapers were full of news about the welfare hotels. *Time* magazine ran a story, complete with photographs of a woman assaulting a hotel guard with a knife, entitled "HOTELS WITHOUT HOPE." [23] This story, along with the others appearing in the papers gave New Yorkers a daily account of what life for the approximately eleven hundred families (about five thousand individuals) trapped in the welfare hotels was like.

The welfare hotel crisis was quick to become a political issue. With the media, the public, and welfare rights groups demanding some relief, the city desperately began casting about for something concrete to do. The issue on which there was universal agreement was that, primarily because of the number of "undesirables"—addicts and the like—who made the hotels their homes or bases of operation, the hotels were a bad place for children. Desirous of providing relief, the city decided to deal with the problem of security. The problem, however, proved to be so complex that any sort of solution demonstrated itself to be double-edged and potentially capable of backfiring. Building security could not, by law, be routinely administered by N.Y.C. police officers. Municipal codes strictly forbade deploying police routinely on private property, unless specifically requested in some emergency. Since by law the DOSS was prohibited from hiring and deploying private guards, the agency negotiated an agreement with the owners of one of the major hotels, in which the DOSS agreed to a surcharge of 50¢ per day per each client so that a security guard could be hired. Within days of ratification the press scored the agreement as a financial fiasco. Predictably, the most temperate was the *New York Times,* whose front page headline stated simply: "CITY IS ASSAILED ON AGREEMENT TO PAY $100,000 A YEAR TO A WELFARE HOTEL TO HIRE PRIVATE GUARDS." The press had learned about the security guard agreement through the office of a congressman who had previously opposed Lindsay in a mayoralty election. The active interest of opposition politicians held forth the promise of a political donnybrook of major proportions.[24]

The advent of partisan politics brought the situation from a moderate simmer to a full boil. City Hall now had to confront an enraged citizenry, the mass media, opposition politicians who discovered an easily assailable issue, and the rapidly coalescing welfare rights organizations which discovered in the welfare hotels the crystallization of years of welfare abuses. Horror stories detailing the inhumane and dangerous conditions in the hotels appeared in the daily papers.[25] Every transaction between the DOSS and approximately forty hotels in which welfare families were placed came under the closest scrutiny. One could expect to pick up his morning paper only to see a headline such as: "WELFARE FAMILY HAS $54,080.00 RENT." The story detailed the condition of a family of nine (one adult and eight children) living in a hotel. The daily rate per person was $11.43, as opposed to $14 for "equivalent" accommodations at the Waldorf.[26]

The cauldron boiled through January and February 1971. Prominent Democratic politicians used the hotel crisis as a platform to call for the ouster of the "Lindsay Whiz-Kid" administration and the return to a more "sensible" and "responsive" state of municipal government.[27] Meanwhile, the city government found itself paralyzed. Although the hotels were receiving more public and official scrutiny than they had ever received before, the conditions, at least as reported in the newspapers, did not seem to be improving. The thorniest issue, however, was what to do with families presently living in the hotel; clearly they (some 1,140 of them) had to be relocated to housing deemed acceptable by the families and their newly found, more vocal allies. Causing the tie-up was the welter of regulations that surrounded each municipal agency. The Housing Department, for example, had housing available in public projects, but refused to admit families in which a member had been convicted of a felony offense, regardless of whether or not he was currently residing with the family.[28] The plethora of contradictory regulations and mutually defeating efforts resulted in the relocation of less than one hundred families in the two month period.

The final incident which was to profoundly affect the families marooned in the hotels occurred on 21 February, 1971. The setting was the Hotel Kimberly, a bleak twenty-story building located on 74th Street and Broadway. Eight year old Tyrone Howard finished his dinner and was sent out to play in the dingy corridor outside his door. Then, in some way—no one is quite sure how—the elevator door opened into an empty shaft and little Tyrone plunged fifteen stories to his death.

The situation was by then at a violent boil and the child's death was enough to cause the cauldron to spill over. The news media carried a complete account of the incident along with pictures of Tyrone and conditions at the hotel.[29] Welfare Rights groups found the death a perfect issue to mobilize a traditionally indifferent population into some kind of activism. A newly completed middle-income apartment development was occupied by the activists and their supporters. (In one case over fifty arrests were made; in another, the people elected to voluntarily leave the premises after receiving a police warning of imminent arrest.) [30] Another group mounted a large demonstration outside the Broadway Central Hotel, where a ten year old boy had died a year and a half before the Howard affair. The hotel was located along the motorcade route feting three astronauts recently returned from exploring the moon. The motorcade was halted by angry pickets brandishing placards with slogans such as : "WHITE ASTRONAUTS FLY TO THE MOON WHILE BLACK CHILDREN DIE IN WELFARE HOTELS." The police had to disperse the crowd before the cavalcade could proceed downtown to City Hall for the planned ceremonies.[31]

The death of the child and the ensuing public outcry galvanized the administration into action. On the level of the commissioner, three agencies were mobilized and a coordinated plan to deal with welfare hotel crises was formulated. The Housing Department moved welfare families presently living in hotels directly to the top of the list for placement in public housing. The DOSS significantly increased the ceiling on the amount of money it could disburse for housing in the private sector by as much as $25 a month in certain cases. The Administrator of the Human Resources Superagency, Jule Sugarman, established machinery whereby he personally could authorize payment of a permanent rent in excess of the established limit.[32] Apparently the operation proved successful. Certain hotels (among them the Kimberly) were placed on the "nonreferral list," (i.e., under no circumstances could welfare clients be sent there) and their existing welfare population was strongly encouraged to find accommodations elsewhere. By July 1971, at least 750 (about 65 per cent) of the families living in welfare hotels on 15 March, 1971 (there were approximately 1,160 families residing in the hotels at that time) were moved to permanent, safe housing.[33] The rest were either expected to find other housing on their own or the several agencies were actively pursuing their cases and permanent housing was expected presently. Simeon Golar, chairman of New York's Housing Authority, was quoted as saying that "cooperation among city agencies in the emergency relocation program has been superb. In a number of cases," he said, "commissioners had even lent their cars and drivers so that welfare families could be shown apartments." [34]

The city mobilized and the welfare hotel crisis was solved—or was it? Later in July, reports trickled in suggesting that while welfare families living in Manhattan's hotels had been relocated, a substantial number of new families were being directed across the river, away from the public eye, into the downtown and/or Brooklyn Heights area of Brooklyn. These documents indicated that as many as four hundred fifty welfare children were living in several hotels in a single area. Middle class Brooklyn residents were enraged, believing they had been betrayed by the mayor for the benefit of the Manhattanites. In response, a top-level aide was dispatched who assured the community that the situation was only temporary, and that adequate housing would be found for these people outside of the Brooklyn Heights community.[35]

By late summer 1971, stories about the welfare hotels had completely vanished from the newspapers. More than eleven hundred families, compromising approximately five thousand individuals, had been vacated from the welfare hotels—hopefully on a permanent basis. However, what effect did this have on the S.R.O. population? Even after the removal of more than five thousand people, a substantial core population remained. This meant that the citywide population was still in excess of 95,000 persons. Although no longer of crisis proportion, the chronic problems besetting the S.R.O. population and the effect that this has on their middle class neighbors are still there. This core population are the old, the infirm, those addicted to either alcohol or narcotic drugs, the mentally ill and others so badly socially stigmatized that middle- or working-class social participation is precluded. These are and will continue to be the peoples of the S.R.O. world.

While journalistic accounts of the S.R.O.'s do give us some idea of what the world of single room occupancies is like, there is some writing which takes us even a step closer. At present we are fortunate in having two sources of information: a number of journalistic writers have used the S.R.O. world as a setting for their work; in New York City, as part of the St. Luke's Community Psychiatry Project (described above), some systematic (that is, scientific) research was conducted on the S.R.O. world. Before we embark upon the larger discussion of the world of single room occupancies it is helpful to take a brief look at some of the work and some of the information already available.

In terms of fictional accounts, the knowledge that we have of the world of single room occupancies and slum hotels comes from two sources. The first author is Julius Horowitz. Horowitz has written a series of books in which the S.R.O. world is used as the backdrop to describe the conditions of underclass life.[36] With sensitivity and compassion, he has been able to show us some of the more degrading and painful aspects of life in the S.R.O. jungle. His work shows a first-hand familiarity with the S.R.O. world and although sometimes some of the cases, information or situations that he writes about appear to be somewhat exaggerated, one gets the feeling that the novel is being judiciously used as a vehicle to call public attention to some of the degradation and outrage built into urban under-class life. For this Mr. Horowitz should be commended.

The second source of information concerning the S.R.O. world comes from a black writer, Robert Dean Farr. Farr, in a very skillfully written book entitled *S.R.O.*, portrays the world of the S.R.O. in symbolic and allegorical terms.[37] As such, the book naturally tells us about more than life in the S.R.O.'s; however, the book is so full of details and vignettes that by the end of it the reader gets the feeling that he has been through the world of S.R.O.'s rather completely.

As an exotic enclave right within our midst, the S.R.O. world, in the future, will no doubt provide the setting for more excellent fictional writing. Not withstanding the occasional violence and ugliness of S.R.O. living, it will be possible for writers to explore and describe the equally good side of human nature; how people are able to care for each other in the face of great hardship and adversity; the spirit of hope and love that, no matter what, seems to persist as a tiny flicker never to be fully extinguished; and, finally, the vitality and humor of people as they strive to cope with a world that often seems to present insurmountable obstacles to the attainment of even their most basic needs.

Systematic study of the S.R.O. world is represented by some of the work coming from the research arm of the St. Luke's Community Psychiatry Project. The principle investigator, Joan Shapiro, presents some general observations concerning the S.R.O. world and the life of the people there in several articles and a book. In these works Shapiro describes kinds of relationships and some general impressions concerning the culture and social organization of the S.R.O.'s she worked in. Shapiro's work, which is discussed more fully in a later chapter, demonstrates both compassion and a good understanding of some of the problems and conditions of the people living in the S.R.O.'s.

While very different, both novel and systematic study point to a single, inescapable conclusion: a viable, intact social world can be found in the S.R.O.'s and slum hotels. As such we come to ask how people who are materially poor, often committed to or regularly engaged in activities that are considered illegal or deviant, and who are unquestionably removed from the mainstream of society, marooned in a single spot in the social structure, manage to build a viable, integrated social system. Interest will be focused upon the rules constructed, the patterns of social interaction that have evolved, and the ways in which this community is able to sustain itself in its larger social environment. In a much larger sense, though, this book will attempt to reach some understanding of how peoples without either the material supports so significant in the larger culture, or access to the formal or informal institutional arrangements, such as could be found within the ecological area in which the poor are normally contained, satisfy the wide and diverse needs upon which everyday life is dependent. The focus will be on the activity of persons in an ongoing system small enough to be viewed as a discreet entity.

The orientation and execution of the research presented in this book is substantially different than the previous systematic studies of the S.R.O.'s. Since I was not tied to any specific service function I was able to range freely throughout the S.R.O. world. Of perhaps even greater significance is the recognition that the presence of a lone, autonomous investigator, committed to the idea of participant research, did less to intrude and ultimately alter the existent social situation than a team of social workers committed to bringing about change in a community.

The plan of the book calls for the gradual introduction of the reader into the world of S.R.O.'s and slum hotels. Our first look, so far, has been through the medium of journalism and sociological analysis; this, of course, presents the most distant perspective. My intent is to bring the reader increasingly closer to the center of the S.R.O. world. Starting, as we did, with the journalistic accounts, our next step will place us in the streets containing S.R.O.'s, viewing buildings from the outside at first, as a tourist would, and then a step closer as we enter the lobbies of several buildings. Stepwise, we get even closer when we speak to those persons charged with determining who will be offered accommodations in the building.

Even closer to the S.R.O. world and its denizens are those persons, designated officially and voluntarily, who provide some kind of service to the S.R.O. population. Such persons are usually seen as "caretakers" and given our perspective on the S.R.O. world, the sociological designation is congruent with our observations. These persons are characterized by their part-time involvement in the S.R.O. community.

Finally, the reader will be introduced directly to the S.R.O. community. This chapter will consider the S.R.O. world from the perspective of its members as they go through their daily lives. Within this chapter the reader will be provided with a detailed sketch of the social life of an S.R.O. community, as seen through both the eyes of its members and the observations of the author who was able to range throughout the larger S.R.O. world.

Having traveled through the various levels to come to rest in the day-to-day community, it then becomes important to extricate ourselves so as to achieve a larger overview. This effort will again consider the sociology of S.R.O. living and offer some public policy recommendations built on our understanding of the needs, problems and life-ways of these people, many of whom are seen as socially irrelevant or even socially terminal.

The S.R.O. World: A Personal Research History

Early in the planning of the study I decided that the research would involve participant observation. This choice was made along two dimensions. The first suggested that it would be the most appropriate way to learn about the S.R.O. community and its people. (We will consider some of the methodological reasons for this decision in the following chapters.) The second was almost a wholly personal one: I have always defined survey-type research as "work"; participant research, on the other hand, has always been "fun" for me and after years of devoted scholarship in the cloistered halls at Yale, the idea of once again getting back "on the street" appealed to me very much. The research idea was approved and the notion of a Chicago-like participant-observation study was endorsed by the faculty. Below, I would like to share some of the experiences I had in beginning and executing the research that was to be turned into *Outposts of the Forgotten*.

In any kind of participant-style research three large problems immediately present themselves. In this study they were: (1) How was entrance to be made into an environment that was essentially alien to the investigator? (2) In order to learn as much about the community as possible, which research roles must be assumed? (3)

What steps would have to be taken to assure the maximum degree of mobility, thereby allowing me to observe as much of the community as possible?

First Days in the Field: Problems of Entrance

Because of the size and heterogeneity of the S.R.O. community any number of roles, at first, seemed possible. Since I had spent, on and off, eight years living in the area and had some impression of the various hotels and tenements, what would be easier, I thought, than to simply move into one of the buildings as just another tenant. This was attempted and after a relatively short stay in the hotel, abandoned. Although I considered myself fairly well acquainted with most parts of the area, I had grossly underestimated the amount of social distance separating its various parts, once the surface was scratched and interaction became necessary. To begin with, finding a hotel or tenement to move into presented much more difficulty than had been anticipated. After choosing several hotels in the area that looked promising in terms of size, informal judgment of tenant population by observing the traffic in its lobby over some time, and their physical decrepitude, the desk clerk in each was approached and inquiry about available accommodations was made. In every case, after a cursory inspection I was dismissed by the desk clerk who stated that the hotel was full, and that no rooms would be available for at least two weeks; and, "perhaps you might try back then?" My suspicion was raised, however, after being turned down the third time, when the man that I noticed behind me emerged from the hotel's lobby and disclosed, when asked, that he had been given a room. On the next attempt I waited until the transition occurred between the day and evening desk staff. The night clerk was approached and told that the day clerk (who it was later discovered was one of the hotel's managers) had promised me a room. Subsequently, a room was offered, a week's rent of twenty-one dollars, a three-dollar linen deposit, and a one-dollar deposit for the room key were all collected, in advance. The hotel seemed ideally suited for research. It adequately met the criteria of population, decrepitude, and size (it was a moderately large one—16 floors and approximately 280 rooms); at last my study was to commence!

However, once ensconced in the hotel, the problems began. I found myself completely unfamiliar with the social situation. I found myself feeling very uncomfortable and, at that time, entirely unable to interact with either the other tenants or the hotel staff. Whatever few interactions were attempted proved to be so stilted and forced that they profoundly affected subsequent ones. In my naiveté I did not fully realize that the S.R.O. world is one that does not appreciate, or even understand, a stranger (especially a white man who does not have a profoundly down-and-out appearance) asking questions. Moreover, I strongly suspect that my extreme discomfort was so drastically apparent to the S.R.O. people that they reacted to it as much as they did to me and my numerous faux pas. After several rather uncomfortable days at the Hotel Cherbourg I abandoned the idea, for the time at least, of simply "going native."

Realizing that direct entrance into the field was momentarily impossible, and therefore the research role of *full-participation* was precluded,[38] I needed a role that allowed for greater social distance. Since independent entrance had failed, a guide or sponsor of some sort would be needed to gain entrance into the S.R.O. world. Having failed to establish rapport with any S.R.O. people I did not even look for a guide there. Since the Upper West Side of Manhattan contains a Federal Urban Renewal Area, it seemed likely that VISTA (Volunteers in Service to America) workers assigned there would have already established ties and rapport with community people, and could make the personal introductions necessary to initiate participant-type research.

As it worked out I did not meet with any VISTAs until later; however, I did come into contact with several of the organizations then attempting to serve the S.R.O. population. It was through one of these, the Mid-Manhattan Health Services Project, that I learned about an on-going, multiagency, social service project conducted at the "Hotel Enfer." Central to the project was a team of four New York City Department of Social Service caseworkers (and a supervisor) who drew its entire caseload from the hotel's tenant population. Other social service agencies/organizations helped by providing back-up services. For example, a registered nurse, from the Visiting Nurse Service (which is a municipal agency) spent one working-day at the hotel; a psychiatric social worker from a quasi-private agency similarly spent one-half day per week at the hotel; a psychiatrist, from a hospital in whose catchment area the hotel was located, was a regular participant in the project's staff meetings and consulted on difficult cases; and a paraprofessional, himself a former alcoholic, employed by the same hospital, led a weekly therapy group aimed at assisting tenants with their drinking problems. In addition, resources and personnel of other social service agencies were available and were, in fact, intermittently employed.

Since the project had been in progress for more than two years, the caseworkers seemed to have excellent rapport with a large cross section of tenants (both their own clients and nonwelfare persons), hotel staff and management; it seemed like an excellent place to begin. I introduced myself to the then acting project coordinator and gave him an account of the type of research that I was interested in doing. We then agreed that he, and the other workers, would assist me in my study in return, quid pro quo, for the utilization of my services in a way yet to be determined. After some negotiating, it was mutually decided that after a time of more or less unstructured observation in the hotel, both our interests would be best served by having me assume a model caseload and service the DOSS clients as their caseworker. Although I would not have official standing, I would deal with the clients as though I did. The decision was less problematic than it may sound, however. My educational qualifications were considerably higher than the majority of the DOSS personnel. My academic major in sociology was preferred by the DOSS (in preference to say, English, Classics or Art History). My age, social class and ethnic background was similar to a majority of the caseworkers employed by the DOSS. The training deemed essential for successful execution of the caseworker role was instruction in rather simple bureaucratic procedures and was very quickly learned. The turnover of caseworkers, per client, was normally so high that the transition from one worker to another (in one case an informant reported eighteen different workers in the last fifteen years) was almost completely institutionalized and was usually accomplished without any incident whatsoever—provided the welfare checks continued to arrive regularly. Lastly, I agreed to take the job in good faith, which I defined as acting as much as an advocate for the client as possible so that no one's position would be injured by my research. Moreover, all of my work would be subject to careful scrutiny and review by the project coordinator since the various documents and forms would be officially filed under his name.

The choice of the field-role of "social worker" proved to be an exceptionally good one for the early phase of the research. To begin with, my presence in the field was immediately fully legitimated. The DOSS caseworker is expected to ask questions about his clients' affairs. Many of the clients appeared to be genuinely pleased to have someone interested in them and would often seek me out for long discussions, usually about life in the hotel, the days before they lived in the hotel, or some special problems that they might have.

Since the DOSS project had been in progress for more than two years the workers had established good rapport with persons other than the welfare clients. I received the same treatment as a worker, and I was therefore able to increase my sphere of activities throughout the hotel. I could, then, legitimately speak with the hotel staff—the maids, porters and other personnel. As important, however, was the fact that I had the same access to the hotel's management as the other workers had. Specifically, this made it possible "to go behind the desk" and discuss, in a somewhat limited way, of course, the functioning of the hotel in terms of security, municipal relations, and tenant admissions. Moreover, in this capacity I was able to hear both sides of the various disputes between the tenants and management.

From the beginning, however, I made it clear to everyone that I was there ultimately researching material for a book that I planned to write about welfare hotels and the S.R.O. problem. This information was greeted positively in almost every case and most people were strongly in favor "of someone telling it like it is, so that the people downtown might find out where it's really at." Suprisingly, however, I never once received an entirely negative response—I was never told that I had no business doing what I was doing and that I should get out of the field entirely. At all times the sensibilities of the informants were carefully considered. Besides advising people about the nature of my presence in the field, I attempted to draw them out as much as possible and make them active participants in the study.

After several weeks of work at the Enfer I discovered that my self-confidence in the field had increased dramatically. I lost whatever fear I had of spending time in the hotel and found that I began spending even more time in the community. While the other workers limited their days at the hotel to the conventional nine to five business day, I was staying at the hotel until late at night and would come in on weekends as well. I found that I was able to respond to a new range of stimuli and was picking up and acting on cues that I previously had entirely missed. It was at this time that I made the decision to expand the scope of my research.

Feeling comfortable at the Enfer, I began thinking about constructing a research instrument to provide some "hard" data about the population. Such an instrument was constructed and I decided to test it by having one person who lived on each of the six floors of the north wing of the hotel, administer it to every fifth room—a sample of approximately sixty persons.

The questionnaire was relatively specific, requiring facts about age, sex, ethnic identification, education, place of birth, length of stay at the hotel, general health, and similar information. The interviewers were volunteers and were offered payment per returned questionnaire.

The results of this single venture, however, were so discouraging that it was decided to abandon the collection of data in this manner. To begin with, the response rate was dishearteningly small—less than 30 percent. Out of the returned questionnaires, some had to be discarded because I discovered that they had been completed not by intended respondents but by an interviewer. In these cases, the interviewer did not even consider his completion of questionnaires as being "dishonest." The converse was considered to be true: "These people", as one of the would-be interviewers explained, "is either too dumb or be lyin' to ya'." Even after an explanation of what a survey was and what it could do, a number of the interviewers remained unconvinced that this was the best way to go about collecting data. Out of the rest of the returned questionnaires, most were done in such a haphazard manner that I seriously questioned the validity of the data. In the few cases that I rechecked myself, I received so much contradictory information that I concluded that expanding the venture would be entirely futile. (The nature of the population is such that intensive, limited duration research aimed at eliciting hard data is just not feasible. Similarly as unfeasible is the hope of dispatching a corps of interviewers armed with a less tightly structured instrument. The population is initially so distrustful that such an effort is almost assuredly doomed to failure.) Interviewing is possible, however, once good rapport has been established with S.R.O. people. Even here, I discovered that efforts to interview those persons that I knew fairly well did not succeed unless the interview was presented in the normal give-and-take context of discussion. At any effort to be more rigid, most persons simply "clammed up" or responded in such a stilted manner that it is problematic whether the data was relevant to anything but a comment on the reaction to formal interviewing.

After several weeks, the limitations imposed by the social worker's role began to be felt with greater force. Since I never really abandoned the hope of "going native"—at least partially—and this would be impossible while being nominally attached to the Enfer Social Service Project, a new focus of activity had to be discovered.

Recalling the difficulty encountered in attempting to gain entrance into some other hotels, I determined that I needed a community sponsor of some sort. Such a sponsor could be found in an organization or group willing to vouch for me. With the aid of the sponsor it would be possible, I believed, to live in a hotel as a tenant. The *United West Side Community* cooperated very closely with me in this regard. This organization is part of Saint Luke's Hospital Department of Community Psychiatry. It is charged with the responsibility of attempting to organize various parts of the Upper West Side area and introducing S.R.O. residents to the full range of medical and social services available to them.

Since the United West Side offices were staffed by local S.R.O. people who were intimately acquainted with several of the hotels in the area, it was possible to discuss the choice of building with them. Moreover, since their people had contact (generally cordial) with the various S.R.O. managers, someone would vouch for me.

This marked the commecement of the second phase of the research. In this role I presented myself to other tenants, hotel staff, and others as another tenant. Here too, I specified that I was writing a book about my experiences; I received essentially the same response that was offered in the Enfer. Now, however, I found that I had almost completely lost my fear of operating in the hotels and, not surprisingly, I discovered that I was able to make friends quite easily with many of the people I met. Following the plan of the research, I intended to move freely in the larger S.R.O. community and actually reside in each hotel for at least several weeks—or for as long as I believed that it was necessary to collect new data.

Part of living in the hotels entailed changing my life patterns to correspond as closely as possible with those of others "natually" living there. For congruity's sake, in the field, leisure clothing was always worn. A conscious effort was made—for the most part I succeeded—to learn the idiom of the population. Within certain limits, of course, I found myself talking and acting like others in the hotels. Minimally, this entailed the usage of ungrammatical construction (which proved to be not at all difficult) and the (almost) unselfconscious employment of certain expressions and gestures.

Almost from the beginning of the second stage, nearly everyone encountered proved helpful in pointing out things that were initially missed, or serious faux pas that could alienate me from others, or in one extreme case, could have imperiled me physically. For example, someone standing on the hotel steps would say: "Now, lookit that dude over there. [Needless to say, before I had substantially acquainted myself with the area I was not even aware of "that dude over there."] He gonna go cop hisself a bag." The man then met with another, went into a doorway and returned to the street a very short while later; shortly thereafter, the participants in this particular exchange admitted the nature of the transaction to me.)

Again, late one very cold night during February, a new friend and I were standing in the unheated lobby of the Hotel Nazir. After mutually complaining about the cold, and cursing the landlord for not heating the lobby, we decided that a drink would certainly be appreciated. Skeets (my new friend) brightened suddenly when another man entered the lobby. As the newcomer approached, Skeets said to him: "C'mon Tony, man, geta taste a 'Up' (Swiss Up wine) together for me and mah man here." Sure enough, the man produced a bottle and we all took a drink. After the second man had left, I asked Skeets whether he *actually saw* the bottle, or merely *surmised* that his acquaintance was likely to have one. He responded, after some rather insistent prodding on my part, that he had *not exactly seen* the bottle. What Skeets did notice, however, even though the newcomer was wearing a long overcoat, was that Tony's right trouser leg was slightly lower than his left, and as he approached he "kept slapping his behind," to keep the bottle from falling out. These cues, to which I was totally oblivious at the time, were perceived and reacted to by others quite easily. As my socialization into S.R.O. culture progressed I came to recognize and understand much of this nonverbal language.

Every effort was made, as well, to reconstruct a life-style that as closely approximated the one lived by many of the people. I was interested in duplicating the life-rhythms found in the population. For instance, in order to bind myself to the welfare routines I had my stipend money sent to me at the hotel on the first and sixteenth of every month. (This is when the DOSS, Social Security, and other disbursement checks arrive.) With the help of caseworkes at the Enfer, I was able to work out a typical budget—living as though I were actually solely dependent on the welfare payments. I made a conscious effort to eat and drink what the S.R.O. people did, discovered how to live on a very limited budget and learned to draw on the various resources available. For certain phases of the work it became necessary to rearrange my daily round so that I slept during the day and spent the entire night "hanging out." In other instances, in order to experience the profound isolation and loneliness of a shut-in, I confined myself to my own room in the hotel for several weeks at a time; here my only human contact was with a messenger who brought groceries every third day or so.

Doing the research in any other way would have been virtually impossible. I was able to enlist the help and support of several community groups, mostly because I demonstrated my willingness to share the same kind of life as the people I wished to learn about. Underclass people today, especially black ones, have come to feel that academic research has too little to do with helping them to realize whatever goals they have singularly or collectively established. Because of this, they are often hostile to such research. Aware of the sensibilities of the respondents, I realized that this phase of my study would necessarily have to undo some of the animus generated by previous researchers who attempted to tell the entire S.R.O. story during the nine to five business day. When either individuals or groups in the community were appraised of what I was doing, the response was always very positive and almost everyone expressed willingness to cooperate with the study.

The final phase of the research necessitated assuming a role diametrically opposite to that of a tenant. Interested in understanding how the welfare hotel functioned as a complex organization it was necessary to place myself in a position that would allow the possibility of observing such an organization from an insider's perspective. A role that would allow me access to the managment and staff of the hotel was needed. I wanted a role that would include me in the normal flow of interaction in a social process, rather than being treated as a complete observer or some-time adversary (as a social worker was). I wanted to be tutored in the ways of managing a welfare hotel. I was also interested in the managers and other employees of the hotels—especially those who had been there for some time. I hoped to determine how they came to define the nature of their work, the way in which they perceived the hotel and its often exotic guests, and their beliefs about a world that seemed to be changing rapidly around them as the municipal government alternated its policies concerning the welfare hotels from laissez faire to extreme concern. I was interested in how the managers perceived and treated the newly felt influx of radical young blacks (especially those right out of prison) into the S.R.O. community, and the concerted efforts of community groups to organize the tenants of various hotels and tenements.

With this in mind, a family acquaintance who owned property on

Manhattan's Upper West Side was approached and advised of my needs. He was sympathetic and introduced me to several welfare hotel owner-managers, one of whom found himself in need of someone to work the late-afternoon-night shift as desk clerk and perform some of the functions of a security guard. The job proved to be tailormade for the research. I found that I was able to informally interview the two owners of the hotel and several employees that I worked with. From the beginning I specified the nature of the work that I was doing, that I was a student and that I hoped to "write a book" about some of my experiences. The information was very well received—especially the part about being a student—and the managers in specific were interested is seeing that I would suceed with my educational plans.

All of my expectations were rewarded in this research role. I was instructed in how to deal with various municipal bureaucrats that would contact the hotel, the police officers who were at the hotel searching for either wanted persons or seeking information, how to maintain control over what could be a somewhat difficult situation and all of the other various and sundry tasks involved in administering a complex organization with a potentially troublesome population. The research role was also able to provide further insight into tenant life. I moved very quickly from "simply another tenant" to "The Man" and found my interaction with S.R.O. people markedly different than before. This last phase of the research lasted approximately fourteen weeks at which time I "officially" left the field after spending more than sixteen months in various roles and places in the S.R.O. community.

Seeing the situation now in retrospect, I am fairly confident that I was able to observe most parts of the community. The research roles that I employed at different times ranged from the complete observer to almost complete participant. I was able to see the community from the standpoint of both participant and controller, client and agent, and outsider.

The New York experiences were more than adequate to prepare me for similar observations in other cities. I found that with the exception of having access to the management of other slum hotels, I could quickly find, enter, and acclimate myself to S.R.O.'s in other cities. As we will see, credibility and hence entrance into the S.R.O. world comes from learning the appropriate symbolic presentation of self.

NOTES

1. Joseph Lynford, *The Air Tight Cage* (New York: Harper and Row, 1966).

2. Harvey W. Zorbaugh, *The Gold Coast and The Slum* (Chicago: University of Chicago Press, 1929).

3. Ibid., chap. 4

4. Ibid., pp. 84–86

5. Arnold Rose, "Interest in the Living Arrangements of the Urban Unattached," *American Journal of Sociology* 53 (1948): 483–493

6. Norman S. Hayner, *Hotel Life* (Chapel Hill: University of North Carolina Press, 1936).

7. William F. Whyte, *Street corner Society* (Chicago: University of Chicago Press, 1936).

8. Elliot Liebow, *Tally's Corner* (Boston: Little Brown, 1966).

9. Steven Roberts, "Ginsberg Assails Welfare Housing," *New York Times,* 4 February 1967, p. 24.

10. Murray Schumach, "New Crime Drive Focuses on Hotels," *New York Times,* 3 December 1967, p.1.

11. Ruth Schwartz, *Serving the Community at the Hotel Endicot,* (New York: Community Services Society, 1970).

12. Francis X. Clines, "Welfare Family of 7 Still Looks for Permanent Home in the City," *New York Times,* 7 March 1969. p.29.

13. Francis X. Clines, "Hotel in 'Village' Step to Nowhere," *New York Times,* 16 July 1970, p. 36.

14. Ibid.

15. Ibid.

16. Ibid.

17. Murray Schumach, "Welfare Cases in Hotels Called a Modern Horror," *New York Times,* 23 November 1970, p. 1.

18. Ibid.

19. Ibid.

20. Ibid.

21. Murray Schumach, "City Plans to End Welfare Abuses Involving Hotels,"*New York Times,* 24 November 1970, p.1.

22. Besides the embarrassment of the mayor at having had welfare clients esconced at the Waldorf while he was telling a tale of fiscal woe, his suspension of the three workers sparked a wildcat job action by welfare workers throughout the city. They demanded that the three be immediately reinstated and all charges against them be dropped. Ultimately, this crisis was resolved by Lindsay delegating full responsibility to his Human Resources Commissioner, Jule Sugarman, who reinstated two of the suspended workers, negotiated an arbitrary settlement for the third, and personally sanctioned the rent that Mrs. Hainesworth had originally requested. (*New York Times,* 28 January 1971).

23. "Hotels Without Hope," *Time* 4 January 1971, pp. 28-30.

24. Murray Schumach, "City is Assailed on Agreement to Pay $100,000 a Year to a Welfare Hotel to Hire Private Guards," *New York Times,* 24 January 1971, p. 35.

25. Michael Knight, "Squalor is a Way of Life at a Welfare Hotel Here," *New York Times,* 28 January 1971, p. 39.

26. Lawrence Van Gelder, "Welfare Family Has $54,808 Rent," *New York Times,* 29 January 1971, p. 39.

27. Schumach, "City is Assailed."

28. Paul L. Montgomery, "Success Reported in Relocating Welfare Families Out of Hotels," *New York Times,* 16 April 1971, p. 41.

29. David Alderman, "Boy, 8, Falls 15 Floors to Death at Welfare Hotel," *New York Times,* 22 February 1971, p. 33.

30. Arnold Martin, "Lives in a Welfare Hotel Go On After a Boy Dies," *New York Times,* 23 February 1971, p. 33.

31. "Protest Interrupts City's Welcome for 3 Astronauts," *New York Times,* 9 March, p. 39.

32. Steven Weisemann, "Welfare Hotel Residents to Get Housing Priority," *New York Times,* 10 March, 1971 p. 25.

33. City of New York, Office of the Mayor, Simeon Golar (Housing Authority Chairman), "Memorandum to John W. Lindsay ... Status Report on Relocation Project for Long Term 'Welfare Hotel' Families," 20 July 1971.

34. Paul L. Montgomery, "Success Reported."

35. Murray Schumach, "Problems in Brooklyn," *New York Times,* 22 July 1971, p. 1; Alfonso Nayvarez, "988 Welfare Families in Hotels Relocated by City Since March," *New York Times,* 22 July 1971, p. 1.

36. Julius Horowitz, *The Inhabitants* (New York: Signet Books, 1960); idem, *The City* (Cleveland: World Publishing, 1953); idem, *The W.A.S.P.* (New York: Atheneum, 1967); idem, *The Diary of A.N.* (New York: Dell Publishers, 1971).

37. Robert Dean Farr, *S.R.O.* (New York: Doubleday, 1971).

38. Buford H. Junker, *Field Work* (Chicago: University of Chicago Press, 1960), chap. 3.

Chapter 2
The Conceptual Context of the S.R.O. World

Theory and its derivative in methodology helps us to make sense of the world, providing a measure of intellectual perspective on any problem under study. As such it relates the observed facts not only to each other but to the observations and experiences of other researchers concerned with other problems. Methodology (as distinguished from technology which uses questionnaires, surveys, and so on) provides the context of our observations. It offers the researcher a more or less well-defined conceptual field or map into which he or she can sort and order the many and varied facts and impressions research generates. It is necessary, therefore, that the conceptual perspective be specified as clearly as possible. Once this has been accomplished it is possible for the reader to readily visualize the process governing the collection, organization, and analysis of data. And so the following chapter explicates the conceptual context which governed my study of underclass life.

Three major sociological concepts figured into the formulation of this study: (1) the culture of poverty, (2) community, and 3) social deviance. Each of these concepts is briefly introduced below.

Since the S.R.O.'s population is overwhelmingly composed of poor people, and they, for the most part, have been destitute for a considerable length of time—in many cases from birth—the concept of a "culture of poverty" is theoretically relevant here. This perspective encourages us to search for some way of seeing the poor as not only indigent but in some way different from the larger body of middle and working class Americans.

One of the ways in which the S.R.O. world might be seen is as a "community." In microterms, then, each building is an isolated community in which one may equate a tenent's rooms to houses and its halls to streets; the entire system bounded by the walls of the building. Or, community might as realistically be described in relatively more macroterms as a set of buildings spread throughout a geographical area. Members of this community are able to move from unit to unit and possess a certain amount of knowledge about the various buildings that compose the community. My interest was directed to locating some sociological definition of "community" that allows the incorporation of both perspectives.

Behavior which could be considered deviant or illegal is common in an S.R.O. Recognizing this, it became necessary to consider the sociological meaning of "deviant behavior." The only commitment I have is the belief that behavior must be considered within the actual context of S.R.O. living. This suggests that behavior be seen in a problematic context so that our appreciation of the situation and aspects of any observed pattern come into focus. This orientation will completely eschew any deterministic approach to deviance, focusing instead on the member in his natural habitat, looking at what he does, how he does it, who he does it with, and how it came to be so.

The remainder of this chapter discusses the relevance of the concepts of social deviance, the culture of poverty, and community to this study, and explains how these concepts were operationalized into an applicable methodological framework.

Social Deviance

The idea or notion of deviance has been an important one in the development of social science. Social thinkers and, more recently, sociologists have wrestled with the idea of deviance in terms of both its conceptualization and its relationship to other social phenomenon. Deviance has been viewed from a large number of perspectives. Some, reflecting simplicity itself, suggest that it is a statistical property inherent in group life and that deviance and minorities are entirely congruent. This, however, is much too simplistic a conception to be useful. Deviance, as I have come to see it, entails some notion of the "pejorative." As such, the quality of deviance and social treatment and/or recognition of deviant members takes on great significance.

Moving from the wholly simplistic, statistical conception to one in which we acknowledge that deviance implies some sort of moral breech, that is, the deviant is seen in one way or another as "morally tainted" or stigmatized, we could admit the idea that deviance has some social utility. When this was considered in a larger, holistically societal context, researchers began asking about the role of deviance in a society. One of the first to reflect upon this idea was the French sociologist, Emil Durkheim. Although he was not writing about deviance, he did see crime as necessary for the sustenance of collective life. The notion found continuity in the work of others, most notably writers such as Kai Erickson, who established that deviance, as a social property, is essential for the maintenance of a society by helping to test and redefine the collectivity's boundaries. This tradition determined that deviance is not in itself a given entity but occurs only at the behest of the audience witnessing the act or the actor. It is the process of witnessing and subsequent judgment and labeling that is here seen as the most theoretically important quality of deviance. In my study of underclass life I became interested in the problematic property of this deviance label and how it would become attached to certain individuals; specifically, why certain people had a greater propensity to have this label affixed to them than others.

Opposed to the conception discussed above, however, is the belief that deviant behavior is simply another type of goal-directed activity essentially indistinguishable from legititmate enterprise. This nonnormative orientation is not a radically new way of looking at deviance. Writers such as Edwin Sutherland, reconstructing the biography of Chic Conwell, saw the life and work of this professional thief in wholly occupational terms.[1] Ned Polsky, writing on the pool hustler, described a way of life very similar to any other profession;[2] and Donald Ball, describing the operation of an illegal abortion clinic, depicts a functioning organization in such wholly occupational terms that there is almost no way to distinguish it, sociologically, from a legitimate medical practice.[3] This orientation stresses the similarity of deviant and legitimate careers and searches for the cultural and social supports that provide the underpinnings of any social activity. In it the deviant (like everyone else) regularly does what he has to do to satisfy the demands made upon him by his needs and in the process organizes his activities into a recognizable daily round. By extension, in certain forms of deviant activity these patterns appear to parallel a legitimate career involving such observable steps as entry, apprenticeship, and retirement.[4]

There is some difficulty, however, in assuming that drug addicts, alcoholics, streetwalkers, and others are in no way different from other members of society with the exception, of course, that they are neither "high" on dope or inebriated regularly. To reject this dimension is to deny that there are any real differences separating the marginal from central parts of society. Recognizing such differences this represents, as Edwin Lemert points out, the "processual" aspect of deviation. Through it, one becomes sensitized to the

> fact that with repetitive, persistent deviation or invidious differentiation something happens inside the skin of the deviating person. Something gets built into the psyche or nervous system as a result of social penalties, or 'degradation ceremonies,' or as a consequence of having been made the subject of 'treatment' or 'rehabilitation.' The individual's perception of values, means, and estimates of their costs undergoes revision in such ways that symbols which serve to limit the choices of most people produce little or no response in him, or else engender responses contrary to those sought by others.[5]

Such a perspective allows viewing the generation of deviance and the assignment of the deviance label (or stigma) in more problematic terms. Attention is directed to those situations in which persons caught in a network of conflicting claims or values choose not deviant alternatives but rather behavioral solutions which carry significant risks of stigmatization. Deviation then becomes merely one possible outcome of their action, but this is not inevitable. It is contingent on the turn of circumstances or convergence of external factors.[6] With this perspective it is possible to examine the varied and often profound differences between those actually "committed" to a deviant career and those persons who only occasionally find themselves transgressing. Moreover, it is possible to meaningfully distinguish careers and career patterns in the legitimate world from those careers that have come to be defined as deviant.

For my conceptualization the crucial variable is definitively *not* the violation of norms but rather the probability of being discovered and consequently exposed to the full impact of the societal control agencies. Attention is directed *not* to the member's act but *rather to the resources (symbolic and otherwise) that he has at his disposal to either disguise the deviation, by maintaining an adequate cover, or his ability to manage the agents of social control delegated to regulate him and his activities.*

The development of this dynamic perspective allowed me to consider the entire social process involved in the creation and maintenance of deviant lifestyles. It compelled my analysis to progress beyond a member's immediate act to an examination of the larger organization of the behavior. Although through the analysis I focus on the symbolic quality of the act and its participants, the dynamic perspective also encompasses the situational aspects helping to shape the interaction and permitted me to be aware of the specificity of any designation grounded in the everyday behavior and definitions of people.

The Culture of Poverty

The biblical admonition "the poor always ye have with you" (John 12:8) scarcely needs confirmation. Every epoch of history and every state and country has had its share of indigents. Yet the question is not simply one of indigence. Writers such as Michael Harrington,[7] David Matza,[8] and Oscar Lewis [9]—to name but a few—have come to see the poor as not simply an undifferentiated mass of persons with an income below some (almost) arbitrarily defined line, but rather roughly stratified into two groups described as "the poor" and "the hard core or disreputable poor." [10] This latter group denotes those persons living on the absolute bottom of the social structure. It suggests that this group is not only poor, but in some way *observably different* from either the "honest poor"—those who are temporarily down on their luck, recently arrived immigrant groups struggling to enter the mainstream of American life, or people who have just overextended themselves. These writers are suggesting that this group has folkways and an ethos of its own; in short, its own culture—a culture of poverty. Below, some of the arguments that favor the utilization of such a concept will be examined.

It appears that the problems confronting those at the very bottom of the social structure are significantly different from those regularly

encountered by either the working or middle classes. We hypothesize that culture arises in response to externally defined conditions
confronting a group of people. As such, culture occurs as the
evolution of a shared set of symbols and meanings which provides a
common understanding of the same environment. Culture becomes
an accepted and known entity. One knows what can be done, when
and how it is appropriate to do it—providing, of course, that one is a
member of that culture.

The welfare hotel and the S.R.O. tenements provide the fertile
ground necessary for the germination of culture. Both social
isolation and a common set of problems are present. Both of these
are given added importance due to the situation imposed by the
location of the welfare hotels in the midst of affluent residential
areas. Unquestionably, a portion of the S.R.O. population were
members of higher classes and then drifted into life in the hotels.
Many others, however, were born into the underclass (some even in
the various hotels in the area) and the move from tenant farm,
tenement, or public institution into the welfare hotel did not
represent a break or exit from the "culture of poverty" in which
they had lived their entire lives.

Oscar Lewis, the anthropologist who originated the concept of a
"culture of poverty" describes it as

> both an adaption and a reaction of the poor to their marginal
> position in a class-stratified, highly individuated, capitalistic
> society. It represents an effort to cope with feelings of
> hopelessness and despair which develop from the realization
> of the improbability of achieving success in terms of the values
> and goals of the larger society. . . . [One must try] to understand
> poverty and its associated traits as a culture . . . with its own
> structure and rationale, as a way of life which is passed down
> from generation to generation. . . . This view directs attention
> to the fact that the culture of poverty in modern nations is not
> only a matter of economic deprivation, of disorganization or of
> the absence of something. It is also something positive and
> provides some rewards without which the poor could hardly
> carry on.[11]

The concept of a "culture of poverty" sensitizes the researcher to
the relationship of the group under study and the larger society, the
nature of a community subjected to material deprivation, and the

attitudes, values and character structure of the individual. Nonparticipation and nonintegration of the poor in the major institutions of the larger society are two of the central characteristics of the culture of poverty. People with a culture of poverty produce very little wealth and receive very little in return.

In the individual, the culture of poverty is manifested by such characteristics as strong feelings of alienation, marginality, helplessness, dependence, and powerlessness. Other traits include a lack of impulse control, a strong present-time orientation with relatively little desire to defer gratification and to plan for the future, a sense of resignation and fatalism, and a very high tolerance for psychological pathology of all sorts. People with a culture of poverty are provincial and locally oriented and have very little sense of history. Primarily, they know and are only interested in their own troubles, their own local conditions, and their own way of life. While they appear not to be class conscious, they are, however, very sensitive to prestige and status distinctions.[12]

The idea of living within a culture of poverty should not be romanticized; neither should we regard the poor as modern-day noble savages. Instead, the concept will be used in this study to call attention to the adaptive functions of human beings: the ability to create a design for living with a ready-made set of solutions for human problems, making it possible to allocate energy resources in other directions. This categorically does not imply, however, that the entire configuration is valued—that the poor are poor because they wish to be and that if choice were possible they would cling to the status quo.

The Concept of Community

Few sociological ideas have achieved the degree of permanence or importance that "community" has. Community occupied a central place in the burgeoning of American sociology. Beginning, roughly, with the Chicago School, there have been almost innumerable studies of either actual communities or theoretical discussions of the concept of "the community" appearing in the professional literature.[13] It is clear, however, that even today little agreement can be reached about the nature of community.[14] Although the concept has proved to be rather ambiguous, it can prove very useful in understanding the behavior of the people living in slum hotels and S.R.O. tenements.

Perhaps the most basic description of a community is this: "a collection of people occupying a more or less clearly defined area. ... A community is not only a collective of people, but it is a collection of institutions." [15] This definition, however, is too simplistic to be fruitfully employed in the study of the S.R.O. problem. A dynamic approach, that is, one capable of viewing community from an interactional perspective, is necessary. Such a perspective can locate and identify a community within a dense (in terms of both people and institutions) urban setting. Essentially, such a concept of community can consider ideas like "social space" and "social differentiation" as resource factors that must be manipulated by persons living within a given locale. In this regard "community," like culture, becomes a problem-solving device for people confronted by the exigencies of an indifferent or even hostile position and/or social environment.[16]

Anthropologically, then, the community is seen in interactional rather than institutional terms. From this perspective, a community is viewed as a type of interactional system possessing the following characteristics:

> Each community is unique (1) in terms of using a set of geographical points (centers) as loci of interaction, (2) in having a given set of interactional group meetings at such centers, and (3) developing a local-interaction culture based on information collected at such centers and distributed primarily to members of the community.[17]

Geographically, the community is a set of centers related to each other by being used regularly by a unique set of associational groups. Socially, these associational groups use the given set of interrelated centers more often than they use any other set of centers.

This can be nicely merged with sociological work that suggests eschewing the traditional idea of "we-ness" or consciousness-of-kind as the distinguishing factor in defining community which is in favor of a behavioral solution such as can be seen in common definition-of-situation. From this perspective community, as a social entity, is seen in largely symbolic terms such that

> the basic social process is that of evaluative interaction; that social units are distinguished by the kinds of situations which

they evaluate; and the defined response of similar units to the same type of situation distinguishes each unit from others in the category. . . . Whatever the breakdown the kind of situation attended to by the unit is the first distinguishing feature of the unit. . . . If communities, our social unit in this instance, do have characteristic individuality indicated by their value systems that arise as the community members interact to define recurring life situations, then two very similar communities can be distinguished by their separate definitions of the same event.[18]

Because of the unusual problems presented by a study of the S.R.O. world it was necessary to employ this sort of interactionist perspective. Since the various hotels and tenements are scattered over a fairly large urban area, the concept of community defined in terms of "place" is meaningless. To simply label each building "community" and stop the analysis there entirely begs the question of conceiving it as an integrated and meaningful social unit. Yet, intuitively, the idea of the single hotel as a community seems right. Unfortunately, the classical definitions considering geography emphasized institutions as well. Institutional services, as utilized by the hotel residents, are neither of their own creation nor for their exclusive use; nor are they controlled and/or operated by the population they serve. Moreover, in most cases (significantly the hospitals), the S.R.O. residents have to leave the geographic bounds of their area in order to obtain the desired service.

Since it is believed that the S.R.O. world can be studied in terms of community, and that as such it produces some characteristic forms of social action, the next task calls for describing some of these forms. Essentially this description directs attention towards three large areas. Each suggests such questions as:

1. Since the community is conceptualized in interactional and not structural terms what are some of the existent social networks? How do they operate to satisfy the various and sundry needs of the community's residents? How did they begin and how do they maintain themselves?

2. How does the community manage to persist as a social unit? What are the forms of social control employed by it to establish and maintain order, thereby allowing collective life?

3. In what way are people grouped or divided? Upon inspec-

tion, is it possible to discern any sort of system of stratification, social differentiation, or status allocation, within the S.R.O. community?

These are the questions which were operationalized in order to study the social organization of this part of underclass living. Immediately below the larger direction of each of these questions will be considered.

Social Networks

Defining community in dynamic, interactional terms obviates the need for description of the usual structures. Our commitment to an interactionist framework demands that we see people bound to each other by common interest or needs. Viewing a community in this way emphasizes the discovery and description of the various "social networks" that compose it. A "social network" becomes a way to describe a set of relationships for which there is no common boundary. Thus:

> Each person is, at it were, in touch with a number of people, some of whom are directly in touch with each other and some who are not. .... I find it convenient to talk of a social field of this kind as a *network*. The image I have is of a set of points, some of which are joined by lines. The points of the image are people, and sometimes groups, and the lines indicate which people interact with each other.[19]

The S.R.O. community will be defined in terms of its various social networks. It is our assumption that these networks are responsible for providing the means of community integration.

Social Control

Central to the question of community is the issue of "social control." Two analytically separable dimensions can be derived from the concept of social control: the problem of social order and the process of control.

The relationship between community and social control was particularly important to the protourbanologists of the Chicago School. Robert Park, for example, was concerned with identifying the mechanisms by which a community composed of several quite different groups could arrange its affairs making it possible for each to maintain its own distinctive way of life without endangering the life of the whole.[20] Hence, social control became the "central fact and the central problem of society." [21] Accordingly,

> society is everywhere a control organization. Its function is to organize, integrate, and direct the energies resident in the individuals of which it is composed.[22]

Control in this sense is situational; ultimately it is the realization of the constantly changing requirements of collaboration within sets of relationships, making it possible for individuals to be inducted into and induced to cooperate in some sort of permanent corporate existence we call society.[23] Phrased in this way, the question of "control" raises a larger issue—the problem of order. The Hobbesian question of the prevention of the war-of-all-against-all is central to the problem of order; attention then is directed towards the organizational question. From this perspective, order can be seen as the realization of the varied patterns and accommodations which the S.R.O. residents have evolved. The weak and the sick must be cared for, and the various and sundry—often exotic—needs of members of the community must be satisfied. Attention is focused upon the establishment of interlocking patterns of noncontractual relationships and the processes sustaining them without recourse to legitimating authority.

Implicit in the question of order is some notion of control and sanction. Control refers to the community's response to those members who, for whatever reason, threaten the collective order. It is important to understand that the control processes that are operating are for the most part, entirely extralegal, thereby completely precluding recourse to the usual agents of social control.

When considering the process of the imposition of social sanctions, three fairly well-defined operations have been recognized:

1. What forms of behavior are liable to control, and under what conditions are they recognized?

2. Who recognizes them?

3. What is the nature of the sanctions imposed, and what are their ramifications for S.R.O. society members and the larger community?

Each of the steps is fully described in demonstrating how the social control process operates within the S.R.O. community.

Social Differentiation

In terms of community, the last issue to be considered will be the system of social differentiation. Social differentiation considers the allocation of prestige and power. In a community as dense, socially differentiated in terms of values, and as socially isolated as the S.R.O. world, it is questionable whether the usual vertical system of stratification, defined by universally accepted symbols, is meaningful. The forms that such a system manifests necessarily reflect conditions found in the community; in the case of the S.R.O. world, a stratification system defined in horizontal terms represents the community situtation most realistically. The dimensions of the system and a description of its operation within the S.R.O. community follow.

Methodology

Having determined that there is indeed an S.R.O. social world my next task required that the concepts or organizing categories be specified. This was partially described in the first part of this chapter where social deviance, the culture of poverty, and community are treated. Here I will further expand on some of the theoretical material presented above, focusing on *methodology* as distinguished from *technology*, which is defined as the mechanics of data collection and does not speak to the process governing what kinds of observations will be admitted. Although the following section is chiefly a methodological discussion, I must necessarily speak to some of the questions of how data were gathered.

Although American sociology has long concerned itself with studies of communities and naturally occurring groups, little thought has been devoted to the research process itself. Since the 1920s and 1930s we have had studies of towns, slums, skid rows, and ghettos, yet we still have little sense of the basic assumptions underlying most research. In this respect sociologists employing "field" or "qualitative" methods have until quite recently, with a few notable exceptions, never come to grips with the basic methodological processes influencing and shaping their work. Their failure to do so has made such studies among the most difficult to undertake in the entire sociological enterprise. Students attempting this kind of study find any number of fine research monographs but no paradigm which would be helpful in starting them. As a result, it is necessary for them to "re-invent the wheel" each time a study is contemplated and attempt to define the salient issues in a vacuum.

A wide theoretical perspective capable of encompassing a greater methodological scope was evolved for this study; it allows for consideration of the widest range of data, thereby neither doing violence to the worlds of the people studied nor falling into the trap of producing soft science or journalism. Such a theoretical outlook is emerging from a perspective labeled "naturalism" or "naturalistic behavioralism"; Norman Denzin provides a concise statement of this perspective, emphasizing its "commitment to actively enter the world of native people and to render those worlds understandable from the standpoint of a theory that is grounded in the *behaviors, languages, definitions, attitudes,* and *feelings* of those studied." He further explains:

> Naturalistic behaviorism aims for viable social theory . . . [and] recognizes that humans have social selves and as such act in ways that reflect their unfolding definitions of the situation. . . . The naturalist employs any and all sociological methods, whether these be secondary analyses of quantitative data, limited surveys, unobtrusive measures, participant observation, document analysis, or life history constructions. He will admit into his analyses any and all data that are ethically allowable.[24]

The larger methodological orientation used in this study reflects this commitment.

The nature of the population, special ecological factors, and the type of research questions posed all indicated that my choice of method was necessarily limited to an ethnographically oriented, community study approach. This following discussion explains the way in which the approach was conceived and the methods I actually used.

The charge most often leveled at the ethnographic method in sociological research is that it does little more than describe what is already clearly apparent and that, after all, the main thrust of the sociological enterprise has been towards the generation of hypotheses and the collection of data to demonstrate relationships between phenomena. Early in the planning stage of the research I discovered that little was known about underclass life in this situation. As such, the deduction and testing of logically related hypotheses was wholly precluded. Consequently, the primary aim of the study was necessarily directed towards system building: identification of the parts, determination of their mutual interdependence, and understanding how the social system is sustained through the interaction of these parts. It was hoped that the study would result in the construction of a model representative of the mode of behavior found within the slum hotel or S.R.O. community. The long-term objectives, once such a model has been realized, are the deduction and empirical testing of hypotheses relevant to general sociological theory (especially concerning deviant behavior and the creation of community) and not solely applicable to the immediately observed situation.

Instead of conceptualizing the population in a "social problem" context, however, attention is more fruitfully directed towards viewing the slum hotel or S.R.O. as an organized social system. William F. Whyte in the now classic *Street Corner Society* project made sense out of a complex, heterogeneous social area by seeing it in organizational terms.[25] The premise governing his research was that although an outside observer first perceived the area as "socially disorganized," it was anything but that. There were rules that could be distinguished if the "proper" observations were made. Whyte discovered that a sociometric orientation made it possible to describe and analyze the entire range of social relationships found in a street corner group. However, by including a more macroscopic approach, the street corner group and the larger social setting in which it operated could also be studied. This latter phase of the research described the self-perceptions of the community, the interaction of the various voluntary associations, and the images community members carried of the outside world.

Similar to *Street Corner Society*, yet employing a remarkably different methodology, is Elliot Leibow's *Tally's Corner*.[26] Rather than a well-defined associational group such as the Nortons (the name of the gang Whyte studied), Liebow was confronted by a loosely integrated group of black men who spent the larger part of their time loitering on a street corner in the heart of Washington, D.C.'s black ghetto. Since the problems were so different (phenomena that figured so importantly in Whyte's analysis—such as leadership—were not to be found on Tally's corner), the methodological approach that served so well in *Street Corner Society* proved inapplicable. To overcome these obstacles Liebow turned to a more anthropological approach. Such an approach both identifies and describes the major parts of the daily life of the native people.

From this perspective the group's structure is rendered into a number of analytically separable systems. The combination and interaction of the several subsystems maintains the group in both space and time. Ethnographic research derives its organization from the situations and rules that are themselves meaningful to the involved people. *Tally's Corner*, for instance, is organized so that the various social categories that the streetcorner men themselves employ—such as "Men and Jobs," "Lovers and Exploiters," "Friends and Networks"—are represented, described, and analyzed.

The real strength of the ethnographic approach lies in its ability to recognize the social categories and classifications that are in themselves meaningful to the population under study. The method might also be seen as one of the most dynamic in its ability to capture the process of social interaction as it is happening. To best accomplish this the researcher should consider a participant type study. This allows him to

> catch the process of interpretation through which [the persons under study] construct their actions.... To catch the process, the student must take the role of the acting unit whose behavior he is studying. Since the interpretation is being made by the acting unit in terms of objects designated and appraised, meanings acquired, and decisions made, *the process has to be seen from the standpoint of the acting unit*.... To try to catch the interpretive process by remaining as aloof as a so-called "objective" observer and refusing to take the role of this acting unit is to risk the worst kind of subjectivism—the interpretation with his own surmises in place of catching the process as it occurs in the experience of the acting unit which uses it. [emphasis added] [27]

Research employing this methodology provides an understanding of the symbolic universe in which a people operates, insight into how commonly held meanings or definitions become attached to actions (or objects and situations), and the parameters within which such action does or can take place. Insofar as an ethnography is written to elucidate the ways of a people, one should never lose sight of the fact that it is people, and the world they build, which concerns us.

The methodology I employed in this study utilized the strongest parts of each tradition. From Becker, Liebow and others committed to entering the worlds of the studied peoples, I've borrowed the idea that research must organize itself around the social categories, classifications and everyday, common-sense meanings evolved by the participating members of the S.R.O. world. Yet, drawing from Whyte's experience, I found it necessary to search for social facts— those more or less objective indicators of underlying conditions. What emerged was a methodology which simultaneously considered the consequences of forces such as "culture," "social structure," "social control," and the like, without losing sight of human beings as acting agents, as members of a community who are continually interpreting, defining, and responding to their own and each other's behavior and thus to the meanings and definitions that are attached to any social situation or interaction.

This synthesis is based on an assumption that there are discontinuities resident within social structure. Absolute reliance on any single methodological approach will, therefore, render whole areas of behavior (i.e., my study's data) invisible. Employing this perspective helped me avoid the traps of sociological or psychological determinism. From the standpoint of this naturalistic oriented methodology, social organization is conceived as a real framework inside of which the acting units (both people and groups) develop their action. Both the framework and the acting units are real and warrant consideration. By simultaneously considering the acting unit, the larger social stage or platform, the S.R.O. society member's methods in dealing with others perceived as similar to himself and with representatives of a larger world outside who confront him in many aspects of his daily round, the portrait of the S.R.O. world will be reasonably complete.

The Sociological Study Of Communities

Our previous discussion has demonstrated that the S.R.O.'s present us with a viable social world. There are, however, two issues germane to this assumption: (a) limiting the scope of study to a manageable unit of analysis; and (b) after delineating the natural boundaries of the world to be analyzed, developing the concepts necessary to examine this social unit in wholistic terms.

Ethnographers have traditionally concerned themselves with groups in which the contiguity of population was, perhaps, one of its most notable features.[28] There were the "small scale" societies found predominately in the "under-developed," "preliterate," or "developing" societies. However, by adopting the traditional ethnographic approach while using the technology for the study of a diffuse, sophisticated, urban setting, a significant obstacle is encountered: determining a unit of analysis which is at once independent and small enough to meet the requirements of the methodology while remaining representative of the larger set of phenomena. Anthropologists who have undertaken studies in developed, industrialized cultures, or sociologists who have undertaken studies in developed, industrialized cultures, or sociologists who have employed anthropological methods in urban research, have typically focused their observation on one of these five social units: a neighborhood, a housing project, a gang or associational group, a community of deviants, or a single family.[29]

Each of these, however, presents significant disadvantages as an object of study. Because the first unit, "the neighborhood," is often too large for complete study, one is often left wondering how many, who, and how representative were those who actually served as informants for the research. Moreover, often it is the researcher who determines that his target area is a "neighborhood" or "community." This judgment begs the question of whether the area's residents or the inhabitants also see it as such and what their perceptions of its social and geographical boundaries are. The housing project, on the other hand, which is certainly a more manageable unit in terms of size, is not usually a "naturally" occurring social entity. Tenants are usually admitted according to statutory regulations, often judged for acceptability on criteria over which they have no control (recall, for example, that in New York City the entire family can be disqualified if a single member has ever been convicted of a felony) and for this reason it is problematic whether, considering the exclusionary criteria employed, the tenantry be considered representative of anything but a rather narrowly defined statistical group. The remaining three units (the gang, the community of deviants, and the single family) are eminently suited to study through participant methods. However, study of the gang and the deviant community provides a view of but a limited segment of the target population, and is additionally suspect because it often restricts itself to but a single area of a person's life. The exceedingly detailed data on only a single family makes it very difficult to extrapolate to a larger portion of the population.

To obviate the various disadvantages in studying the foregoing units, the entire hotel or tenement building was chosen as the unit of analysis. The building is considered to be, unlike the various units described above, not only suitable for study in terms of size but also, if a number of units are carefully selected, capable of essentially representing the whole of the target population. To effectively do this it was necessary to identify a set of boundaries that simultaneously satisfied the requirements of the study's methodology without doing violence to the group's perception of the environment in which it operates.

While the question of boundary definition has been an important one for sociology, little agreement has been reached on how to achieve it. Some writers have conceptualized the process in terms of norms; a group's boundaries can be delineated by ascertaining where and when in social space a specific norm relinquishes its legitimacy. This, then, marks the limit beyond which the normative force of the group no longer extends and therefore people holding to other norms can be seen as members of other systems.[30] For other sociologists the question has been conceptualized in more simplistic terms: the group or little community was isolated in space (or time) and its boundaries were definitively marked geographically, or in some way signified by dimensions over which the group could exert no control.

Another approach to the problem of boundary definition utilized the common-sense definitions held by the population in question. This phenomenological approach is useful in understanding the ways in which people construct boundaries in a large, heterogenous urban area.[31] The use of this phenomenological approach allows the study of the overlapping use of the same geographical space by coterminously residing groups. This perspective permits the investigator to see how a person comes to define the area in which he operates as a "community" and thereby establishes some sense of territory, while not necessarily signifying a limited or solely inclusive notion of "we-ness" or "consciousness of kind." Conceptualized in this way, one is able to envision persons who can justly perceive themselves as "members of a community" while not necessarily belonging to any group, and interacting (in some cases) only minimally with those around them.

The adoption of this perspective focuses attention on a S.R.O. community by demonstrating how people restrict their daily round of interaction to places, persons, and institutions that are generally rejected by the coterminously residing middle- or working-class population. The sense of the community's boundaries derives from the limits indicated by the common-sense impressions of persons within the community.

Within the larger geographical boundaries (loosely set by streets and avenues while being definitively established ecologically) the individual buildings were chosen for study sites by relying on the common-sense impressions of members of the community. The need to observe several sites in the community was established early in the study. Obviously, the welfare hotel or S.R.O. tenement is more than a building with rooms in it—it is a social system. Each building has a somewhat different character because of the difference in tenant population, management personnel and policies, and other factors. For example, when asked about a certain hotel, most people within the S.R.O. community have some notion about it, for example, certain buildings are known to be more violent than others, or "everyone knows" that narcotics are very easily accessible in others. By utilizing this folk knowledge it was possible to construct a model defining some of the *stations* within the larger S.R.O. world.

The recognition of such "stations" suggests the question of social navigation—the ability to move about in a social milieu; and, at the same time, appreciating the significance of the various symbolic markers which delineate the important status positions in the milieu. Thus conceptualized, the S.R.O. community takes on a fuller character: it becomes an almost self-contained world. A person enters (sometimes at birth—but not necessarily so), occupies several more or less well defined status positions (usually accompanied by changes in physical situ), and ultimately exits.

Envisioning the single welfare hotel or S.R.O. tenement as a part of a larger community suggests an additional methodological perspective. Such a methodology makes possible the study of the S.R.O. community in a wholistic fashion. In his book *The Little Community*, Robert Redfield deals with some of the conceptual problems involved in the methodology of community study.[32] The book offers several pivotal concepts permitting an investigator to view a little community in wholistic terms. First, for instance, the little community can be perceived as a whole, as a boundaried entity small enough so that all of the members of the group or any cross section can be studied; it can also be seen in systemic or structural terms, or described in terms of a typical biography, or the kind of person it produces. In order to be adequate, a community study must demonstrate understanding of the arrangement of individuals, spaces, times, functions, and social processes and the effects of these.

While much of the above has already been incorporated into this study's methodology, Redfield's discussion, "The Little Community as an Ecological System" merits special attention.[33] In his work in the small, technologically backward villages of the Yucatan peninsula, the ecological system defined the interrelationship of man and nature. It described those concurrent regularities, both natural and artificial, which were encompassed in man's relationship with the world. The system is not a static one, but its organization regularly responds to both external and internal changes. This concept calls attention to the regular, temporal transformation of the system. This system is likened to a dramatic or literary composition; there is a cycle (annual, but not necessarily so) in which there is a cast, a prologue, a development, and a denouement. Every year the community lives the play, but its last act in any one cycle may be different from the last act in the next.[34]

The concepts of the ecological system and ecological time are particularly relevant to the study of the S.R.O. community. Given the reality of the American political situation much of what happens to an underclass population is entirely beyond its control. Unorganized and effectively disfranchised people have little influence over politicians and bureaucrats attuned to the needs and wishes of a different segment of the population. Housing ordinances, zoning regulations, delivery of vital services, and police activity all strongly affect the nature and quality of S.R.O. life, yet the S.R.O. community has about as much control over these as the Central American Indians have over the amount of rain that falls on their maize.

The concept of "ecological time" is also relevant. Using the perspective it provides, the regularly occurring events over which the community has little or no control can be studied and organized. For example, while few members of the S.R.O. community participate in the electoral process and even fewer look to it for redress of grievance, the period preceding elections precipitates major alterations in activity for many persons in the community. Persons engaged in illegal occupations or those committed to a life-style dependent upon illegal goods find operation exceedingly more difficult before election time when promises have been made to "clean up the streets" by removing the addicts, prostitutes, bums, and other undesirables.

In describing some of the life styles of members of the S.R.O. community the concept of ecological time is equally useful. An addict's life style, for example, would be amenable to such an analysis. A complete cycle is built around the regular acquisition of his drugs. Other definable parts of the cycle involve the strategies that must be employed to "cop" or secure drugs, and the various ploys needed to assure the certainty of their enjoyment free from fear of apprehension or harassment. The concept calls attention, as well, to the vicissitudes in the availability of drugs. During "panics," for example, when drugs are very scarce, drastic disruptions in the addict's daily rounds necessarily occur. Conceptualized in this way the concept of ecology was found to be very useful in the study of both the S.R.O. community and the life-styles of its members.

NOTES

1. Edwin H. Sutherland, *The Professional Thief by a Professional Thief* (Chicago: University of Chicago Press, 1937).

2. Ned Polsky "The Hustler," *Social Problems* 12 (1964): 3–15.

3. Donald Ball, "Ethnography of an Abortion Clinic," *Social Problems* 14 (1967): 293–301.

4. Travis Hirshi, "The Professional Prostitute," *Berkeley Journal of Sociology* 7 (1962): 33–39.

5. Edwin Lemert, "Social Structure, Social Control and Deviation," in *Anomie and Deviant Behavior,* ed. Marshall B. Clinard (New York: Macmillian, 1964), pp. 81–82.

6. Ibid., p. 12.

7. Michael Harrington, *The Other America* (New York: Macmillan, 1962).

8. David Matza, "Proverty and Disrepute," in *Contemporary Social Problems,* ed. Robert K. Merton and Robert A. Nisbet (New York: Harcourt, Brace and World, 1961), pp. 619–70.

9. Oscar Lewis, *La Vida* (New York: Vintage Books, 1965).

10. Matza, "Poverty and Dispute."

11. Lewis, *La Vida,* pp. xliii–xliv.

12. Ibid. p. xlv.

13. Maurice Stein, *The Eclipse of Community* (New York: Harper and Row, 1960), chap. 1.

14. See for instance: A. B. Hollingshead, "Community Research: Development and Present Condition," *American Sociological Review* (1948): 136–46; Richard L. Simpson, "Sociology of the Community: Current Status and Prospects," *Rural Sociology* 30 (1965): 127–49; Willis A. Sutton, et al., "The Concept of Community," *Rural Sociology* 25 (1960): 297–303; George A. Hillery, "Definitions of Community: Areas of Agreement," *Rural Sociology* 20 (1955): 111–124; George A. Hillery, "A Critique of Selected Community Concepts," *Social Forces* 37 (1959): 236–42.

15. Robert E. Park, *Human Communities* (Glencoe, Ill.: Free Press, 1952).

16. In terms of definition of community this idea has been previously advanced. Although he, for the most part, does not consider the interactionist perspective, Albert Reiss wrote of "community ... as a collective response to conditions of life in a particular territory. We shall say that community arises through sharing a limited territorial space for residence and for sustenance and functions to meet common needs generated in sharing this space by establishing characteristic forms of social action. Albert J. Reiss, "The Sociological Study of Communities," *Rural Sociology* 24 (1959): 118–30.

17. Morris Freilich, "Towards an Operational Definition of Community," *Rural Sociology* 28 (1963): 122.

18. Richard E. DuWars, "The Definition of the Situation as a Community Distinguishing Characteristic," *International Journal of Comparative Sociology* 3 (1962): 263.

19. Elizabeth Bott, *Family and Social Networks* (London: Travistock Publishers, 1957), p. 34.

20. Stein, *Eclipse of Community*, p. 17.

21. Robert F. Park, *On Social Control and Collective Behavior*, ed. Ralph Turner (Chicago: University of Chicago Press, 1967), p. xi.

22. Ibid.

23. Ibid., p. xii.

24. Norman Denzin, "The Logic of Naturalistic Inquiry, "*Social Forces*" 50 (1971): 166–67.

25. William F. Whyte, *Street Corner Society*, 2d ed. (Chicago: University of Chicago Press, (1955).

26. Elliot Liebow, *Tally's Corner* (Boston: Little, Brown, 1966).

27. Herbert Blumer, "Society as Symbolic Interaction," in *Human Behavior and Social Process: An Interactionist Approach*, ed. Arnold Rose (Boston: Houghton Mifflin Company, 1961), p. 188.

28. The formulation of this section owes materially to a discussion of the problems of urban ethnography by Dr. Alan Harwood, in "Neighbor Medical Care Demonstration" mimeographed (Bronx, New York, 1968).

29. Elena Padilla, *Up from Puerto Rico* (New York: Columbia University Press, 1958); see for example, Herbert Gans, *The Urban Villagers* (New York: Free Press, 1962); Gerald Suttles, *The Social Order of the Slum* (Chicago: University of Chicago Press, 1969). Peter Willmoth, "Class and Community at Dagenhom" mimeographed (London: Institute for Community Studies, 1960); see for example, Lee Rainwater, *Behind Ghetto Walls* (Chicago: Aldine, 1970). Whyte, *Street Corner Society*; see for example, Liebow, *Tally's Corner*. Maurice Leznoff and William Westley, "The Homosexual Community," *Social Problems* 4 (1956): 257–63; see for example, Albert J. Reiss, "The Social Integration of Queers and Peers," *Social Problems* 9 (1961): 102–20; Howard Becker, *Outsiders* (New York: Free Press, 1963). Oscar Lewis, *La Vida* (New York: Random House, 1965).

30. Kai Erikson, "Notes on the Sociology of Deviance," *Social Problems* 9 (1962): 307–14.

31. H. Lawrence Ross, "The Local Community: A Survey Approach," *American Sociological Review* 27 (1962): 75–84.

32. Robert Redfield, *The Little Community* (Chicago: University of Chicago Press, 1953).

33. Ibid. chap. 7.

34. Ibid.

Chapter 3
A Descriptive Portrait of the S.R.O. World

The quality of life of those living in slums, welfare hotels and S.R.O. tenements differs radically from that of their more affluent neighbors. In part, their physical environment can be held responsible. Below, some of the physical aspects of S.R.O. living will be examined. Specifically, the nature of the accommodations, the facilities provided, and their ramifications on social interaction will be discussed.

Using the concept of "community" discussed in the previous chapters, this chapter will consider the S.R.O. community and the units or "stations" that are to be found within its boundaries. These stations will be differentiated and described. At the entrance of each station, however, a gatekeeper is located to control the flow of human traffic. As such, this gatekeeper occupies a pivotal place in the S.R.O. world. The functions, modes of operation, and social characteristics of these gatekeepers will be investigated.

Ecology

You know, I just can't seem to put my finger on it—but there's something just right about the S.R.O.'s being there.

This was the impression of a young, midwestern VISTA worker newly assigned to the urban renewal project on Manhattan's upper

West Side. Whether or not other residents of the area would agree with him is very doubtful at best. It has been estimated that there are approximately one hundred thousand units of S.R.O. and S.R.O.-type housing in New York City and almost one-third of them are to be found between West 59th and West 110th Streets. The experience of other cities across the nation is similar. While the absolute size of the S.R.O. population is smaller, there is some tendency towards concentration in certain parts of the city. The way in which the housing turns into S.R.O. accommodations is similar; very few, if any, buildings are built to be S.R.O.'s, instead, through one or several renovations they are so transformed.

Returning to New York City, it is illustrative to note that one quarter of the city's S.R.O. buildings contain more than one hundred units, while one half have from ten to ninety-nine units. The average building on Manhattan's West Side is larger than the citywide pattern, and contains relatively more S.R.O. units per structure. Thus, the lone person, and the problems generally associated with him, is more concentrated on the West Side. A large number of S.R.O.'ers living in an area further increase the social isolation of the S.R.O. tenants through their being labeled as "neighborhood nuisances." Once this label has been affixed, the mobilization of the higher status residents is likely and the larger community pressures for the elimination of the S.R.O. resident's bothersome presence.

Description

If one were to walk down a street on Manhattan's West Side, how would one be able to recognize an S.R.O. building or welfare hotel? From the outside, most buildings in this area look approximately the same. They are evenly covered with the same layer of soot and grime, which has quietly been depositing itself year after year from the industry on the east, and New Jersey's oil refineries on the west. Externally, little dilapidation is visible. Most of the buildings were constructed during a period when housing was expected to last forever giving the structures a massive, solid facade. Those buildings, originally constructed as hotels, still have signs affixed to them, with legends such as:

HOTEL MOUNT ROYALE
Transients and Permanents Accommodated
CLEAN AIRY ROOM-KITCHENETTE SUITES
ROOMS FROM $2 PER DAY & UP

S.R.O. hotels are unlike skid row flop houses in which one typically has to climb a flight of stairs to reach the lobby, which is located on the second floor. (Street level in the skid row hotel is characteristically taken by businesses.) It is interesting to note, however, that both present a basically nondescript appearance. Often, the only external clue to their identification is the presence of several persons, some shabbily dressed or in various stages of intoxication, loitering around the entrance way. If, however, several buildings cluster on a single block, one of them will become the focus of the street sociability and business transactions. Many buildings are recognizable, at least during the warmer months, by the accumulated refuse, or "airmail" as area residents call it, of broken bottles and other trash that is simply thrown out of the windows. Ultimately, this accumulation of refuse becomes such an eyesore that after the landlord receives repeated police citations it is removed, then only to begin accumulating again.

As soon as one enters the lobby of an S.R.O. building, any resemblance to a conventional apartment building stops. The lobbies of conventional, higher class buildings in the area are usually comfortably furnished with several pieces of old yet elegant furniture. The lighting in the lobby area is subdued, focusing social activity on a well-lit panel of mailboxes located in close proximity to the elevators.

Conversely, the lobby of a welfare hotel impresses one by its starkness: the absence of any furniture is striking. The management has removed it to discourage any loitering or sociability in the lobby area. In some buildings, one is struck by the decaying remnants of past grandeur—broken, soiled marble colonnades, cracked mirrored paneling and ornate but damaged tile mosaics decorating the floors present the flawed props for lobby dramas.

The most striking feature, however, presented by the S.R.O. or welfare hotel lobby is the caged enclosure through which business is transacted. In some hotels, the precautions are so elaborate as to include electronically operated doors, bullet proof glass with a narrow opening, set at right angles to the base panel, through which mail or communications can be passed, or thick plexiglass carousels to move material between tenant and management. Looking through glass or bars from the lobby into the enclosed areas, one sees the wooden pigeonholes into which mail is sorted—most residents, however, seldom inquire about mail since they receive it so infrequently. Prominently visible from the outsider's perspective is an armamentarium of baseball bats, taped pipes, nightsticks, heavy clubs and even firearms, hanging in mute anticipation of any sort of trouble. In some of the larger hotels, which in their halcyon days hosted affluent guests, the large safe with its interior divided into separate locked compartments to provide security for the guests' valuables, stands with its doors thrown open, benignly accumulating the dust and cobwebs of disuse.

When a building is converted into an S.R.O. the enclosed area is situated so that it commands a view of the street entrance. In theory this was done to make it possible to control traffic through the hotel. All the hotels prominently display signs over these areas proclaiming that no visitors are to be received after 10 P.M. (In some, no visitors are allowed at all.) The lobby is further secured by a system of mirrors that reveals the presence of anyone standing in any part of the lobby. These have been installed by managers fearful of robbery or other violence. Looking directly out through the bars or protective screen of the manager's cage one sees the door to the street, and then, by inspecting the mirrors, one observes the rest of the lobby and the entrance to the elevators. The lobby area is brightly lit with glaring high-watt bulbs that make it and everyone in it visible from the street.

S.R.O.'s, roominghouses, and some hotels each have different floor plans. Predictably, the plan of each floor is dependent upon what the original structure was like. We have provided a generalized floor plan for those buildings that were converted from apartment houses, whether they are officially listed as S.R.O.'s or hotels.

There are, however, certain aspects of S.R.O. living that transcend any given unit or building. The walls of every S.R.O. building can be characterized by their dreary color: walls are unfailingly painted either a shade of dark green or brown. In addition, the omnipresent grime tends to quickly permeate even the newest coat of paint and soon it too has a dulled, dismal appearance. Hallways are generally poorly lit; burned out or broken lamps are not promptly replaced; or, the fluorescent lighting is so defective that the area is bathed in the eerie, flickering glow of the dying lamps. Windows in hallways are glazed with heavy, opaque glass, covered with so much grime and old paint that they allow little light through. Many others have had the original glass replaced by metal sheets after they were broken. Some floors still have the remains of the carpets that they had before the hotel began accepting welfare tenants. On these, water damage and ingrained grime has obscured all but the faintest remains of their original color and patterns, giving the floor a grubby, lackluster appearance. Fixtures, such as railings and staircase railings are likely to be dirty to the touch and have been painted and repainted so many times that the ornate designs of the iron work are almost imperceptible.

In most buildings, the limited, poorly paid staff of maids and porters finds itself unequal to the task of cleaning the constantly accumulating garbage. Common trash cans on each floor overflow with unsightly and noisome garbage through which vermin can be seen scurrying. Dirt is the omnipresent companion of the S.R.O. dweller. Garbage is often simply thrown into the halls, as well as from the windows. The level of hygienic abuse is primarily a function of how much the manager will tolerate. Some managers demand a higher level of cleanliness than others, and specify that if a tenant is not willing or able to meet it he will be evicted from the building.

Dogs kept for pets or protection by some tenants often present an additional source of uncleanness. While most pet owners observe the amenities involved in maintaining an animal in an apartment dwelling, others refuse to walk their animal outside of the building during spells of severe weather (or in some instances, during an alcoholic bender). Instead, it is simply released in the hotel corridor for its daily exercise and attendant functions with the inevitable consequence of aggravating an already unpleasant situation.

Perhaps one of the most striking memories that I retain of the S.R.O.'s that I worked in was that of two infant black girls, one completely naked and the other in a torn pink shift, playing on the floor of a hotel corridor, littered with broken bottles, garbage and dog feces; cockroaches were crawling on the walls and the entire scene was bathed dimly by the flickering light of a dying fluorescent lamp.

Social Adaptions to the Physical Environment

As dreary and colorless as one finds the S.R.O. corridors and halls, it would be incorrect to describe the S.R.O. as bland and devoid of variablility. A DOSS caseworker who had spent more than two years working in the Hotel Enfer described an impression he had:

> Harvey, I know you're not aware of it yet, but when you get to know this place you'll find that each hallway has its own smell. Man, I'll be willing to bet that you could take me to a place [in the hotel] blindfolded and I'd still be able to tell you exactly

where we were. Sometimes it's the smells that really get me, man.

The S.R.O. building is considerably less neutral than its higher class counterpart since there is very seldom any effort made at standardizing or removing smells. Often the smell of an entire corridor is dominated by a single tenant. A certain corridor, for instance, was recognizable through the smells of a women who had had a colostomy; or, the corridor in which the notorious "cat-lady" (a woman who kept more than two dozen cats in a small room) lived was at times almost impassable.

Because many S.R.O. people have come to define the environment in which they operate as actively hostile, they have learned a set of skills which they believe can aid in their protection. People learn how to listen, or conversely, how to not hear, a lot more carefully than the middle-class person who has to confront a different type of isolation. At least partially responsible is the way in which the S.R.O. units are constructed. In many buildings the only separation between the individual units are partitions fabricated from a single layer of plasterboard. With conditions such as these one must be careful that his public recognition of others does not appear to be constructed upon information which may be construed as having been received in an illegitimate manner. In the S.R.O. world one's public or social face is accepted literally; members do not look back into another's background or history to validate his claims or social presence. For example, if several persons are conversing together, and another, well known to each singularly, enters the room and directly attempts to penetrate the conversation, anyone already in the group, who might resent the intrusion, need only say, "Am I talking to you?" This will effectively insure that the newcomer's social presence is not acknowledged, thereby removing him from the conversational sphere. In terms of this interaction, then, he is expected to remove himself, and whatever he might have learned from having overheard the conversation is to be treated in the same manner as information that might have "come through the wall."

The S.R.O. world is a noisy one. There is a constant background of random sound: the phonographs, radios, clanking pipes, loud laughing or strident arguing, all blend into an omnipresent cacophony. Punctuating this, however, are episodic incidents that S.R.O. people readily respond to. For example, I was sitting with several people in a common room in the Enfer, when from somewhere above there was a loud noise, sounding as if a sizeable object had hit the floor. The room got very quiet and a moment later someone said: "That was too heavy to be a body." This struck me as very funny and I began to laugh. However, since no one else laughed, or even smiled, I quickly stopped. A little later the faux pas was carefully explained to me. The comment was offered in all serious-ness, therefore my response was deemed to be entirely inappropri-ate. On many other occasions there were opportunities to observe the ability that S.R.O. people have to distinguish different sounds; some tenants, for example, could positively identify the several individuals in a group outside of his door by their footsteps alone.

S.R.O. Living Facilities

The living facilities provided by S.R.O.'s place significant con-straints on the satisfaction of one's most basic needs. In a conventional apartment unit one finds a kitchen sink, electric refrigerator, four burner stove with oven, and storage cabinets, making the preparation of food possible. These facilities are wholly lacking in the S.R.O.'s. If private kitchen facilities (i.e., in the tenant's room) are provided, they consist, more often than not, of an older model electric or gas two burner range. Most rooms do not provide refrigerators. Because of the absence of refrigeration, an S.R.O. building can be distinguished during the winter months by the array of food-stuffs precariously perched on the exterior window sills. Room sinks are of the type found in older bathrooms: a shallow bowl with separate hot and cold spigots. Although the New York Housing Code clearly specifies what facilities must be present in a room to be rented as a unit with "cooking facilities," landlords have discovered that the only essential item is the hot-plate. For most tenants the sleeping or rooming accommodations are the primary consideration; complaints are seldom voiced vo-ciferously enough, if at all, to affect the addition of other facilities or the reduction of rents.

Since private storage and preparation of food is precluded for most S.R.O.'ers, they might be expected to use the common facilities located in the communal kitchen. Like other public areas in the S.R.O.'s, this communal kitchen has no one who is directly responsi-ble for its up-keep. Because of this, most evidence a state of extreme uncleanliness, are vermin-infested, and are littered with discarded refuse and trash. Although a refrigerator and storage cabinets are provided, a cursory inspection finds them empty. Residents are very reluctant to store any food in these common areas because of the absolute certainty of having their food taken by someone else. As one resident reported:

Respondent: She-it baby, I won't put nothing there. I rather buy my grub every day. If some nigger don' get it, them rats'n roaches will.

Interviewer: But aren't you entitled to use these facilities—don't you even complain to the landlord?

Respondent: Mr. Turkel—what he care? He just say that every time he put a new box in here with a new lock, someone up and come and break it off. He doesn't care. And man, I don't wanna catch nobody messin with my shit—I just don't want no hassles, ya dig?

Ideally, the communal kitchen should provide a focal point for group life (like the kitchen in Mrs. Grundy's folksy rooming house); instead it is avoided by most residents. Since it is a public area, access is freely available. One can never be sure of whom he might encounter in the kitchen and therefore, whether his person or property might be placed in jeopardy.

The bathrooms are equally noisome. Since only a poorly paid porter is directly responsible for their maintenance, most are in poor condition. All show evidence of extensive water damage, such as paint and plaster falling from the walls and ceilings. Floors are filthy and often partially inundated with water from leaking pipes and malfunctioning facilities. Amenities such as toilet tissue are seldom to be found. Because sanitary facilities so often malfunction, an entire floor is forced to rely on a single set of accommodations. In these cases residents complain of the landlord's seeming hesitancy in repairing broken equipment. In reply, landlords report that the tenants break the facilities faster than they are able to repair them.

For most residents, their complaints are subordinated to concern about physical security. Public areas such as bathrooms and kitchens are accessible to anyone. One can never be certain that someone is not lying in wait in the lavatory. Among older and female residents this is a frequently stated fear. Many S.R.O.'ers can recount incidents in which either they, or an acquaintance were so accosted. The trip and return from the bathroom, especially at night, is one that provokes much anxiety for these S.R.O. people. The moment when the person has his back to the corridor, as he inserts and turns his key in the lock to open his room, is when he is particularly vulnerable. One outspoken woman, at a tenants' meeting dealing with the problem of security at the hotel, stated:

> Youse people, [referring to the social workers leading the meeting] youse don't know nothing.... Couple a week ago some muther trieda duff me [assault] when I came back from the john. I told the Man, and he say he'd take care of it—course nothing happened. Now, I tell you, I just don't go out at night— no how! Got me a piss-pot 'neath my bed.... [At this point there was an appreciative chuckle from the audience. Encouraged by this she went on.] Yeah, that what this whole joint is— a piss-pot! [This was answered with several enthusiastic "right 'ons!" from the audience.]

Lavatories are used by persons who are not tenants of the building. Addicts who have "scored" in the hotel will often use a hotel lavatory to "shoot-up," since their dealer will refuse to allow his customers to congregate in his room and use it for a "shooting gallery." Occasionally, if the drugs are exceptionally good, addicts will drop into a stupor right in the lavatory and remain there until some of the effects of the drug have worn off. (Occasionally the drug proves to be so powerful that the user actually dies from an overdose.) During the winter, homeless people or those so inebriated that they are unable to return home, will wander in and use the hotel bathrooms, especially the bathtubs, to sleep in. Since most hotels lack any effective internal security, and few tenants are willing to do anything on their own, their use of the facility is not precluded.

In response, S.R.O. people have adjusted their life-rhythms to this situation. Some report having structured a daily round so that they can attend to all functions at times, and in ways that they assume to be the safest. For example, when I was confronted by the problem of making a before-bed toilet, and not wishing to travel to the next floor because the facilities on my floor were out of order (it was more than three weeks before they were fixed), I discovered that the sink right in the room served as well for urination as it did for washing.

Individual rooms found within an S.R.O. or welfare hotel vary from large and spacious to those with cubiclelike proportions; the room specifications are dependent upon how the building was renovated. In a hotel on Riverside Drive, for example, on a single line of rooms, the room overlooking the river was large (measuring about twelve by fifteen feet) and airy, dominated by three dormer windows. The room closest to the elevator, (the one I stayed in) on the other hand, had only a very small window and measured a scant six by eight feet. The room was so small that only a bed and a straight-backed chair could be accommodated.

Vermin are always present in an S.R.O. dwelling—cockroaches are so numerous and common that most tenants have learned to ignore them. The insects seem impervious to even the most determined pesticide spraying—merely returning the following day. Rodents are common and S.R.O. dwellers seldom leave food unattended; mice are accorded little, if any, notice. In some buildings, mothers slept with their infant children and forbade older children to bring any food into bed with them for fear of rats. Stories of small children molested by rats are not uncommon; many S.R.O. people will keep clubs and brooms within handy reach.

One tenant reported that when he complained to the manager about seeing a rat in his room, he was simply told to plug the rat's hole with steel wool. The tenant plugged the hole and a few days later he discovered a new hole within inches of the first. When he complained again, the manager suggested that the tenant speak to his caseworker about it. The caseworker was contacted and she promised to look into the matter. After several weeks, the tenant simply gave up. The experience of this resident is in every way typical.

If the caseworker had filed a formal complaint with the Health Department, the city would be obliged to intervene. This would entail dispatching an inspector to the building. The inspector will investigate and if evidence of rats is discovered (usually by the presence of fresh droppings), he will issue a warning. The landlord then has two weeks to correct the problem before the premises is reinspected. If the violation has not been eliminated in that time, a summons (which carries the possibility of a fine upon conviction) may be issued. If the summons is not answered, the landlord may be liable to arrest and the revocation of his permit to operate an S.R.O. Legal action appears to present little threat for S.R.O. landlords. Landlords often speak of how crowded the court calendars are, and how it can take up to two and a half years to get to court. If represented by counsel, and if the attorney requests additional time in order to prepare a defense, the process continues for at least another three months. With this much time, as one landlord philosophically said:

> Who knows—God willing I should be alive in three years—by then, who knows, I'll sell this joint, and then what? I should live and be well, and I'll worry about it then.

The municipal housing code specifies that every owner or leasee of an S.R.O. building must obtain a permit annually from the Department of Buildings, authorizing the operation of the S.R.O. Issuance of a permit is conditional on the absence of building violations. In theory, the need to secure such an annual permit would compel all S.R.O. operators to maintain their property at a minimum level and ameliorate any conditions which violate the housing code. In fact, though, many S.R.O. buildings are currently operating without a permit. The existence of manifold violations prevented them from obtaining permits, but operating without a permit is simply another violation. Since landlords pay little attention to control agencies, partly due to the cumbersome and ineffective nature of enforcement machinery, little is (or probably can be) done to improve the living condition in the S.R.O.'s.

S.R.O. rooms tend to reflect the characteristics of their occupants less than those of higher status persons. The S.R.O. *room* is less of a vehicle for the presentation of self than the *person* of the S.R.O. dweller. Materially impoverished, the S.R.O. dweller has little furniture of his own. The furnishings of an entire room, characteristically consisting of a bed, a chair, and a bureau, have been provided by the management. The furniture and the overall conditions of the room are entirely congruent—both are dilapidated. Rooms are poorly lit, the major source of lighting generally being an overhead fixture, often flourescent. The walls and ceiling are painted the same dark, characterless green, grey or beige as the corridors, and are in need of repair. Due to water damage, walls and ceilings generaly show large cracks and areas of peeling paint; and, during the winter, often feel clammy to the touch. Carpeting is old and threadbare, showing ingrained stains and dirt. Wooden floors are broken and linoleum is often worn and old.

Stations of the S.R.O. Community

In the preceding chapter we briefly discussed the quality of "social navigation", that is, the ability to recognize symbolic markers within a community and orienting one's geo-social action towards them. The most important of these symbolic markers are the recognized "stations" found in the S.R.O. world. These stations are actual S.R.O. buildings that can be distinguished from each other. Indigenous S.R.O. people recognize the different buildings for what they are, and fairly consistent value judgements are held throughout the larger community. Below we shall examine the characteristics, qualities and organization of these S.R.O. stations.

All S.R.O. buildings, however, are not identical; some are considered by S.R.O. people as "better" places to live. Two major criteria are considered in this evaluation: (1) the appearance and facilities of the building; and (2) the matter of security. The latter far outweighs the former as a determinant of desirability and choice. In many ways, the condition that the building is in is a function of who has access to it. If we were to construct a continuum, the opposing poles of the S.R.O. world are signified by those buildings considered "open"—anyone may enter at any time; to, "closed"—one's person and packages are searched upon entry for the possession of alcohol, or whatever else the manager has declared as contraband. In this second group, rules regulating the entrance of nonresidents into the building are not only stated but rigidly enforced.

The "openness" of the building determines the quality of life for the residents ensconced there. Openness, however, is defined in two ways. In the first, an "open building" is simply one in which there is more than one entrance and there is little or no control placed upon who enters or leaves the building. Anyone, therefore, has unimpeded access to the building, its residents, and their possessions. Such buildings are often the scenes of violent street crime, in which the perpetrator will loiter outside of the hotel until a likely victim is spotted. The crime—typically a "grab and run" (purse snatching) or "yoking" (mugging)—occurs with the perpetrator(s) fleeing into the hotel. Generally, he does not remain there but will exit from the building via another entrance which fronts a different street. Understandably, the victim or civilian witnesses are extremely reluctant to pursue anyone into an S.R.O. building. In other instances, "people from the outside," as building residents describe them, "come into the building to bust into people's houses [burgle their rooms] when they not there." In addition to free access to the hotel or buildings from the street, the open buildings do not enforce the municipal rule requiring that the original apartment door be locked and only people living in that wing have keys.

The second and even more significant factors determining an "open" building is the manager's willingness to give a room to almost anyone who can pay for it. The "closed" S.R.O. or hotel, conversely, demands that its prospective tenants meet certain standards of dress (such as clean, not overly shabby clothing), deportment, employment or finances, before a room will be rented to them.

Stations within the S.R.O. world are defined through these characteristics. The most feared, the most notorious hotels or S.R.O. buildings, are those that are the most open. When talking with S.R.O. people in New York City, names such as Harvard, Whitehall, the Mount-Royale, the Marseilles and others, are mentioned time and again. A veteran of one of the most infamous describes his brief sojourn there:

> Got outta the joint [Manhattan State Hospital] and the Welfare sent me uptown [to the Harvard]. 'Vestigator said it was cool ... she called up a couple of hotels and this one had room. Man, I didn't know nothing ... soon as I walked up to the place I had a feeling, you know, like something just ain't right. The man cashes my check and I get a room. They got all these dudes just hanging' in the lobby, and this cat droppin' into a deep nod right there. Man, I knew it wasn't cool then. Man, just outta the joint and this place ain't gonna do me no good. One day I come back from the bathroom and this dude in my room, lookin' all around. He sees me and whips out this shank [a knife]. I say, it's cool, baby, it's cool—man, I sure that motherfucker was gonna cut me—I backed outta that room fast and hauled ass right downstairs. Got my shit together, man, and told Miss L. [the caseworker] I hadda get outta that joint ... then I came here. Man, I be sleepin' in the subway trains 'fore I go back there.

Most S.R.O. dwellers, even if they haven't had firsthand experience with these hotels, have at least a very strong impression that they are to be avoided if at all possible.

These open buildings tend to be populated by those people who have had difficulty finding accommodations elsewhere. They are the ones most likely to continually manifest bizarre and unusual behavior and/or the most regressed alcoholics or addicts. These open buildings prove to be the most dilapidated and the dirtiest.

In contrast, the "closed" buildings are characterized by the rigid exclusion of those persons considered by the management to be a poor risk. Public access to these S.R.O. buildings is radically circumscribed. Only one entrance is provided and a key is needed to open the front door. The manager (or his agent) is on duty at all times and all strangers are excluded. Visitors must be collected at the desk, and often a sign-in-sign-out policy is in effect. Inside, each wing of rooms is kept locked and often a listing of that corridor's residents is posted. This population tends to be less mobile, quieter and less likely to be considered a neighborhood nuisance. These S.R.O.'s tend to have greater proportions of whites, orientals, and students. In New York City, certain landlords are especially interested in recruiting tenants of Haitian and/or Dominican nativity. They assume that many are in the country illegally and consequently make a much more pliant and docile tenant because of their understandable reluctance to seek any sort of official assistance in dealing with housing complaints. Members of these groups recruit newly arrived, fellow countrymen by word of mouth, stressing that the managers will not ask any questions when renting rooms. Many of these immigrants report that the presence of their countrymen living in close proximity is an advantage to the newcomer, especially if he wishes to call little attention to himself. A parallel phenomenon is in operation in the southwest where many Mexicans can be found.

The wholly "open" and wholly "closed" S.R.O.'s represent the polar extremes of the S.R.O. world. Between these two are the majority of buildings in which the management attempts some sort of restrictive admissions policy and ongoing control of behavior. Since the buildings can be located on a continuum, observers (cf. Shapiro, above) tend to attribute a "personality" to each building. While each building or hotel should not be seen as a distinct step on a scale, groups or clusters of similar buildings can be identified as differing steps by indigenous S.R.O. people. These clusters are not defined geographically. On one side street, for example, one of the most notorious buildings in the area could be found: the hotel was reputed to be a major point of distribution for heroin on Manhattan's Upper West Side. Almost directly across the street was an S.R.O. building of the "closed" variety which had been designated by the local police precinct as a "model S.R.O." While the "open" hotel always had people loitering in front of it, trash regularly thrown from windows, and many of the building's residents were well known to the police, the closed building presented a radically cleaner, quieter appearance and was never mentioned as a source of nuisance or anxiety by higher status residents of the area. Stations, in the S.R.O. world, are wholly socially defined.

Initial Contact with the S.R.O. World: The Gatekeepers

Since few questions are asked of one who is attempting to procure S.R.O. accommodations, and there is hardly ever any attempt at verifying a prospective tenant's claims, one's place of entry into the S.R.O. world is not necessarily a determinant of which station he might next progress to. Entrance and mobility depend, instead, upon the observable conditions of the person, the resources which he can mobilize, and the impressions and consequent judgment that the gatekeeper he first encounters makes about him.

It is these gatekeepers who occupy a pivotal place in the S.R.O. social structure. By a differential admissions policy, they ultimately decide what the character of the building will be. Although legal title to the building might change hands frequently, or the landlord may rent the property to different individuals or groups to manage, the building retains its character because the individual(s) who specifically handles the gatekeeping function generally remains with the building regardless of its change of higher management and/or ownership.

Many of these gatekeepers, whose official title is "room clerk" or "bookkeeper," have many years of tenure with the hotel. They demonstrate a notable similarity in their sociodemographic characteristics. In the eleven New York City hotels and buildings which I intensively studied, eight of the gatekeepers were Jewish women, between forty-fifty and sixty years of age, foreign-born, who had either been interred in the Nazi concentration camps (most still retain the tatooed number on their left forearm.) or fled their native lands immediately before the occupation. They came to the United States right before or directly after the war, found employment in the hotel, and have remained since then. The other three gatekeepers were men, but in all other background characteristics they were identical to the women. None live in the hotel in which they work; however, one who was a sabbath observer had a room reserved as part of her contract.

In all of the hotels, the admissions function is relegated entirely to these women. If a person should inquire about a room when the usual gatekeeper is off duty, he will be told that either the establishment is full and he should try somewhere else, or that rooms are only rented between the hours of 8:00 A.M. and 6:30 P.M.; if he is still interested, he is advised to return the following day.

The gatekeeper has a realistic picture of the existing conditions within the hotel. She demonstrates a sophisticated outlook regarding the admission of an individual who differs significantly from most of those already ensconced in the hotel. Her primary loyalty is to the organization and she clearly recognizes that the presence of such an individual could mean trouble for the establishment. Trouble is defined as calling additional notice to an already tenuous situation by police or other control agencies. The gatekeeper, in the successful execution of her role, must be able to make a number of almost instantaneous judgments about the suitability of a prospective tenant. One described her role in this way:

> This place ... you know ... it's no Waldorf, we got all sorts here. Some of them are O.K. We also got some *ganuvim* [thieves] here.... It's not as bad as some, let me tell you. You asked why I didn't give that man a room ... the little Puerto Rican fella? I didn't give him a room on account of he looked like too much of a *mensch* [gentleman] for here. That Clarence [referring to a particularly suspect tenant] would take one look at him and he would just eat him up alive.... Let me tell you, the biggest favor I did that man today was to tell him that we were full up.

Judgments are made in the opposite direction as well. An individual will approach the gatekeeper and she might judge that his appearance indicated that he was an addict, or perhaps too "tough" for the hotel. The gatekeeper's is the last word, there is no appeal and once she judges someone as ineligible, there is almost no way he can get accommodations at the hotel.

One woman who had been working at a hotel for eighteen years recounts some of her experiences and some of the cues that she looks for when interviewing a prospective tenant.

Respondent: *Boychick,* you just listen to me. When I first started here I was really a *greener* [new comer].... *Gottinu* what I didn't know ... but that was years ago. When

I first came here there was an entirely different element, but who's to say ... times change and now Mr. Bloom and Mr. T., they have to make money too.... Ah, but I've seen it change. The *Schwarzes* [black people] ... all the *Schwarzes* they all know they can't pull nothing over Bea.... I know from all their *stiplach* [tricks].

Interviewer: But Bea, exactly what do you look for?

Respondent: You remember that boy that was here yesterday ... the colored boy who wanted a room?

Interviewer: The one you thought was a narcotics addict?

Respondent: He couldn't fool me ... I know he was taking needles. [Here she paused, nodded her head with a knowledgeable expression on her face and mimed someone using a hypodermic syringe on his left elbow.]

Interviewer: But how exactly did you know?

Respondent: How do I know, how do I know anything. I use my *kepela* [head]. You look at him, he's so skinny you'd think he'd never eaten.... Also, you remember how warm it was yesterday? Who would wear such a heavy sweater on a day like that? I know, there's no fooling me—he was on needles.

It was problematic, of course, whether or not the prospective tenant was an addict. What was not at all problematic, however, was that he was defined as being an addict, and solely on the basis of this judgment was denied accommodations at the hotel.

Some gatekeepers are adept at structuring the interaction so that the prospective tenant is forced into making some revelation about himself. One woman, when confronted by young, black males who inquired about accommodations, would take out the stack of F.B.I. wanted posters that are routinely sent to large hotels, and begin leafing through them with the prospective tenant standing directly before her. On at least several occasions, she reported, the prospective guest suddenly remembered that he had already obligated himself for accommodations elsewhere. Another gatekeeper confronted the prospective tenant with the house rules, presenting them as stringently as possible. If his response was not satisfactory— usually measured in terms of docility—she would discover that the hotel was full.

Since the gatekeeper is often the most visible of the hotel's management to the tenants, it is she who is most likely to be the recipient of information about what might be happening in the building. She, of course, has direct access to the management and her judgments can be crucial in having a tenant evicted. Within the S.R.O. social system it is these persons who perhaps wield the most power. Since they persist even in the face of management/ownership changes, they assure that the nature of that building's population retains continuity over time, even though many of the individuals who had originally peopled it have left. It is in this way that the character of the several S.R.O. stations remain constant and the community retains its integration.

The S.R.O. Population: Brief Notes on its Sociodemographic Composition

At the outset of *Outposts of the Forgotten* we suggested that the typical population of the nation's S.R.O.'s are socially terminal. At this time, this should be qualified to some extent. The material in this chapter treated some of the differences between the "closed" and "open" S.R.O. buildings. The closed buildings contain a much more intact population, one that aspires to upward mobility. For this group the S.R.O.'s provide a relatively inexpensive and non-restricting (in the sense of time commitment) residence. The notion of social terminality, however, figures considerably more important tantly into our picture of the open S.R.O.'s. These are the buildings that contain a preponderance of social casualities: people with no place to go, people that we as a nation would rather forget. To complete this descriptive portrait of the S.R.O.'s, a look at some of the social and demographic characteristics of this population is appropriate.

Valid, reliable data about this population is hard to come by. The population is not one that is seen as deserving of indepth research. What data we do have generally reinforces part or all of our assumptions having to do with the nature of this population. For instance, we see that nonwhites are strongly overrepresented in this population. A majority of the S.R.O. population in New York is black. Also, the population tends to be older; in a large way we are considering people who are well into the middle and even older age cohorts. Some researchers have observed that the white population tends to be even older than the nonwhite, especially the black, population. The hypothesis employed here suggests that the white person has a greater social distance to travel than the black before he finds himself living in S.R.O.'s. Questions such as these will hopefully provide direction for future S.R.O. research.[1]

In the economic sphere, the population is, of course, a poor one. S.R.O. people tend to be employed in low status, low paying occupations or not employed at all. Their family backgrounds tend to reflect this as well; only a minority of people come from higher status backgrounds.[2]

There is a certain amount of ambiguity considering the proportion of people who are receiving public assistance or welfare in the S.R.O. population. One New York City study suggested that more than three-quarters of the population in the surveyed hotels were welfare recipients. (This figure is probably biased because people who were gainfully employed, even in marginal occupations, probably were invisible to the social workers.[3]) Other research has estimated the proportion of people receiving some sort of welfare or public assistance at around 40 percent.[4] An additional proportion, probably as high as 15 or 20%, receive some sort of fixed-income such as social security, veteran's benefits, or other kinds of disbursements. This places some very severe economic restrictions on the population.

Some of the most telling statistics, however, have to do with health. Unfortunately, here too systematic research is unavailable. It is apparent through nonsystematic observations, interviews with health professionals (such as public health nurses and social workers in the community), as well as from the small amount of research data we do have that the population is not a healthy one. In addition to widespread reports of nonspecific poor health, aches and pains, frequent upper respiratory infections, and digestive disorders and the like, substantial proportions of the population report more serious difficulties: cardiac and vascular problems are quite common, people report that it is because of a "heart condition" that they are incapable of working. People with physical debilities are quite common in the S.R.O. world. It is not uncommon to encounter amputees, deaf, and wholly or partially blinded people.

The same can be observed for mental health. Here, too, we are lacking in any objective measure or assessment. In the population, reports of mental hospitalization(s) or extensive psychiatric treatment are so common that little question or stigma is attached to mental illness in the S.R.O. world. Other indicators of mental difficulties seem to abound as well: alcohol abuse is very common.

The social workers attached to the St. Luke's project projected that some 90 percent of their case loads, that is, people in the hotels, had some sort of problem with alcohol.[5]

If data (again, for the most part unsystematic) from other cities is considered, essentially the same pattern emerges. Depending upon the area of the country, one substitutes, for instance, Spanish Americans for blacks, or one substitutes Native Americans (Indians) for other nonwhite groups. Regardless of the locale, it's clear that the core population of the S.R.O. world contains poor, unhealthy, predominately nonwhite and underclass people. This is a population that is excessively troubled, that holds little hope of being able to initiate any kind of significant change or self-improvement. It is a population to whom we are reluctant to provide anything but the barest supportive services, believing that there is little that they can benefit from what resources we would be willing to expend upon them.

NOTES

1. Barbara Hoffberg and Joan Shapiro, "S.R.O. Service-Research Project," mimeographed (New York: Columbia University Urban Center and St. Luke's Hospital Center's Division of Community Psychiatry, 1969), pp. 26–27.

2. Ibid.

3. Ibid.

4. Center for N.Y.C. Affairs, op. cit., pp. 7–8.

5. Barbara Hoffberg and Joan Shapiro, "S.R.O. Service-Research Project."

Chapter 4

The Caretakers: Helpers and Exploiters of the S.R.O. World

Following the design of the research, we are becoming increasingly more involved with the S.R.O. world. Our interest began on the most distant level when we considered ecological statements about the spatial distribution of S.R.O.'s within a larger urban area. We then examined newspaper accounts of various aspects of the S.R.O. problem, followed by a shift to a closer, more detailed portrait of what physically constitutes an S.R.O., starting from a street-level glance to a walk through the halls, and then into some of the rooms. The chapter to follow advances even a step closer to the S.R.O. world: it will consider those persons who enter and operate in the S.R.O. world on a part-time basis. S.R.O.'ers look to these persons for support, assistance, and occasionally guidance. They might best be described as serving in the role of the "caretakers" of the S.R.O. world.

This chapter first examines and discusses the meaning and operationalization of the sociological concept of "caretakers." From there, several different types of caretaking and caretakers regularly involved in the S.R.O. world will be considered. In this discussion we will develop a dual perspective, initially seeing the S.R.O. world through the eyes of the cared-for and then those of the caretaker.

Caretakers and Caretaking

Social scientists interested in the study of communities have postulated that every society has "caretakers"; that is, institutions or individuals who offer various services and different kinds of care to its members.[1] In *The Urban Villagers*, Herbert Gans's study of a community located within a metropolis, the concept of "caretakers" was considered with the intention of deriving an operational scheme for its use. The sociology of "caretaking" is similar to gift-giving in the way Georg Simmel saw the exchange.[2] Both are similar because they are not altruistic acts, but, rather as the embodiment of reciprocal relationships in which the caretaker provides service in exchange for a material or nonmaterial return.[3] This achieves even greater significance when we realize that the relationship of the beneficiary to his benefactor has become almost fully institutionalized, and in most cases (perhaps the most notable of which is the urban poor) the shift has been from "charitable" individuals to complex organizations. One ramification of the formalization of this relationship has been the legitimation of "officially" labeling the recipient of assistance (or care) with designation that is meaningful to both the caretaking organization and the larger society.[4] The imposition of any such social label can have a profound and enduring effect on the designated person.

In describing the interaction of the caretakers with the community, the following typology proved helpful.

> 1. The *service oriented* who helps the client achieve goals he cannot achieve by himself.
> 2. The *market oriented* who gives the client what he presumes the client wants, and as such is similar to a commercial relationship.
> 3. The *missionary* who endeavors to have the client adopt his own norms and values.[5]

In addition to orientation, caretakers might further be divided into the dimension of external or internal. *External* caretakers are persons whose role or occupation demands that they physically enter the S.R.O. world only intermittently. While they are normally active in the area of providing service to other residents, they will only enter the S.R.O.'s when called upon to perform a specific service or function. The *internal* caretakers, conversely, are those who are there all of the time. Their occupational role is constructed primarily around the S.R.O.'s Caretaking activity, as it affects the S.R.O. world, should not be viewed in an overly limited context. Not only do the caretakers respond to demands made upon them by their profession and/or occupation, but much of what is done, as well as how it occurs, reflects the delicate political balance affecting the S.R.O.'s as well as the larger, more affluent community.

The manifestations of this delicate balance might best be seen through the interaction of the S.R.O. caretakers and the larger community. While the caretakers' primary orientation is towards doing something *for* the population they serve, another group is oriented towards doing something *to* the populace which has been defined as troublesome. This other group is committed to the *containment* of the S.R.O. phenomenon and the S.R.O.'er. On the policy level, these persons and/or groups endeavor to prohibit conventional, non-S.R.O. housing from being renovated into S.R.O.-type units. On the social level, they wish to limit the sphere of personal autonomy enjoyed by the S.R.O.'er solely to the confines of the welfare hotel or S.R.O. building. This second group has been designated as "containers." "Containers" are most often persons who have organized into civic improvement groups or block-associations with the expressed purpose of limiting the operation of S.R.O. dwellers and combatting the urban blight brought about by S.R.O.'s expanding into new areas.

The interaction of the groups increases the possiblity of role strain which is built into the caretaking role.[6] Containers look to caretakers to provide the social machinery to effect the actual restrictions of the S.R.O. dwellers. In many cases, then, the caretaker recognizes that his definition-of-situation within the role definition is established for him by the socially more powerful container. Since this is the case, his client's needs and best interests become subordinated to another goal, which necessarily encourages a very different type of interaction between caretaker and client. Behaviorally, the structured strain points clearly to the two worlds in conflict. Each group (S.R.O.'ers and high status area residents) has articulated its needs and/or wants, and looks to the caretakers for their satisfaction. Since the caretaker is (at the very minimum) partially controlled by one group and has to regularly interact with the other, he feels the most profound effect of this structured strain. As such, he can be seen in a truly marginal position.

When the interactions of these groups are considered, two separate dimensions should be considered:

> 1. The mechanisms that allow persons separated by much social distance from the S.R.O.'s to still exert a tremendous impact on the quality of life there; and
> 2. The mechanisms responsible for defining the interactional and/or social boundaries of the S.R.O. world.

Both of these questions are relevant to several of the sociological questions raised in the preceeding chapters. The construction and maintenance of boundaries is undoubtably a major concern for any group; the group must be able to define "safe" areas of operation. Both caretakers and containers play a significant role in the creation and maintenance of these boundaries. In addition, we have discovered that the caretakers are often instrumental in the formation and maintenance of social networks. It is the interaction of these caretakers and containers which constitutes the embodiment of exogeneous forces at work, constructing, maintaining and (partially) regulating the S.R.O. world.

External Caretakers

S.R.O.'ers spend much time discussing "The People Downtown." The people downtown are the various functionaries charged with providing some service for the S.R.O.'er. These functionaries are radically distinguished from "The Welfare," that is, the Department of Social Services, which dispatches a corps of (DOSS) investigators (now called "caseworkers") who make at least the pretense of providing social work services.

The people downtown are faceless. Periodically, however, S.R.O.'ers are compelled to deal with them, in such contexts as the necessity to claim or adjust Social Security disbursements, pensions, and Veterans benefits. The arrival of an official looking, windowed envelope evokes fear and anxiety in most; they wonder "what do they want now." Since many S.R.O.'ers find it difficult to understand the communication, which is invariably written in bureaucratese, it is ignored. Subsequent letters generally receive the same treatment and the S.R.O.'er is then shocked if the stipend that he is used to receiving fails to arrive.

Few S.R.O.'ers have much understanding about the nature of a bureaucracy, and "those people"—the bureaucrats—are seen as being imbued with malevolent omnipotence. These perceptions are soon transformed into a feeling of alienation which manifests itself, typically, in two of the recognized facets of the phenomenon: a subjective belief that one is *powerless;* and the perception that one's actions are irrelevant to any outcome, or *meaninglessness.* In both of these it is a condition of "normlessness" which causes the member to seriously question the utility or efficacy of any specific behavior.[7]

For the S.R.O.'er confronted by a situation he neither understands nor feels he can overcome, the response to the attendant alienation is essentially an adaptive one. The member begins casting about for a definition-of-situation which will allow him to integrate the information about what is happening to him into his existent belief system. Some of these adaptive patterns will be discussed below.

The simplest, perhaps, is a straightforward resignation to a situation that is perceived as impossible. One young man, for example, who was attempting to have the Veterans Administration acknowledge his claim of service-connected physical disability described it:

> Those people . . . those people just twist and turn you. Just turn you around in any direction at all. Any shape . . . whatever they want . . . it really doesn't make any difference. They don't really care. You don't make no difference to them . . . it's all the same, anyhow.

For this young man, the alienation manifests itself as a feeling of hopelessness. Although he understood that his desires and needs were not being adequately met, he expressed neither rancor nor the will to do anything to change the system. Instead, his feeling of powerlessness is turned inwards and he accepts the inevitability of losing both the battle and the war. These persons tend to scale down their lives and express a willingness to live within the confines of rules that they neither believe in nor understand.

For other S.R.O.'ers "the system" assumes anthropomorphic proportions. Much like Don Quixote, they occupy a good part of their time tilting—though in imagination only—the bureaucratic windmill. Their talk invariably concerns lawsuits which are due to be instigated imminently, or the implication that a new, even, higher official has interested himself in their case and full restitution is at

hand. Some carry on their person, at all times, all of the correspondence between themselves and the intransigent agencies. The
context of the communication is accorded little importance; the
official letterhead and inside address, ascertaining that it is indeed
the property of the embattled member, are the most significant
parts.

Within the S.R.O. community those in litigation have their
position within the social structure well demarcated. They define
themselves as being somewhat different than other S.R.O.'ers. They
use the accumulating file of official correspondence to set themselves apart. Since the litigious state is defined as an almost never-
ending one, the member hardly need wonder about what next to do.
Although his social position within the S.R.O. world is assured,
most remain acutely conscious, even jealous, of the social distance
they have established between themselves and other S.R.O.'ers.

The social marginality of those in litigation can be perceived, as
well, by their attraction to persons coming from outside of the
S.R.O. world. They look to any outsider, especially if he is white, to
further validate their claim of distinction. Inexperienced DOSS
personnel are often deceived by their superficially elaborate
schemes and grandiose claims, believing them to be among the most
intact of the S.R.O. dwellers.

This initial i fatuation, however, quickly turns to disenchant-
ment, which, in turn, leads the professional(s) to abandon these
persons and their needs. The young, middle-class social workers
report that they experience particular frustration by their client's
seeming acceptance of the *form* of bureaucratic exchange without
an understanding of either the process or a real commitment to
positive change. When a caseworker was interviewed concerning
her refusal to accompany a client to an agency hearing to act as his
advocate, she reported:

> Worker: Why didn't I go downtown with Rundell? You really
> don't understand yet ... Rundell, Clarkson, Monk,
> and those others we were talking about—I just don't
> want to waste any more of my time. They really
> don't know what they want. I remember going
> downtown for a fair hearing, we [the client and
> worker] had talked about [it] for weeks before. And
> you know what happened? We arranged to meet
> downtown. I even gave him money—out of my own
> pocket—to get his clothes cleaned. But he didn't

show, I waited and waited and then I finally just
gave up—I felt like such a fool.

Interviewer: Perhaps he just got lost on the way downtown? Or
couldn't find the office?

Worker: No, that wasn't the trouble. He didn't even try to go.
... I found out he spent the day up in 407 [the room
of a friend] drinking wine and generally carrying-on.
No, the fact is he didn't even bother to try. The next
time something like this happened I decided that I
would personally accompany the client downtown.
I made the necessary appointments, we [the worker
and client] prepared the case, and I didn't let him
out of my sight the entire day. We got downtown,
checked in and had to wait. When our case was
finally called, Hugh [the client] made such an ass out
of himself that I was embarrassed to death. After the
hearing all he could say was: "Well, Mrs. Klein,
guess I really showed 'em this time—ain't nobody
messin' wid me no more—no how!" I couldn't even
tell him that all the time we spent preparing had
gone to waste and that the hearing officers probably
didn't have the faintest idea about what he was
ranting and raving about—what good would it do?
And just as I had expected, we received word [one is
advised of the decision by mail] that his case had
received a negative disposition.

Interviewer: What happened then?

Worker: Funniest thing ... I was sure that Hugh was just
going to freak out. But ever since the hearing he's
been running around the hotel—talking to anyone
who will listen about his great "triumph." When we
found out about losing the case, he just didn't seem
bothered at all—he didn't even stop telling the story
... I just don't understand these people.

Within the confines of the S.R.O. world, however, his behavior is
quite understandable. The S.R.O.'ers seldom look to official bodies
or agencies for redress of greviance; few seriously expect that any
such efforts could be fruitful. The recognition of the litigation itself,
however, does provide a place for them within the S.R.O. community. For many, the on-going legal process becomes a way of life.

One is able to overcome the feeling of simply marking time and perhaps convince himself that he actually seems to be going somewhere. Winning, for the most part, comes to be defined as secondary to sustaining the process. Moreover, the winning, in effect, occurs outside the boundaries of the S.R.O. world, while the member looks solely to his community for support and sustenance. It is not so much that winning removes him from the community, but that the winning terminates the process; and with the removal of his access to the process a condition of personal disorganization or *anomia* can be precipitated.

Affirmation is the third adaptation to the alienation experience. This adaptation takes the form of an almost childlike belief in the "goodness" of the system. While persons exhibiting either of the former adaptations report a feeling of tension or opposition between themselves and "the system," "affirmers" look to the system in a much more positive way. They are unlike working class groups whose support of the system, and their place in it, is built upon strong ideological and traditional underpinnings. The unquestioning acceptance and childlike trust manifested by the affirmers arises as an adaption to the alienation they feel. The system is not perceived within an Orwellian "Big-Brother-is-watching-you" context, but rather as a benevolent, almost indulgent parent. One elderly woman was interviewed right after she (and many others) had received notification that Social Security disbursements would be lowered:

Interviewer: Mama, do you know what this letter says?

Respondent: It's ... eh ... a letter ... it's a letter from the Social Security.

Interviewer: The letter says that your payments will be lower in the future—almost $10 a month less.

Respondent: Eh ... is that what the letter says? They take care of their Mama ... they always take care of their Mama—I don't worry none. ...

No amount of probing during the course of the interview could elicit a response that was any different. While the woman was at times outwardly hostile to the hotel's management and occasionally hostile to DOSS caseworkers, she had an unshakable confidence in the goodness and/or fairness of the large bureaucracies. Rational judgment and indignation about inadequate allotments, and cutbacks on allotments were all subordinated to an affirmation of the

system's munificence. It appears that the alienation and its attendant *anomia* engendered the creation of such a belief system. This
belief system found mutual reinforcement within the S.R.O. world
by bringing together members willing to share a similar definition-
of-situation.

Realism is the last and least often encountered response to the
most distant caretakers. It is a frank understanding of both the
political and social realities of the situation. When members of this
group are interviewed, one hears neither the hopelesness nor
bravado characteristic of the other groups. One elderly man, for
example, would carefully read the social security information
column carried in one of the syndicated papers. He was able to
report fairly recent and apparently accurate developments in the
laws relating to social security and veterans' benefits. He had a clear
picture of what his rights were and the processes that would be
necessary to alter his present status. For him and a small number of
others, the "people downtown" were neither good nor bad but part
of a cumbersome, complex organization, with which they realized
only coexistence was possible.

Although the potential for action and effect on the S.R.O. world is
greater by the city and state bureaucracies than the federal agencies,
S.R.O.'ers tend to report even greater social distance from them.
While the Veteran's and Social Security Administrations are seen as
having something tangible to offer, state and municipal agencies,
ostensibly created to protect their citizens, are viewed with extreme
cynicism. S.R.O.'ers freely express the belief that the various
inspectors and agency representatives are "all on the take" and that
the hotel owners and/or managers completely "have them in their
pockers." One resident reported:

Respondent: Lookit here, you don't know yet! You don't know
but the half of it man. Mr. T. and Solly they got the
whole thing really together. That 'spector which was
here yesterday, how come you think he didn't go up
to the fourth floor? They [the managers] just said
"now look here, you give us a break here, and you
know we take care of you."

Interviewer: Did you hear all this yourself?

Respondent: Sho 'nuff did! I back behind the office there, cleaning
the toilet. When Solly saw me they all got quiet and

> then started talking Jewish. I knew they didn't really care—guess the 'spector got a little jumpy.

S.R.O. residents express virtually no anger or bitterness at the apparent corruption. Collusion between muncipal personnel and hotel management was considered to be the norm; so much the case that few residents could envision a situation in which someone was not paying-off someone else. Since subcultural expectations regarding living conditions are so minimal, the same rancor or quiet despair characterizing the reaction to caretakers responsible for financial sustenance is just not generated and/or sustained. The relationship between S.R.O. residents and distant state and city bureaucracies might best be characterized as an unspoken conspiracy of mutual disregard; anything else would prove unworkable.

Service- and Market-Oriented Caretakers

Some people, through either fate or design, come into direct contact with the S.R.O. world and its inhabitants in a caretaking capacity. While many of these transactions are governed by purely commercial norms in which the terms and context of the exchange are set well in advance of the incident, as great a number involve a complex social interaction in which each party attempts to establish control by evolving a specific definition-of-situation.[8] Most of the caretakers involved in these interactions would fall into the "service-" or "market-oriented" categories.

In addition to the orientation of the caretakers, a temporal dimension must be considered. For many providing the caretaking services, the S.R.O. community represents but a small part of their public. These caretakers are active in the S.R.O. world only intermittently: they arrive when needed (or demanded), provide service, and leave. Conversely, for other caretakers, through happenstance or choice, the S.R.O.'er is the only public they serve. These different types of caretaking situations will be discussed from both the perspective of the caretaker and the cared-for.

For the S.R.O'er, as well as for many other under- and lower-class groups, attitudes and interactions with the police often carry ambivalent definitions. The lower classes, for example, request the police to perform a variety of services. Police are looked to for help in times of trouble, crisis, and indecision.[9] With equal frequency, police are regarded as "The Man," and as such are observed warily;

many S.R.O.'ers fear and distrust the police and are extremely reluctant to cooperate with them in any way.

The police view the S.RO.'er and his world with the same ambivalence. The law enforcement officer, responding to a call for noncriminally related assistance (that is, medical) in a typical slum hotel, finds himself both compassionately touched and repelled by the conditions in which he finds the people living. Many officers, however, define the S.R.O's population as a threat to their physical safety. This implies that every response to a call from an S.R.O. will be dominated by this definition of situation. Police, for example, are routinely dispatched to the locale in which medical assistance has been requested. The officers are expected to assess the severity of the situation and then put in the request for an ambulance, if such is indicated. Even on a routine call like this, made during daylight hours, the officers enter the buildings carrying their nightsticks. Some officers have even been observed loosening their service revolvers in their holsters as they enter a hotel lobby.

Interaction between S.R.O. residents and police is dominated by the social distance separating them. S.R.O. residents report that the police are generally hostile, are not interested in helping them, will verbally abuse them, will purposely not hear or will misunderstand their requests, and will generally treat them in a manner they define as contemptuous.

In one such typical encounter, an obese, elderly black woman, who was almost paralyzed by a chronic arthritic disability, had fallen off her bed. She was so incapacitated that it was impossible for her to even crawl across the floor to the door. For almost three days her only source of nourishment was obtained through rags tossed into the sink (located at the side of her bed) and then squeezed into her mouth. After the fall, she had become almost entirely incontinent and was forced to lie in her own excreta. Eventually she was discovered by one of the hotel's maids. The maid quickly notified the social service office in the hotel and the worker who was dispatched immediately placed a call for medical assistance. Recall that since an ambulance cannot be called directly, but only by a law enforcement officer, the call for the ambulance brought two uniformed patrolmen to the scene approximately twenty minutes later. The senior officer, a very large man, strode into the room and towered over the woman lying on the floor. Although her agony and distress were readily apparent, she brightened visibly when she saw the policeman. He responded, however, by looking down at her and inquiring in a loud, almost belligerent manner, "What 'cha doing on the floor, honey?" Then his partner in a low but still audible voice said:

> You go back to the car and call the ambulance. I gotta get out of here ... the fucking place is worse than a pig sty. If'n I don't get out, the smell is gonna make me puke all over the place.

When other residents of the hotel heard the recount of this incident, none expressed surprise. To the contrary, most responded with a "What else do you think could have happened?" or "If you think that was something—let me tell you about...." Little or no anger or disappointment was voiced against the police. Police are, in effect, considered as a class: they are neither good nor bad per se, but they are to be avoided—and approached, albeit cautiously, when needed.

Police attitudes towards the S.R.O. population exhibited the same kind of ambivalence. While violence and crime are unquestionably part of their concern, they invariably find themselves confronting the ugliest and worst parts of life (and death) in the S.R.O. world. In order to keep functioning in the S.R.O.'s police have to learn how to turn their feelings off. An interview with an experienced patrolman who had done service throughout the city revealed the following:

Interviewer: We were talking about duty in this precinct ... how it differs from tours elsewhere—could you tell me some more about it?

Patrolman: OK, you get used to a lot of things in this job. You never know if you're gonna get blown away when you go through a door. But that's all over when you draw one of these gigs [referring to police work in ghetto/poverty precincts]. Somehow you get used to people hurting each other ... the cuttings, bustups ... it ain't really too bad 'til you hear it happens to one of the guys [fellow officers]—then you get pissed because you know it could have been you.

Interviewer: I hear you ... but how is work here different?

Patrolman: I don't know if it's really different ... there just seems to be more of it. OK, you remember that dead junkie we had a coupla weeks ago? [the interviewer allowed that he did.] It's we got stuck with it.... It wasn't our job after we called the hospital, yet we still got stuck with it.

Interviewer: Why don't you tell me about it.

[Here the officer sat back, took a long drag on his cigarette, and his face clouded for a moment before he began talking.]

Patrolman: OK ... we knew the guy, he had a pretty good habit, he knew his shit so I think somebody gave him a "hotshot" [heroin to which a powerful poison has been added; or of such a strength that a fatal overdose is almost a certainty]. OK, you guys gave us the call 'cause somebody complained about the smell. OK, the guy musta been dead for more than a week. . . . He was blown up to twice his size and his skin was beginning to crack. . . . Jesus, bugs crawling all over him. . . . He still had the needle stuck in his arm ... what a mess. . . . Mike [his partner] got sick as soon as we got that door open. OK, we called for the wagon [the ambulance] and the guys from downtown [the coroner's office]. The boys come on up and flatly refuse to touch the guy. . . . We all knew that as soon as somebody would move him he would just blow up all over the place.

Interviewer: What did you do then?

Patrolman: Well, we stood around and argued about who would bag the guy [a large plastic bag is used to contain decomposing bodies in situations like this]. Finally I said to Mike "OK, what the hell, we can't stand around here all day, let's go get it over with." What a mess! Mike stands at the bottom of the bed with the bag held open and I pick up the front of the bed so he'll slide into the bag. . . . Whew! This was one helluva mess!

It's not that this kind of incident is unique to work in the S.R.O. world but that police work seems to involve the disposition of more of them. Police officers report that the only way they can maintain themselves in the environment is by removing any possible emotional effect from their work.

That episode begins to point to the complexity of police relations with, and attitudes about S.R.O'ers. On the most basic level, most officers report a dissatisfaction with the concentration of S.R.O.'s and welfare hotels located in the area. They see the buildings in much the same way as many of the area's other residents: as concentrations of criminal, mentally ill and seriously troubled persons whose mere presence is a threat to both the solidarity and safety of the neighborhood. For the police the presence of the welfare hotels is seen as yet another complicating variable in servicing an extremely high density, heterogeneous, and at times racially tense area. In an interview, a high ranking police officer advanced what he considered the majority police opinion that if the S.R.O.'s (and their bothersome population) "would just slide off into the Hudson [river] no one at all—especially us—would miss them." The police, however, have recognized the permanent existence of the S.R.O.'s in the West Side and have taken steps towards coexistence. One of the precincts servicing the area has established a public relations officer who is charged with providing liaison between the police and the various grassroots community organizations. This officer occasionally visits a community service project created to aid S.R.O. residents in a certain locale. During the holiday season precincts have opened their doors to neighborhood children, providing refreshments and toys. Although the police claim the parties are open to *all* of the area's children, it is problematic whether many of the children living in the S.R.O.'s and welfare hotels ever find their way into them.

For most police, however, the social distance separating them from the S.R.O's and their people proves an almost insurmountable barrier to meaningful social interaction. The police, in order to remain effective in their work, have had to drastically separate themselves from the S.R.O.'ers and their way of life. From the S.R.O.'er's perspective, this social distance and its interactional concomitants can be illustrated by the "safe-buildings" incident.

The residents of one hotel became extremely anxious because within a one month period two brutal murders had occurred in the building. The first was the result of a drug transaction in which a seller was shot and killed because he had reneged on a large deal by substituting dilutant for the entire quantity of heroin he had promised to deliver. The second, however, was the one that thoroughly enraged the S.R.O. community. A popular young woman, who was almost seven months pregnant, was brutally beaten and stabbed (the wounds were in the abdomen) to death. As expected, the crime thoroughly shocked the community's collective conscience and members began demanding "that something should be done." Since the area of law enforcement is entirely outside the capabilities of S.R.O. dwellers to affect, the community was forced to turn to a preventive response. The social service staff contacted the local police precinct house (which coincidentally was having a "safe-streets month"), and asked what might be done to assure the physical safety of the hotel's residents. The public relations officer was delighted to hear that the Enfer's (the hotel) residents were interested and promised to arrange for a police "security specialist" to come to the hotel to address the residents. In anticipation of the meeting, the caseworkers began making large posters announcing the event. Interest was running so high that other residents in the hotel approached the social service staff amd inquired whether, even though they "were not on the welfare," they might attend the meeting. The hotel's management was interested in the meeting; besides authorizing the use of the large ballroom, they agreed to contribute funds for the evening's refreshments.

The evening arrived and the attendance was well over one hundred and fifty people; some even came from other hotels. The police arrived: the community relations officer who was a sergeant, two other sergeants, and the lecturer, a captain. None of the policemen were in uniform. Most of the group were flashily dressed (the captain was wearing a pink ruffled shirt and an iridescent blue suit) and were white. The officers spurned the social service staff's offer to tour the building so that they might get some picture of what conditions were actually like, saying: "all these joints are the same anyway."

The meeting was then called to order and the captain proceeded to deliver a prepared talk. His speech touched upon basic security factors which, if followed, would help assure the citizen's safety in a wide variety of situations. The captain proved to be a dynamic and forceful speaker. He gave numerous examples illustrating each of the points he was making and could periodically punctuate his talk with amusing anecdotes concerning doormen, cab drivers, delivery men, several recent fine-arts thefts, and a famous jewel robbery which he had worked on several years ago.

The talk, however, was not well received. From **the** outset it became very clear that the talk's content was almost entirely irrelevant to problems of S.R.O. or welfare hotel living. Few S.R.O.'ers, for example, regularly take taxi cabs "home from an evening at the theatre." Even fewer welfare hotels have doormen who can be told what time the resident is expected home and should be alerted for his or her arrival. The captain was very definite in telling female residents that they should remove their first names from their mail boxes in order to stymie attempts to prey on lone women. What the captain failed to realize, however, was that one of the most distinguishing features of a S.R.O. or welfare hotel is its complete absence of publicly accessible mail boxes. The lecturer mentioned recent security advances such as pick-proof magnetic locks. S.R.O. residents, however, rarely have enough money for the implementation of such devices and, moreover, most breaking and entering occurs through "raw jaw" methods of simply kicking the door down after ascertaining the room is empty. In almost every aspect, the lecture was prepared for and directed at the middle and upper-middle class residents who share the area with the S.R.O.'ers. On the part of the hotel's residents, little or no usable information was received.

The final part of the incident occurred during the question-and-answer period. Few questions bearing directly on the talk's content were raised. People concerned about the hotel's narcotics problem were given platitudinous answers about how the police were doing everything that could be done. Other residents complained that police were very slow in answering calls for assistance, saying that often two or three calls had to be made before any help arrived. These too were treated in the same way.

Complicating a situation that was already beginning to evidence strain were parts of the audience who were becoming increasingly more inebriated as the evening progressed. Those familiar with the S.R.O. world have come to recognize that the drinking of alcoholic beverages is to be expected at any sort of gathering. Consequently, professionals have come to expect and will tolerate a certain amount of moderately erratic behavior. The police, however, do not possess this familiarity and its concomitant tolerance. From the beginning of the meeting, one could observe the pint bottles of wine being passed back and forth in the back of the room. The guests and speakers noticed this as well, and one officer remarked to a social service staff member that it was making them all (that is, the police) rather uncomfortable. It was during the question-and-answer period, though, that the full difficulty was realized. Other than extemporaneous comments and loud and occasionally raucous responses from the floor, the police endured the general level of disorganization fairly well.

The meeting assumed an entirely new tone when one man asked a rather difficult legal question concerning criminal liability involved in a self-defense action, and the police speaker declined to give an answer, saying he was not competent to speak to the issue. The issue proved handy to crystallize the nascent feelings of resentment towards the police. Some of the men began talking about having "guns in their rooms," saying "just let anyone come messin' wid my door and they'd be iced right there." The other people at the meeting clearly understood that the basis of each claim derived from an elaborate ceremony of bravado; each man attempting to out do the others. Since many of them had been drinking for several hours, some of the claims were extraordinary. In addition, having the police (the symbols of authority par excellence) as a captive audience, forced to listen to whatever claims were being made, tended to exacerbate the grandiosity of the comments being made. While the other residents recognized what was happening and treated it as a performance staged for their entertainment—at times even spurring the participants on with shouts of "Right On!," "You tell 'em, baby" and the like—the police treated both the claims and the audience response with absolute seriousness. When one man, for example, claimed to have a "Thompson submachine gun" in his room, the officer responded by earnestly saying that the possession of such a weapon violated several laws (he quoted the appropriate statutes), and made the individual liable for a long prison term if caught and convicted. This continued until the social service staff realized that the situation was gradually deteriorating. At that point the meeting was adjourned. The police left, expressing their disappointment and dissatisfaction with the way they thought things had gone, one reporting that the social service staff "sure had a load of weirdos to look after." Similarly, the hotel's residents were very disappointed with the evening, some reporting that the police "had worked some sorta number on them" and "weren't a shits-bit interested" in either their concerns or problems. After the police left, the men active in the final part of the meeting went around recounting and embellishing some of the stories and "giving skin" (that is, slapping each other's upturned palms) congratulating each other.

On the level of person-to-person interaction, a similar pattern of noncommunication can be observed. When talking with S.R.O.'ers, police officers seldom establish or maintain direct eye contact. This was observed during some personal dealings I had with the police. Throughout the length of the interaction, the officer avoided any eye contact, looking over my shoulder instead. When a concentrated and persistent attempt was made to hold the officer's glance, he signified his absolute desire to terminate the encounter. When interviewed about this phenomenon, most S.R.O. residents will report its occurrence; few, however, appear to be at all bothered by it. This, along with many other factors relating to the police, is simply taken for granted.[10]

Medical

Like other underclass and poor people, S.R.O.'ers have only limited access to medical care. For the S.R.O.'ers in this study, the bulk of either emergency or acute services was provided by the emergency rooms of two large hospitals, each of which had part of the Upper West Side designated as its catchment area. S.R.O.'ers complain about very long waits to receive medical care, the discontinuity of service deriving from seeing a different physician at each visit, and the impersonality of care organized around the utilization of emergency rooms and hospital clinics. In this way too, S.R.O.'ers are like the other poor people.

In addition to the hospital-based services available, S.R.O.'ers have supplementary sources of medical care. This care is provided in two ways: the first is through the offices of medical caretakers, such as physicians, visiting nurses, specialized social workers, and pharmacists; and the second is through a folk-derived system which incorporates a combination of folk and scientific elements. These caretakers, their work and orientation, will be discussed directly below; the operation of the indigenous curing system will be examined in the following chapter.

For S.R.O. residents, service-oriented care, if available, is provided by visiting nurses and psychiatric social workers involved in the aftercare phase of treatment. The visiting nurse's caseload is composed of those persons who, upon discharge from a hospital, require regular aftercare, but are not as yet ambulatory enough to make clinic visits. The visiting nurse's duties are quite similar to nursing in any other setting. In the hotels, nurses regularly administer hypodermic vitamin therapy, change surgical dressings, and execute any doctor's orders. A special service provided by the nurses in the hotels is visiting newborn infants and their mothers. The child's development and progress is monitored during the first several weeks along with the mother's postpartum recovery.

The persons providing psychiatric aftercare are primarily M.S.W.'s or master's level clinical psychologists. While these workers seldom administer any therapy per se, they monitor the ex-patient's posthospital adjustment, assess the adequacy of his medication (which was most often major tranquilizers), provide generalized assistance (such as filling out forms, contacting potential employers, etc.), and provide whatever counseling appeared to be indicated at the time of the visit.

While both the visiting health nurse and the psychiatric social worker each have a predetermined caseload, if any special assistance by persons not on their caseload is requested, they usually respond within loosely established limits. In these cases, informal counseling, with an appropriate referral, was the service most often provided.

In most S.R.O.'s, these caretakers arrive at regular intervals, execute the specifics of their indicated tasks (that is, service the persons on their caseload) and depart for another building and the patients there. Part of the reason that they do not provide more services to the general community is that there is simply not enough time. The caretakers cannot take time to convince someone that he either *does* have a problem, or that help, which the S.R.O.'er might define as acceptable, is actually available. Instead, the interaction is necessarily limited to a quick, essentially impersonal referral to an agency or institution. To the S.R.O.'er who lives in an intensely personal-oriented world, such behavior is deemed entirely unacceptable. The source of the referral and the manner in which it is introduced are often the major criteria used by the S.R.O.'ers to determine the appropriateness of the advice offered, or even the quality of the service which he can expect to receive.

The case of a hotel in which a social service project had been established was somewhat different. The caretakers in that situation were charged with providing service to the entire building. In order to best effect this goal, all the specialists as well as the full complement of Department of Social Service caseworkers (five altogether) converged on the building on a designated day each week. During the course of one of these work days, special interest discussion groups for the hotel's residents, led by one of the workers, would be held; the caseworkers would make special referrals to the medical personnel (who, at the time of the study, were limited to a visiting nurse and a psychiatric social worker); and a tenant's meeting and free supper—open to anyone residing in the building—would be held in conclusion of the day's activities. The philosophy underlying the program was aimed at transforming the hotel into as much of a therapeutic community as possible. According to this plan, all of the participating professionals were to work with the DOSS caseworkers, and with each other, so that effective, individualized treatment plans for the residents might be formulated and carried through.

It was believed that this could be best accomplished if the entire morning was devoted to a staff meeting and case conference. This time was used to discuss plans for future activities and problems involved in the management of difficult cases. In addition, the staff meeting was expected to function in ways similar to an encounter or sensitivity training group by improving the intrateam communication. It was anticipated that this exercise would have a salutory effect on the entire staff (especially the DOSS caseworkers) by establishing an atmosphere more conducive to efficient interpersonal functioning, which, in turn, would reduce or resolve any personal incompatability, philosophical differences, and any other such problems.

The theory, however, never achieved realization. The professionals claimed that too much time was being spent in conference. When the project was younger, and several different private social work agencies were actively involved, a much higher level of coordination was required. Now, however, with just a few agencies actively involved (and their involvement limited to part-time staff placements), the attempt to maintain the previous level of organization was unrealistic, even counterproductive. The professionals reported that rather than spending the entire morning involved in a case conference of which, they believed, but a small part was at all relevant to the work they had to do—their time at the hotel could be more fruitfully utilized directly by its residents.

The permanent DOSS staff, similarly, had ambivalent feelings about the meetings; while there was a vague agreement that the meetings were in some way "necessary," no one was able to quite define why or in what way. Decisions and case assignments were made in a fairly routinized way, since the caseworker's administrative prerogatives were steadily constricting. The improved functioning-through-human-relations plan was ineffective as well. While the plan called for improvement in the organizational ambience through openness and honesty, the time allocated to this exercise proved to be too little and too far apart. Rather than being meliorative, the meetings proved to be more disruptive to the organization's functioning. Animosities, jealousies, and various personal dysfunctions affecting organizational functioning were raised. Once these problems surfaced, however, the group did not have the requisite skills to resolve them, and the group's integration was further threatened.

S.R.O. Residents' Views of the Service-Oriented Caretaker

From the cultural perspective held by the S.R.O.'ers, many of the service-oriented caretakers were invisible until the S.R.O. residents' lives changed in some way. For example, during an interview a resident mentioned that "the lady in the house [room] next door" had seen the visiting nurse yesterday. There was little or no shared information on how to get the nurse or any common understanding of what the nurse might be expected to do if. summoned. Conversely, the level of shared information was extremely high about the movement of outsiders within the spatial boundaries of any S.R.O. community.

On the personal level, S.R.O.'ers had little information about or understanding of the services that they were receiving. This observation was reinforced on several occasions when I accompanied a visiting nurse on her rounds. Her patients would ask about a specific medication they were receiving, and were simply told, "It's medicine ... it's good for you, now just take it." By denying the patient an active part in his own treatment and recovery, the social distance separating the caretaker from the cared-for was again reaffirmed or even increased.

The interaction between the S.R.O.'ers and social workers is even more ambiguously defined. While the S.R.O.'er is able to define the nurse as part of a greater institutional complex in some way connected to illness and disease (that is, things that are real), the social worker and her role cannot support as concrete a definition. In the S.R.O. world a very clear distinction is made between DOSS caseworkers—"investigators" as they are called—and other social workers. DOSS personnel have a specific function: it is the DOSS worker who is defined as being responsible for their biweekly stipends. For most, however, the relationship between their individual worker and the larger institutional set is at best ambiguously defined. The most common mode of interaction uniting client and worker is defined almost wholly in transactional terms: the relationship that they enjoy is essentially a fiscal one.

Money, however, is very clearly the common denominator and all but the most naive workers seem to recognize this. This was revealed during an interview with a worker who had been with the DOSS for a little more than a year:

> Remember we were talking about putting together some sort of plan for each client? Well, I really couldn't say it before, but you know, it's all just a lot of BS [nonsense]. The clients don't really care—I don't even think they listen to half of what we say to them ... all that they're really interested in is their checks. I guess if they weren't so uptight and we didn't have our little ego-games, they'd just tell us to shove it.

Other social workers in the field do not have this fiscal responsibility. They define themselves as "professionals," all either have an M.S.W. or higher academic degrees, and they see themselves in one way or another as "treating" or changing their clients. These professionals are committed to the belief that through the use of any or several modalities—such as "casework," "group work" or "community organization"—they have something to give to their clients. S.R.O.'ers who are the recipients of these services often have much more difficulty in actually seeing what it is that the caretaker is trying to do for them. Often, the definition of what constitutes "help" from the S.R.O. resident's perspective is radically different from the social worker's: the S.R.O.'ers see "help" as money or jobs—while the social worker defines "help" as treatment of some sort. Social workers working in S.R.O.'s have reported that the lack of mutual understanding is the first—perhaps even the most serious—obstacle that they have to overcome.[11]

Conversely, there is much subcultural information to draw upon when one has to have dealings with the DOSS. Certain workers, for example, are known to be "easier" than others and some are known to be "regular S.O.B.'s." Residents report that there are physicians in the area who, for a nominal fee, will falsify medical records, thereby making it possible to receive welfare assistance. I was directly referred to one such physician, a psychiatrist, who for a fee of fifty dollars would certify that a patient was temporarily incapable of work. Since the rewards offered by other social workers are much less tangible, the level of information surrounding them is significantly lower; the amount of *anomie*, therefore, affecting interaction between S.R.O.'ers and these helping professionals is necessarily greater.

Market-Oriented Caretakers

While the public health nurse, DOSS personnel, and professional social workers adhere closely to a service-oriented model, other caretakers do not. The major remaining sources of exogenous medical care are furnished by private physicians, private clinics, and pharmacies, all of which operate on an almost wholly entrepreneurial model. In the past, the medical entrepreneur has traditionally overlooked the poor as a worthwhile market. In the late 1960s, however, changes in the social security laws, the popularization of prepaid medical plans, and the extension of other medical financial assistance (in New York City primarily in the form of "Medicaid" and "Medicare") to a much larger population, made the poor active consumers of medical services.[12] The work of these market-oriented medical caretakers, their definitions of the S.R.O. world, and the perceptions that the S.R.O.'ers have of them will be discussed below.

Although a private physician is compensated through Medicare or Medicaid for his professional services, not all practicing physicians are willing to accept S.R.O.'ers as patients. Physicians complain that the four and one-half dollar ceiling (excluding medication or special services) on each visit is unrealistic.[13] Many physicians complain, as well, that often the government is too tardy in paying its bills—some report that waits of six months to a year to have their accounts fully settled are not uncommon. In interviews, some of these physicians intimated that they believe that taking "welfare cases" as patients would adversely effect their practice. Thus, for the S.R.O. resident, along with other underclass peoples, the choice of practitioners is extremely limited.

The physicians who do service the S.R.O. population tend to be old—in more than one case, doctors had come out of retirement when the medical assistance laws were put into effect—and they had very small, active practices. In interviews they reported that they had watched the neighborhood change around them and most of their patients had either left the area or died. In an interview with a physician who drew almost his entire practice from the S.R.O. hotels in the area, some of these factors were revealed. The physician was in his middle seventies, his office was in a large greystone building that still had some of the trappings of erstwhile elegance, but was now in serious disrepair; his office was in similar condition. The waiting room, although of stately proportions accented by its high ceiling and large arched windows, now had a musty quality to it. The furniture, curtains, and carpet were old and threadbare. Prints hanging on the walls, portraying great moments of medical science, had long since lost their colors and had faded to shades of yellow and grey; so too had his examining room. The furnishings were a style one seldom sees nowadays: a large nonfunctioning autoclave dominated one side of the room, an ancient refrigerator the other, the glass on some of the instrument cabinets had been broken and never replaced.

During the first interview, Dr. Sharps (the physician) claimed that he was "only interested in doing good"; that he, alone was continuing to "wage his personal war against disease and human suffering." However, in later interviews a more intimate note was elicited.

Dr. Sharps:	You wanted to know why I am still practicing. You think an old codger like me should get out of the business already, don't you? [Here he stopped and chuckled to himself for a few moments.] Well let me tell you ... I'm seventy-four years old and never felt better in my life. I retired a while ago but when Sara [his wife] passed on I just didn't know what to do with myself. Finally I said, "OK, enough's enough and I came back to work. This Medicare, I know a lot of other men [doctors] fought against it tooth-and-nail, but I have no complaints.
Interviewer:	What do you think of your practice now, doctor?
Dr. Sharps:	My practice, what do you mean my practice? Ah, how things have changed! I can remember ... now, this is going back twenty maybe thirty years now.... I can remember when it would be full of kids out there. [He waved his arm to refer to the waiting room.] Now, now I hardly see any at all.
Interviewer:	Other than few children, what are your patients like now?
Dr. Sharps:	You know my patients ... you have brought in enough by yourself. I still see some people in the neighborhood that I've known for years.... That's why I still have the same office set up—even when I was retired I still saw a few people. Most, though, just aren't here now. Not a week goes by now that I don't hear of somebody dying.... God Almighty, it seems like they're just dropping like flies....
Interviewer:	I'm sorry, I'm not sure you understand me. How do you feel about your patients now; how do you feel about what you're doing?
Dr. Sharps:	What's to feel? A patient is a patient.... They don't know anything anyway.... These colored, most aren't bad people, you know.... They're different than we are ... or just drunk all the time.... They really don't understand, some just ignorant ... but I get along with everyone. They don't need much—I do whatever I can. Again, what's to feel. They [the DOSS caseworker] call me, I come—just you make sure that they have their Medicaid card, and its up to date. A few times I remember running out and

they don't have their card or it expired and I
wouldn't touch them. Now, I know better, I just tell
you to get their cards ready. That way I can get in
and get out fast. Now, I make out ... it's not the
greatest. But, between what I put away in the past
and the money I get now I've got no complaints.

For this physician, his work in the hotels is clearly defined in
entrepreneurial terms. Although the attitudes are never explicitly
voiced, even the most casual, disinterested observer gets the
impression that this physician, and others I interviewed, define their
current patients and practice in pejorative terms. Like the S.R.O.'ers
themselves, the world has passed them by, and both are trapped in a
slowly stagnating eddy of the social structure. Both have lost the
strength to marshall the resources necessary to move themselves
back into the mainstream.

While most S.R.O.'ers are probably cognitively unclear about
what constitutes meaningful or quality medical care, the majority
report that they do find something remiss in the service they are
currently receiving. Most report serious failings, on the part of the
practitioners, in both the material and nonmaterial aspects of the
medicine. Both the S.R.O.'ers and other members (such as DOSS
caseworkers) tend to view these physicians with almost total
cynicism: "He's just in it for the money," "He don't really give a
hoot for the peoples," are rather typical of interview comments
directed at the doctors. From the S.R.O. resident's perspective the
following encounter with a physician would not be seen as atypical:

Interviewer: Clyde, what happened when you saw the doctor
                yesterday?
Respondent: I wasn't feeling too good yesterday, had a pain all
                'way through here. [He indicated his abdominal
                area.] Asked Miss L. [his caseworker] to call up a
                doctor. That ole joker, Doctor Sharps, he come, shit,
                he didn't know nothing till he read my Medicaid
                card. Then he say, "What's wrong?" I shows him
                that I got a pain here, and he say, "You'll live,
                soldier." Then he writes me a 'scription and goes.
Interviewer: Do you think that he treated you well?
Respondent: That doctor ... he outta here so fast. He don't even
                take off his hat and coat—he even left his glove

> on. . . . He don't look at me, just stands there an' taps
> his foot. . . . He weren't there but a minute.

Several weeks later the man was admitted to a hospital with a hemorrhaging stomach ulcer. His report of the medical treatment that he received from Dr. Sharps was almost identical to that of others in the community. S.R.O.'ers found it difficult to understand how a physician might examine them and make a diagnosis without the use of any medical instruments at all; often without even removing his leather gloves. Moreover, S.R.O.'ers indicated that they thought they were treated discourteously by this and other of the physicians willing to come into the hotels.

The DOSS caseworkers and others involved in generalized caretaking activities for the S.R.O. community experienced the same sort of ambivalence. Most, being middle class, had received good quality medical service so that they clearly perceived the discrepancies in the medical services available in the S.R.O.'s. Since their clients were in need of medical services that they were not able to directly provide, the exceedingly scant availability of resources in the community forced them, in order to meet the demands made upon them, to utilize services of practitioners they held in very low regard. It was these ecological constraints that had the effect of casting the physicians and other caretakers in a symbiotic relationship. Not only did they utilize these services for their clients, but they found themselves fulfilling an active case-finding function for these physicians.

The dynamics of this relationship was explained during an interview with one of the Enfer's DOSS caseworkers:

Respondent: Sharps, Blindel and that other lady doctor you see around her sometimes—you know, the one with the heavy accent—sometimes to hear them talk you'd think we've got a city full of Schweitzers! I, personally, wouldn't let them touch my dog if she were sick. I just don't know, they seem to work hard enough jumping in their Cadillacs and running from building to building. . . . I just wish they'd do something once they arrive.

Interviewer: Tell me how you feel they treat your clients.

Respondent: God, you've heard that often enough. . . . There's really nobody who's happy—or even satisfied with what's going on. It's like we're all acting out a giant script ... you know, going through the motions, almost believing it, but not really. ...

Interviewer: I'm sorry, I'm not sure I understand what you're saying.

Respondent: Well, the clients aren't happy, they say they need a doctor and then they grumble when one of these guys shows up. The other workers really don't like the way the doctors treat them. ... They say a client is ill and all the doctor does is ask about their Medicaid card. I don't know ... they say "beggars can't be choosers"—well I guess that's true enough here. I used to wish for something better. ... It used to embarrass me every time a client would complain. Now I just don't seem to hear it anymore or I just forget it a second after they leave ... what else can I do?

For many of these caretakers, being bound into this enforced symbiotic relationship engendered a large measure of role conflict. This conflict was ultimately resolved through the lengthening of the social distance separating caretakers from cared-for and increasing the amount of alienation the caretakers experienced about their work.

The Clinics

Less directly involved with providing medical caretaking service to the S.R.O. community itself, but more oriented towards the Upper West Side in general, were the several private group-practice clinics that had recently emerged. These practices are structurally similar to other group ventures, however, they recruit the bulk of their patients from persons who receive Medicare or Medicaid benefits. The clinics occupy storefronts on some of the larger avenues in the area. Lettering painted on the windows identifies the storefront as a medical clinic. In addition, these organizations, unlike the other medical practitioners in the area, have made a strong attempt to solicit the business of the Puerto Rican and other Spanish speaking peoples; each has prominent signs indicating that Spanish is spoken within, and has carefully recruited bilingual personnel to fulfill gatekeeping functions. As of yet, however, they have had but a minimal impact on the needs of the S.R.O. community.

In a large measure, this reflects the unwillingness that S.R.O.'ers have to leave the confines of their community. Like other culture-of-poverty people, S.R.O.'ers tend to be very suspicious, to the point of avoidance, of things that they are unfamiliar with. As such, these new group practice clinics have not permeated the shared culture of the S.R.O. social system and are, therefore, for the present, avoided. The irony here is that these organizations can provide a higher, more comprehensive level of medical care.

The Pharmacies

The remainder of market-oriented medical care comes to S.R.O.'ers through the many pharmacies located in the area. While the large self-service, supermarket like pharmacy has made some inroads into the Upper West Side, enough of the small, independent, "corner drug store" operations still remain to provide the type of personal-oriented services S.R.O.'ers are comfortable with. While the pharmacy is, of course, stringently regulated as to the types of medications which can be dispensed, it is often only the pharmacist who will be consulted in the event of subacute illness. Most often, cases are diagnosed and treated using over-the-counter, proprietary preparations. Several cases, however, were observed in which pharmacists dispensed antibiotics (tetracyclines) without physician's prescriptions. Not as common would be the dispensing of small amounts of minor tranquilizers and hypnotics to well-known customers complaining of "nerve trouble" or insomnia.

Owners and Managers: Major Caretakers of the S.R.O. World

Each of the caretakers discussed above could be classified by his main orientation to the S.R.O. world. Therefore, it was relatively simple to distinguish those who fulfilled service-oriented functions from those whose focus was primarily entrepreneurial or market oriented. Although there will probably always be a measure of functional autonomy manifesting itself as an overlap, the place that each caretaker occupies in the S.R.O. social structure can be reasonably well defined. This level of definition, though, is much more difficult to specify when considering the functioning of the managers and/or owners of the various. S.R.O. buildings. A tremendous amount of contradiction and strain is built into the manager's role. The manager is not simply a "building manager," responsible for the upkeep and maintenance of property; neither does his role specify that he function to maintain a high level of social control, such as a prison warden or the superintendent of a mental hospital;

nor that he provide therapy and support like a live-in counselor. Instead, to merely persevere in the S.R.O. world, he has to successfully fulfill a myriad of functions—both material and social. His training and experience directly equip him for only a scant number of these functions. This *anomic* situation has prompted one S.R.O. researcher to comment that: "The managers of these S.R.O.'s are contantly under stress. They consider themselves real estate businessmen, but they are in reality untrained directors of staffless institutions." [14]

Both the social characteristics and modes of operation of members of this group were looked at. My study is particularly concerned with understanding the definition the managers have constructed about themselves, their role, their work, and their definition of the S.R.O. world and its people. Lastly, I seek to bring the definitions that the S.R.O.'ers themselves have come to hold of these managers, and the nature of quality of the social interaction between the two into focus.

One becomes a manager of a welfare hotel or S.R.O. tenement in any of several ways: the real estate can be owned outright by an owner-manager; he can be one of several partners who own the property and he is delegated (or chooses) to manage it; the property can also be wholly owned by an individual or corporation and the manager leases the property and returns a share (percentage) of the rents received to the owners; or, the manager can be a paid employee of the owner, his salary computed on the basis of a percentage of gross rents, or otherwise contractually established. Although the scope of this research did not delineate the full extent of these patterns, several observed regularities can be described. In New York City, the last pattern, manager-as-employee, was found to be the least common. This encourages the speculation that the work is so demanding that nothing but a very high profit incentive would induce the kind of committment required. Prevalent in the larger buildings is the pattern of a separate property ownership which is then leased and operated by others. The most common pattern, however, in the moderate and small buildings, is the manager-as-owner or part-owner. In other parts of the country, manager-as-employee was a somewhat more common pattern. It was rare, however, to find a straight salary situation; generally there was sone profit-sharing arrangement. Differences in the social and demographic characteristics of persons occupying each of these managing situations were observed. In the cases of manager-as-leasee, the persons most often were native-born Americans (generally second generation). They report having had experience in the hotel business and often are simultaneously involved in other real-estate ventures (especially higher status hotels) as well. In one situation studied, one of the managers spent his time commuting between a large welfare hotel and a well kept, reputable (endorsed by the American Automobile Association and cited by Holiday Magazine) establishment located in Midtown Manhattan. In interviews he reported that although the higher status hotel was in many ways more pleasant, he still enjoyed spending time ar the welfare hotel because "something [was] always happening."

While these large hotel managers strike one as being very typical of middle level business executives, the owner-manager working in Manhattan does not. Overwhelmingly, these men tend to be immigrants. Most report coming from Central European countries. Of these, most are Jewish and came to the United States shortly after World War II. The majority report either having been in German concentration or forced-labor camps during the war; one often sees the tatooed identification number on their arms. This group is clearly middle aged, with a mean age of approximately forty-six years. Most manifest the syptoms of stress-related illness: stomach ulcers, heart disease, and other such conditions. The majority report having attempted other business ventures and then slowly settling into this aspect of the real estate field. As one recalled it:

Respondent: You want to know how first I broke into this business? Let me tell you, this now, it's a good business—a young man like you with a *Yiddishe Kupf* [Jewish head] could do really well. How much, how much will you make being a professor? [The interviewer suggested a figure here.] Let me tell you, that's just peanuts! When I came here [the United States] after the war, and I didn't know what to do with myself. In the old country I was a diamond cutter. But here I didn't know from nothing, so I lost some money. Then somebody said: "Abe, what you should look into is real estate. I have got a couple of good tips for you—and who knows ..." Well, to make a long story short, I went into something. And then, once you're into one thing others just come up. Now, me and Zalman [his partner] we own between us lotsa property. Not only this joint—*Gottinu*, the *Tsuriss* [trouble] this place gives.

Interviewer: Where was your first building? Was it like this one?

Respondent: Ah, the first ... no it wasn't like this one, it was downtown [meaning below West 72nd Street]. It was smaller, a nice place, older people they lived there, not so many of the *Schwarzes* [blacks] then. You wanted to know from where the money came from. . . . I'm not ashamed to tell you, at first most of it came from the Germans. You know, the reparations money they paid because of the camps. Then, thank God, business has been good.

The experience reported in this interview is typical of the Upper West Side's other small owner/managers. Most came to the United States shortly after the war, attempted to reestablish themselves into the same type of business they engaged in, found conditions somewhat different here and ultimately drifted into the real estate field where, as part of their diversified holdings, they found the ownership of S.R.O. type housing to be profitable. Although no hard data exists at this time, one does receive the sense that it was these war reparation payments that made possible their first business ventures. One perceives the same sense of marginality when managers in other parts of the country are considered. In places like Miami, Chicago, and Los Angeles, several of the people interviewed suggested that they first got into the hotel/real estate business in New York City and then moved. In other cities the pattern it more of a drift from marginal enterprise to marginal enterprise with work in smaller, slum hotels as yet another step in this pattern of drift.

The S.R.O.'er looks to the manager of his building to fulfill a wide variety of functions and to satisfy diverse needs. Unlike the dweller in a conventional hotel, apartment house, or even roominghouses, most S.R.O.'ers have defined their building-unit as the major focus of their daily round. Since the building's manager is the single caretaker most likely to be most often present, he necessarily becomes a major focus of social interaction. Much like the fictional Pawnbroker who had his shop in Harlem,[15] the S.R.O. manager manifests the full range of emotion possible in dealing with his tenants. He fluctuates from cruelty to extreme compassion, from indifference and contempt to warmth and sympathy, and from love to hate. As with the other caretakers, but perhaps even more so, an enormous gulf of socal distance separates him from his charges.

These managers tend to view the worldly and social deprivations of their tenants with ambivalent attitudes. On the one hand, they are conscious of the conditions characterizing their buildings and the ramifications of the multiple social problems and pathologies affecting the residents. On the other hand, however, one can observe a certain flatness of effect characterizing their response. For some, when interviewed about attitudes concerning their tenants, a racial explanation was offered. Blacks and other nonwhites were seen as inferior to the others: "We did it, why can't they;" or "The Jews have had thousands of years of oppression, they [the blacks] don't even know what they are yelling about" are often characteristic responses. For others like the Pawnbroker, the absence of effect is offered in more personal tones: "I have had more suffering here [holding up the smallest joint of his little finger] than they've known in their entire lives." While the veracity of this statement is, of course, unmeasurable, the tenacity with which this belief is held assures that the social distance separating the two will never be diminished.

The S.R.O. resident, because he has less recourse to fiscal and social assistance than the middle- or working-class person with whom he shares the area, finds himself turning more often to the building manager who has many more resources at his command. Managers, at their own discretion, can extend the tenant a line of credit, thereby making it possible for the tenant to live above his means, using his rent money for the purchase of goods and services not otherwise available. Managers will occasionally assist residents with small loans, helping to tide them over in cases of need. S.R.O.'ers, however, tend to look at these efforts with ambivalent feelings. The criteria by which the manager disburses any sort of assistance is never clearly articulated, and the attendant ambiguity functions to confirm the S.R.O. resident's belief that he is at the mercy of entirely gratuitous forces. From the manager's perspective, his formal role demands that he maximize profits, that he operate, at least in theory, solely as a real estate businessman, and that "the welfare department should take care of the needs of these people." The absence of viable alternatives, however, casts manager and tenant so closely together that his role definition consequently takes on a broader definition.

The caretaking role extends to virtually every area of S.R.O. living. In the closed S.R.O.'s, the manager, or his agent, performs rigorous gatekeeping functions, assuring that the building's residents will not be threatened by any discordant elements. The managers of these closed buildings regulate the traffic through their domains so very closely that in some buildings, when an outsider wishes entrance, the tenant is summoned and must personally escort his guest to and from his room. Others are so strict about outsiders entering the building that no guests are allowed. While the legality of this is of course questionable, residents are advised of this rule upon admission and are made aware that noncooperation will mean eviction. Since physical safety and cleanliness are two of the qualities most sought after in S.R.O. housing, most residents consider the rule not too high a price to pay.

Some managers have adopted an even more generalized caretaking stance. The S.R.O.'ers are seen by them as scarcely able to maintain themselves. These managers look to the unhygienic and often inhumane physical condition of their own and other buildings as validation of this belief. Some claim that they have even had to teach certain residents how to use a toilet and shower. Most report that in the early ventures in S.R.O. housing, they took a much greater interest in the lives of the residents, attempting to provide moral, spiritual, and social guidance to their tenants. As time progressed, however, they report experiencing an ever-increasing feeling of cynicism. The people living in their building were variously described as: "hopeless," "just like animals," "mishugoyim" (crazy), and "not worthy of anything." Most of these managers have almost entirely derationalized their caretaking functions and administer assistance solely on an ad hoc basis.

His visibility and lengthy hours in the S.R.O. building thrusts the manager, often unwillingly, into the caretaking role. At times he must actively intervene in the lives of his tenants: interrupting domestic quarrels, arbitrating disputes, and occasionally even providing a measure of physical protection for them. All of these occurrences take place without his tacit approval; each time he finds himself embroiled in a difficult situation he resolves "this will absolutely be the last time," and yet the frequency of reoccurrence only serves to reemphasize the tremendous amount of uncertainty of his role.

In the event of acute illness or some other medical emergency, often it is the building's manager who is first summoned. Since in most buildings only he has a telephone—public pay phones in all but the best closed S.R.O.'s are regularly vandalized to a point beyond repair—it is up to him to make the call for medical assistance. Here the manager places himself in a position of uncertainty. Recall, as previously stated, a call for medical assistance is not answered by an ambulance but by police, who then summon an ambulance if they feel the situation warrants it. The police, however, are dispatched directly from the precinct in which the building is located. The manager fears, probably quite realistically, that if too many "crank calls" (for clear nonemergencies) are made, he might lose the respect of the police, with the result that their response to any subsequent call will be less than prompt. If, however, he does not summon assistance, he might find himself legally culpable in the event that the resident's condition worsens, or if he dies. The manager, therefore, must make an instantaneous judgment and act on it. Often what will happen is that the manager can "cop-out" by delegating the call to someone else, usually a tenant, and when the police do arrive, if the condition proves trivial he can claim ignorance. Of the three alternative actions possible: a direct call, a direct denial, or a "cop-out," the last is the one pattern most often chosen.

The Manager and Other S.R.O. Caretakers

In other social situations with ecological and social constraints similar to those found in the S.R.O. world, researchers have noted the need for patterns of accommodation on different levels. These accommodative patterns often take the form of social interaction that can be characterized by the semblance to symbiotic relationships through which people are able to mutually achieve the satisfaction of needs that could not have been addressed individually. Since the manager's position is so pivotal in the S.R.O. world, many such patterns necessarily revolve about him and I was able to define the nature and dynamics of some of these relationships from an organizational as well as an interactional perspective. Below we will consider some of these findings. The brief interchange which follows is rather representative of the relationships of some managers with certain residents. The scene was recorded at the desk of a hotel where a new resident was in the process of complaining about his accommodations.

> *Manager:* I know all about you, Leroy. Don't you think that for one minute you will get away with here what you're always doing. One trouble, and you're out! Do you understand?
>
> *Tenant:* What you mean, man? You don't know me, man . . . I never been here 'fore in my life, man!

While Leroy was correct in stating that he was never a tenant in the building before, and he had never seen the manager, he is incorrect in assuming that because of this the manager does not know him. This knowledge is come by in one of two ways. In New York as elsewhere, the real estate business is characterized by a fairly rapid turnover in ownership. S.R.O. property is particularly liable to this, with most "operators" (as these real estate businessmen now describe themselves) wishing to buy a building, squeeze the maximum amount of profit from it, and then "get out" (sell the property) before it becomes necessary to invest any additional money in it. As such, operators often call one another suggesting business transactions of various sorts. As part of the preliminary business protocol, small talk is always made around generalized laments concerning municipal difficulties, breakdowns in physical plant and stories and ancedotes about particularly troublesome tenants. The latter, however, tends to overshadow the former two. Operators are understandably reluctant to divulge any information which could conceivably bias a business deal. The information that the physical plant is absolutely ready to collapse or that the city, for some reason, is interested in enforcing building or health codes more stringently would be considered prejudicial to any sort of business venture. The one given, in the S.R.O. word, is that tenants represent at best a bothersome presence and are in some way considered an occupational hazard of the business. As such, they become the subject matter of the business smalltalk. Those persons seen as particularly troublesome or difficult, become such frequent topics of conversation that at almost any given time they can be located in the S.R.O. community.

Many operators whose properties are in reasonably close proximity meet informally for lunch and then spend an hour or two visiting on the street afterwards. During this time, much information about housing conditions, tenants, municipal matters, and so forth is exchanged. In New York, if one should pass one of these informal, street corner gatherings, he would be likely to hear some Central European language (Hungarian or Polish, most often) or Yiddish being spoken. S.R.O. residents passing on the street report a certain amount of anxiety about what "the man" (landlord) might be saying in his native tongue. It is clear that reasonably well functioning, informal information networks exist among this group of caretakers.

The police and the S.R.O. hotel managers enjoy an accommodative relationship that might best be described as symbiotic. Police on almost every level (from foot patrolmen to detectives) who are familiar with the area, appreciate the pivotal position that the manager enjoys in the S.R.O. world. It is often the manager who informs the police that a person who is wanted for questioning, or who is suspect, is either "holed up" or has been seen about the building. With the assistance of the manager, the "collaring" or apprehension of the individual is facilitated. The manager can also provide information that the police consider necessary in conducting an investigation. The interaction between the police and the manager is extremely cordial; while it is problematic whether they actually like or respect each other, each clearly realized the utility of the relationship.

The S.R.O. manager uses the police in a variety of ways. On the most basic level he expects the police to perform for him what they do for others in the area: to expeditiously arrive when summoned, accept his version of the story, and then act in such a way that his interests might best be served. In addition, managers look to the police to go beyond the specfications of their jobs and provide special services. A manager, for instance, will attempt to manipulate his interactions with S.R.O. residents, making it appear that his will has the force of the law behind it. A clear demonstration of how this occurs can be seen in the way one manager handled the process of eviction. As can be expected, most tenants have very negative feelings about eviction. Moreover, of late, with the steadily diminishing supply of S.R.O. housing, an eviction can cause considerable hardship, and the probability of resistance, either active or passive, is relatively high. Having managed the property for a considerable length of time, this manager had carefully cultivated relationships with a number of uniformed police officers who were willing to assist him in making these evictions. The police would accompany this manager to the tenant's room, announce themselves with a forceful knock on the door and a loud, "Police! Open Up!" When the door was opened, they would remain there while the manager delivered his ultimatum or order. For most tenants, the presence of two fully armed, large, uniformed police officers is enough to discourage any sort of resistance and they will docilely comply with the order.

Other S.R.O. managers report that they have fully ingratiated themselves with the local precinct and look to the police for a wide variety of services as well as very prompt response to any call. In turn, they have been able to convince the police of their complete willingness to cooperate in any investigation as well as offering special inducements. As one manager explained it to me during the time that I was being "broken in" to the desk clerk's position at the hotel:

Manager: You wanted to know for what we are saving that room? That room, it is reserved for the boys from the police station over there. I'll tell you, if somebody ever comes in and says he's from the [precinct] house and he wants 404, you just give him the key. No questions asked, just give to him the key and then you look somewhere else.

Interviewer: What do they use the room for?

Manager: *Gottinu* ... for a college boy you're just not so bright sometimes! Just don't ask so many questions. You listen, give to him the key, that's all!

Not all hotels provide such a special service. In all, however, managers and uniformed officers—both patrolmen and sergeants—interacted freely and easily. Police, when entering a hotel (unless on some emergency call or in pursuit of a suspect) would stop behind the desk to chat with the manager for a few moments. The presence of police officers was particularly noticeable around the holiday season. Although any sort of financial exchange between police and managers was never observed, on more than one occasion, managers who were interviewed complained that they were "giving the police an arm and a leg." What this might translate into, in monetary terms, is of course, unknown, but other reports suggest that some police were almost "on the payroll." Although there was some complaining, every account manager indicated that the extra assurance and security he received was well worth the expense.

Relationships between the S.R.O. managers and the DOSS personnel, from the level of caseworker to (unit) supervisor, are probably some of the most difficult and at times tenuous in the S.R.O. world. DOSS personnel are municipal government employees. Most are young, the job description requires that they hold at least a bachelor's degree, and most tend to be rather idealistic—at least when they begin their job. In the S.R.O. world, as in other depressed areas, the "welfare worker" enjoys a protected, privileged status—at least during the daylight hours. His symbol of identity is the black, loose-leaf casebook in which he keeps his records. The appearance of this book assures that the (white) person carrying it has a legitimate reason for being where he is, and reports of workers being molested are extremely rare.[16]

The hotel manager is aware of the status that the caseworker occupies in the community. He is similarly cognizant of the fact that for many tenants, almost all of their resources (not the least of which is their rent) are channeled through the office of the DOSS worker. The manager comes to view the DOSS worker as one of the few positive resources that he has access to. For many managers, the DOSS workers come to be defined as allies in the manager's struggle with his tenants. The manager's definition of the caseworker as a positive resource is supported by several factors. In many cases the worker and the manager share the same ethnic and class affiliation, and managers are not reticent in emphasizing this in their pleas for assistance from the caseworkers. Most workers have a well-scrubbed, earnest appearance which projects an air of rational professionalism. The manager who has defined his position as essentially beleaguered, quickly attempts to co-opt such a person into a sympathetic stance.

It is the manager's belief that a caseworker's support eases the problems of dealing with intransigent tenants. He assumes that the worker has a measure of moral suasion over his client and if need be, "can talk some sense" into the client. In addition, the construction of a manager-worker coalition tends to further isolate the S.R.O.'er, facilitating the application of control sanctions by the manager.

Organizationally, full enlistment of the worker's support and cooperation can be extremely rewarding. This occurs in several ways. Most S.R.O. buildings, with the exception of the very best of the "closed" ones, have some difficulty with their vacancy rate.[17] The manager who has developed good relations with the DOSS has a continual source of referral to his building. Not only referral, but referral with the assurance that the tenant's rents will be paid.

As would be expected, managers prefer a referred tenant to an unknown person off the street. In some instances, the relationship between manager and the DOSS is so institutionalized that the hotel will accept a person for tenancy only *after* he had been cleared by the DOSS in terms of support, and can actually demonstrate to the manager that he is on the welfare rolls. In one hotel studied, persons making inquiry about accommodations would immediately be referred to the DOSS office. In this situation, the DOSS personnel were delegated an important preliminary gatekeeping function.

For the manager, one of the most desirable arrangements between himself and DOSS workers involved a fiscal understanding. Welfare money is distributed directly to the client. This fulfills the fiction that the money is to be used in a "therapeutic" way; that the worker and the client have evolved a "fiscal plan," and that through it, the client is learning how to manage his resources. Managers, however, report generalized discontentment with this system. They complain that the tenant will simply cash the check and then spend his allotment before he pays the rent. Managers consider it to be in their own best interests to convince the worker that tenants are incapable of effectively managing their own money, and the only way that the managers can be assured of receiving their rent payments is by having the check made payable to *both* the tenant and the manager. The tenant, therefore, can *only* cash the check with the manager, who is then able to immediately deduct the money that the tenant owes. Naturally, in order for a manager to be able to effect this arrangement, he must insure that the worker is willing to accept his definition of the situation (which includes the manager's evaluation of the tenant) and not the S.R.O. resident's.

The place of absolute centrality that the S.R.O. manager can occupy in the S.R.O. world's social system can best be realized by the understanding that (with the exception of some covert, individual adaptions) he effectively controls the entrance and flow of materials and persons (i.e., institutional representation) into the S.R.O. world. "The Hotel Enfer Doctor Affair" provides a good illustration of this.

As previously stated, the only medical care available to S.R.O.'ers is provided through either the offices of private physicans working in the area, private clinics, or hospital emergency rooms. In the hotel in which I was playing the role of DOSS caseworker, medical care was universally acknowledged to be the single most urgent need of the tenants. In order to provide quality medical services to this population, we evolved a strategy which called for bringing a doctor (or doctors) into the hotel and establishing a regular "sick call" in an on-site "miniclinic" for the hotel's residents. After several staff meetings, I was delegated the responsibility of locating a physician (or physicians) who would be willing to participate. In addition, I was charged with coordinating complementary social service efforts at the hotel. This latter task, for instance, required that the entire DOSS staff be kept advised of all developments, expediting the cooperation of the visiting nurse in aiding the doctor, planning for an adequate referral system, and serving the liaison function between the social service staff and the hotel's management.

The first efforts to find interested practitioners were directed towards the general hospitals which included the hotel within their catchment areas. The possibility of having these hospitals increase the level of services provided was explored. For a while, a physician from one of the hospitals' Department of Community Medicine had been making monthly visits to the hotel. This level of effort, however, was deemed inadequate by all involved. The residents claimed that the infrequency of doctor's visits precluded service when it was really needed, and both the visiting nurse who coordinated the effect, and the DOSS staff, found the demands too great and the time allocation too little to adequately serve the needs of the hotel's residents. When asked about the feasibility of intensifying this program, that is, allowing the participating physician to visit the hotel more often, it was learned that the hospital's directors had already decided to entirely terminate the service. With the closing of this avenue, the involved staff then decided that it would be necessary to locate practitioners elsewhere. Attention was then focused upon the academic sphere. We surveyed those persons involved in biomedically oriented social research and asked them to refer us to any of their colleagues currently practicing medicine who might be interested in participating. Several leads were followed up until a physician in one of the medical schools in the city expressed some interest in the project. The idea appeared particularly attractive to him since he had recently associated himself with a private group practice clinic located on the Upper West Side, just a few blocks from the Enfer.

Members of the social service staff and this physician began planning for service delivery. The plan evolved for a "minisatellite clinic" which would be established inside of the hotel. This small unit would fulfill the initial diagnostic function and furnish treatment for minor ills. Concurrently, second stage planning was developing around a system which would effectively link the satellite and mother clinic, thereby allowing for more extensive laboratory, diagnostic and/or treatment services. The DOSS staff, after consulting with the hotel's management, agreed to surrender one of the rooms the management allotted to them for administrative purposes; this room would be the locale of the miniclinic. The young physician who would actually be operating the miniclinic came to the hotel to meet with the DOSS staff, the visiting nurse, assorted other caretakers, and the hotel's residents. During this time period, the mother clinic had an examining table and an instrument cabinet delivered to the hotel. Morale was running high among both the DOSS workers and the hotel's tenants. People congratulated each other, believing that at last something was "really going to get done" and some meaningful changes would actually occur. The presence of the medical equipment for all to see was taken as proof positive that something was underway.

The optimism, however, proved to be short lived. One week before the miniclinic was due to open, one of the managers approached members of the DOSS staff and began voicing reservations about the idea of the clinic. A physician acquaintance of the particular manager had suggested to him that the miniclinic in the hotel would make the participating doctors rich, and the manager was more than willing to believe him. Although the manager was never specific, he suggested that the annual revenue possible from the operation of the miniclinic would total in excess of a "couple of hundreds of thousands of dollars"; therefore, he said, "no one was going to pull something over on him."

In subsequent interviews he reported that he originally thought that the clinic would be staffed and administered by "a couple of young interns who were trying to break into the business," not by "people who were trying to make a buck off him." Although the participating physicians expressed a willingness to pay rent for the space they would utilize, at more than the going rates for rooms that were presently returning no profit, the manager absolutely refused this possibility. After some negotiations, he proposed that the only arrangement acceptable for any clinic operation in the hotel would involve a rental fee computed on the basis (that is, a percentage) of the remuneration that the miniclinic received from the various agencies subsidizing medical care. The managers assumed an intransigent stance on the issue. The doctors then rejected the proposal, stating that such an arrangement was absolutely unacceptable on legal and ethical grounds.

The negotiations continued past the date that the miniclinic was due to begin operation, and then broke down entirely. When I left the field, roughly one year later, nothing had been resolved and the more than one thousand residents of the Hotel Enfer were still without the kind of medical care that such an on-site operation could have provided.

In many ways, the "Doctor Affair" is very typical of the long-term, organizational relationship between the S.R.O. manager and the S.R.O. social system. While managers often tend to exhibit a good deal of psychological sophistication in dealing with tenants (for example, effecting complex manipulations directed at maintaining relative power differentials) they tend to demonstrate little, if any, of the same sort of sociological or organizational acumen. Organizational management is viewed from a rather narrow cost-benefit frame, emphasizing immediately realizable fiscal profits. The notion that profits might in some way be related to living conditions, and that by improving the overall ambience the vacancy and turn-over rate might be improved, seems to have little influence on the organizational decisions made.

Managers and Social Control

The S.R.O. manager must have some method of regulating the behavior of members of those groups he regularly interacts with. For the first major group, the S.R.O. residents, this control can be virtually of any means. Often these forms of regulating behavior are reminiscent of those found in some kinds of "total institutions." Although there are some striking similarities between S.R.O. and total institutions, some caution should be exercised when the concept is employed. To begin, control in total institutions must be broken into two somewhat distinct situations. The first involves the situation in which the "kept" has been remanded to the "keeper" by an external authority which is superior to both. The second defines the keeper and the kept as tied together through mutual agreement, (usually) without recourse to any formal, sanctionable contract. The former is best exemplified by prison or legal/judicial commitment to a state mental hospital; while the latter is exemplified by a voluntary (that is, nonjudicial or self-) commitment to a private sanitorium. Both are, without question, "total institutions" in that they satisfy all of the members' needs, treat their inmates with a good deal of standardization, and manifestly have a program designed to change the inmate in some way.[18] One important dimension that distinguishes the two is the nature and types of social control which can be applied. In the former, controls, as would be expected, can take almost any form, from subtle, psychological manipulation to physical coercion employing the threat or actuality of violence. In the latter, however, the range of control is severely restricted. Since the bond between keeper and kept is defined in wholly voluntary terms, the keeper must be able to convince the kept that "he is, indeed, better off where he is," and that the rules and controls imposed upon him are "for his own good," these rules being neither gratuitous nor capricious. The controls and sanctions employed, therefore, must necessarily be of a more subtle, manipulative character. Control directed at S.R.O. residents conforms somewhat more closely to the voluntary model.

For the second major group, the caretakers, the control processes must be viewed in wider terms. In this situation, the problem of maintaining order, control, and of managing uncertainty are most fruitfully considered in organizational terms. This concluding section on the caretakers of the S.R.O. world focuses on the various patterns of control employed by S.R.O. managers by first examining the nature and quality of control-oriented social interaction occurring between S.R.O. managers and the other community caretakers. Second, we shall consider some of the questions and processes employed in maintaining intra-S.R.O. social control.

In order to effectively administer their S.R.O.'s, managers find it necessary to enter into informal, collusive agreements with other caretakers. Above, I discussed one such adaption with the police. In this adaption, the manager, in effect, contracted with individual officers for policing and services over and above those legally specified. Managers have learned that such arrangements are both possible and useful with other caretakers as well.

In the case of the police, the interaction comes to be defined within the context of an informal contract; both parties have established what is expected from the other and will continue to "produce" as long as the other does. The nature of the interaction, then, can be seen as an equilateral exchange. In addition, this encourages the speculation that this quality of reciprocity contributes to the continuing stability of the relationship.[19] It is very probable that the extralegal (or even illegal) nature of the exchange admits even another dimension. The fact of this extralegality and the conspiracy involved to sustain it generates a kind of social inertia. This inertial condition helps to sustain the relationship by making it difficult for either partner to opt out of the exchange without experiencing some anxiety about discovery.

Since the interaction is based upon individually initiated contracts and does not have an overtly recognized normative foundation, it must somehow be redefined and/or renegotiated each time new personnel find their way into the system. When new people are introduced into such a social system, their behavior tends to be somewhat nonpredictable. Behavior which is nonpredictable carries with it a high probability of being labeled as "deviant" by the remaining partner(s). In order to cope with this, it is likely that social control mechanisms will be activated. A good illustation of this was provided through an incident involving the eviction of a tenant who had been drinking for several days and was becoming progressively more troublesome. I was then employed as the hoel's desk clerk/security guard, and following usual procedure I called the precinct house directly (this, in itself, is a rather unusual procedure in as much as all calls for police services are supposed to be handled through a central number) and was advised that a car would be dispatched. Presently, an officer unknown to either the manager or myself arrived. (Later it was learned that the officer had only recently been assigned to the precinct.) When we advised the officer that we wished his assistance in the eviction, he refused to cooperate, and in the most vehement of terms stated that he was a police officer and that he "wouldn't do anyone else's work for them" and that his presence during the eviction was not "part of his job." The manager on the scene made no attempt to convince the officer to cooperate; instead he apologized for the misunderstanding. Soon after the officer left, the manager turned to me and said, in a knowledgeable way, "Don't worry, I now know what to do." A little later, another call was placed to the precinct house, this time by the manager himself. Shortly thereafter, two known officers arrived and the eviction progressed as expected. Several weeks later, when I again had occasion to call for police assistance, the first officer from the previous episode arrived. This time, however, when he was told about what needed to be done he proved extremely cooperative and did all that he was asked to. After the police left, I asked the manager about the change in the officer's demeanor. He reported that shortly after the last incident had transpired, he (the manager) called "some of the boys down in the station house, and they talked to him [the noncooperative officer] sure good." What is most significant, however, is that the manager himself did not employ any sanctions, but only activated the control mechanism whereby others, more likely to have a greater affect on the truculent member, might effectively do so.

Necessarily, the S.R.O. manager must affect different (social) control patterns with other caretakers. Since the occupational group within which these other caretakers normally operate does not share the same degree of integration as do the police, the use of certain control mechanisms is precluded. This necessarily demands that the manage take a more direct part in the administration of sanctions. In the S.R.O. world this involves the evolution of a system based upon the giving or withholding of money. In some service situations, because personnel have come to expect this extra money as almost normal remuneration for their job (although it is never reported to the Internal Revenue Service, as in the case of a waiter's gratuities), the amount is computed in along with their salary when any consideration of their financial worth is made.

Naturally, most have very strong feelings concerning this extra source of income and will not do anything to jeopardize it.

S.R.O. Managers and S.R.O. Residents

The control mechanisms employed by S.R.O. managers in dealing with their residents are considerably more complex. Considering the dimension of the establishment and maintenance of order, managers attempt to evolve patterns of accommodation which, if successful, will assure the predictability of behavior. On the simplest level, this involves the exchange of pleasantries and the expected amount of civil interaction required by a given social context. In addition, the manager often will assume a stance of noblesse oblige and through it give certain tenants small monetary loans and provide extra services. In partial return, the manager expects from these tenants a certain amount of cooperation in maintaining both the physical premises and the order of the S.R.O. Both of these are seen as control operations in that the manager expects these chosen tenants, in addition to behaving in the desired way, to exert a measure of influence over the other residents in the maintenance of these functions.

In addition to any informal controls exerted by these persons, the manager expects these chosen tenants to serve as informants, informing on other tenants involved in any wrongdoings. Managers refer to such a resident as a "confidential man." In reality, however, the "confidential-man system" works poorly because so many of the residents only feign the appearance of requisite respect for the manager's wishes and property. As one would expect, such tenants are simply "playing it cool" in the expectation that they can maximize their material position by balancing their loyalties between their peers in the S.R.O. community and the S.R.O. manager.

While the system may not provide the manager with a large amount of readily usable information, it does give him a pool of potential building employees. S.R.O. employees, such as desk clerks, security guards, porters, and maids are overwhelmingly recruited from the building itself. The attainment of such a position, in which one enjoys reduced rent, a small stipend, and fuller participation in the social life of the S.R.O. is regarded as a very positive goal by many of the residents. An overview of this dimension suggests that positive sanction involves the resident in a movement along a bipolar, horizontal status plane, defined by a "formal" status position on one axis and an "informal" position on the other. Within the S.R.O. world, attainment of a formal status with regular rewards and benefits is defined as more valuable than an informal one. An informal status position is characterized more by its quasisymbiotic nature. An example of this can be seen by a S.R.O. manager's regular calls upon a former prize fighter in the event of trouble. Within the context of such a relationship, the resident believes that he might be able to request and receive a superior room or a few days grace if the rent might be late. Through the formalization of status, however, the resident receives these privileges *plus* a more central, secure position within the S.R.O. community. Moreover, the formalization of his status allows him a measure of power over his erstwhile peers. It should not be forgotten that the S.R.O. employee retains his position only at the pleasure of his employer, the manager. As one would expect, this provides the manager with a considerable degree of leverage since the conditions of the employment are almost always removed from the notice of any official (that is, government or union) regulatory bodies.

Positive sanctions improve the member's material and social position within the S.R.O. community. Negative ones, however, can present him with an acute danger. Several somewhat dissimilar styles of negative sanction were regularly observed. On the most basic level the manager has the threat or actuality of physical force to effect (social) control. Since the S.R.O. world intermittently has a violent side to it, the use of force as a vehicle of control can be well disguised. Use of this extreme sanction is exemplified through an incident which occurred during an attempt to organize a S.R.O. building.

A local community action group was attempting to organize several of the S.R.O. buildings in the area. A part of the group's overall strategy involved the identification of (at least) one tenant in each building who would serve as building coordinator. This coordinator would be responsible for distributing literature, informing other tenants of meetings, and in general sustaining a high level of interest in the group's activities. As one might expect, most managers would view such efforts with a large amount of antipathy. The resistance, however, is seldom or never manifested at the organizational level; recognition of such groups seldom occurs. Instead, persons, especially S.R.O. residents aligned with them, come to be defined as "troublemakers." Given this definition-of-situation, managers have little difficulty effecting sanctions on single individuals. An interview describing one such occurrence is reported below.

Interviewer: Can you tell me about some of the events that led up to your moving from 351 [the building's street address] to here?

Respondent: She-it, that a long story, man. I started listenin' to them folks at the "People for Action" office and they been making some sense. So I say "OK, I'll do it, I'll be tellin' peoples at my building what's happenin." And Mr. G. [the manager], man, you never saw nobody that uptight. He say to me, "You can't be botherin' all the other peoples wid that shit, here!" I just don' say nothing ... next time he sees me he start in again—I say "Be cool," he tell me if'n I don' stop I gonna be put outa the building.

Interviewer: What happened then?

Respondent: I went over an' told the "People for Action" folks and they say to me—"How long you been living in the building here?" I say 'bout four-five months— then they say—the man, he can' put you out. ... All you gotta do is keep paying your rent. Then I goes to pay my rent and the man he won't take it. I'm hip, you know ... I say "it's cool" and just split.

Interviewer: Did you pay your rent for those weeks then?

Respondent: Shit yeah, I paid-up. I waited 'til the man he leave and the night man, he there, and then I layed it on 'im. I say that I didn't have the rent together during the day, so I want to pay it in now so I don' get ripped-off.

Interviewer: But you still haven't told me what made you move.

Respondent: I'm getting there man, just be cool. The next day I sees the man and I can tell he pissed ... I know he want my ass outta there something bad. Nothing happens then for a couple of days, then he sees me putting up a sign for a meetin' and up comes and pulls it down. Next day I'm coming outa my house [room] and this dude come up to me and say he don' want me messin' with his woman no more. I say, "Be cool, brother, I don't know your woman." Then this other dude he start yellin' on my head 'bout some shit. And afore I know it, we all mixin' it up. Man, they kicked my ass good that day. Lookit here—[he pointed to prominent scars on his chin and under his eye]. I got cut bad.

Interviewer: Why did you get beat up?

Respondent: She-it, you knows why, didn't have nothing to do with no bitch. The man [the manager] he was gettin' so uptight that he done got these dudes to duff [assault] me.

Interviewer: Did you go to the police?

Respondent: Yeah, I went to the police, I told them what happened. Then they wrote everything down, I know they ain't gonna do nothing.... They just think it's a bunch a crazy niggers drinkin' and fighting. Anyway, I got to thinkin' that it just not worth gettin my ass kicked. The people, they stupid, they don' care what the man works on them. ... Why should I?

While this incident probably represents the extreme limits of sanctions employed, it does demonstrate the willingness these caretakers have to employ them. Most often, "security personnel" are hired directly from the building and these men tend to be the largest and most aggressive. In most cases, the manager signifies to them his willingness to "look the other way," thereby assuring that a modicum of order will be maintained in the building.

Most often, however, managers employ a range of sanctions which fall between subtle psychological manipulations and outright force. The one most used is the threat or actuality of the "lock-out." Here the resident is warned tht unless he changes his behavior, pays his bills, or does what is expected of him, his "door will be plugged." Technically this entails placing half of a lengthwise-cut key in the lock, thereby precluding the tenant from inserting his own key and opening the door. (The plug can only be removed by using the other half of the key, which the manager has.) For the lone S.R.O. resident in particular, the possibility of not having a place to go to, in addition to not having the resources necessary to secure another one, places the individual in a very difficult, perhaps even painful, situation. The lock-out is an especially useful device because it entails a minimum of risk on the manager's part, and it does not necessitate any immediate, direct confrontation between manager and resident. Consequently, displaced residents must interact with the manager in a situation over which the manager has complete control. If the resident wants entrance to his room and access to his possessions, he must do what the manager requires.

It is important to recognize that the manager's ability to affect control, through the imposition of negative sanctions on the tenant, rests upon differentials in terms of their access to the large, formal agents and/or agencies of social control. The manager, in affecting these penalties, finds himself able to do things that are of questionable legality; he understands that S.R.O.'ers do not have the same access to police, courts or regulatory agencies that other residents of the area have.

An S.R.O.'er, requesting assistance from a police officer in the case of a grievance with a manager, will invariably be quoted the letter of the law. Recall, however, that while police officers have been enlisted to perform extra legal services, S.R.O.'ers asking for assistance are made to feel the entire weight of due process. In one such incident, a resident had been locked out of his room. As one would expect, he believed that he had been treated unfairly. The resident decided that the best course of action would be (much like the manager's) to bring a uniformed police officer along when he presented his demands to the manager. I accompanied the resident to the precinct house where, upon our arrival, we were denied access to the building by an officer loitering on the steps. The policeman demanded that we state our business to him before entering the station house. The resident then explained the situation to the officer. The officer advised him that before a policeman could legally enter a private building he had to have either a complaint charging that a crime had been committed, a warrant, or be in pursuit of a suspect. In the case of a dispute between tenant and landlord, such as this one, the officer "could do absolutely nothing." If, however, the tenant would "go to Centre Street" (where the various law courts are) and "get the judge to give him a paper, then he would be happy to serve it."

If the content of the interaction was to be examined, one might conclude that the embattled resident (or "mark" in this case) had effectively been cooled out.[20] The officer's remarks and suggestions precisely followed the letter of the law and his demeanor, while hostile, clearly fell within the boundaries acceptable for interaction between police and citizens. The prospect, however, of approaching the hotel's management through appropriate legal channels to seek redress of grievance, is one not at all easily entertained by S.R.O.'ers. In this encounter, as in so many others between S.R.O.'ers and authority, the S.R.O.'er quietly drops out of sight after little more than a perfunctory protest.

If one were to characterize the interactional patterns between caretakers and the cared-for in the S.R.O. world, the only conclusion possible is that the exchange is anything but equal and that the balance of power clearly rests with the caretakers. Caretakers have at their command both a significantly higher level of social organization and considerably greater access to many and varied resources. All of the patterns evolved are reflections of this inequality.

NOTES

1. Herbert Gans, *The Urban Villagers* (New York: Free Press, 1962).

2. Simmgl, Georg. *The Sociology of Georg Simmel.* Translated by Kurt H. Wolff. (New York: Free Press, 1950), pp. 379-95.

3. Gans, *Urban Villagers,* p. 143.

4. Lewis Coser, "The Sociology of Poverty," *Social Problems* 13 (1956): 140-48.

5. Gans, *Urban Villagers,* p. 143.

6. Bruce J. Biddle and Edwin J. Thomas, *Role Theory* (New York: John Wiley and Sons, 1966), p. 62.

7. Melvin Seeman, "On the Meaning of Alienation," *American Sociological Review* 24 (1959): 783-91.

8. Erving Goffman, *The Presentation of Self In Everyday Life* (Garden City, N.Y.: Doubleday, Anchor Books, 1963).

9. Albert J. Reiss, Jr., *The Police and The Public* (New Haven: Yale University Press, 1971).

10. The same sort of distancing has been observed in total institutions in which a large degree of social distance separates inmates from keepers. In prisons, for example, an inmate who looks a guard directly in the eye can be held in low regard by his fellow prisoners.

11. Joan H. Shapiro, *Communities of the Alone* (New York: Association Press, 1971).

12. Evelin M. Burns, *Health Services for Tomorrow* (New York: Dunellen, 1973), pp. 39-79.

13. This was the fee in 1970-71; it may have been raised since.

14. Shapiro, *Communities of the Alone.*

15. Edward Lewis Wallant, *The Pawnbroker* (New York: Signet Books).

16. A thorough search of the *New York Times* index revealed only two reported incidents of a case worker being molested while on duty, and one of these occurred not in the field but in a DOSS center.

17. With the constant shrinkage in S.R.O. housing this is just beginning to change.

18. Erving Goffman, *Asylums* (Garden City, N.Y.: Anchor Books, 1961).

19. Alvin Gouldner, "The Norm of Reciprocity: A Preliminary Statement," *American Sociological Review* 25 (1960): 176; George C. Homans, "Social Behavior as Exchange," *American Journal of Sociology* 62 (1956): 597–606.

20. Erving Goffman, "On Cooling the Mark Out: Some Aspects of Adaptation to Failure," *Human Behavior and Social Process*, ed. Arnold M. Rose (Boston: Houghton, Mifflin Company, 1962), pp. 482–505.

Chapter 5
The Social Life of an S.R.O.

The larger plan of this study has been steadily bringing us closer to the heart of the S.R.O. world. Initially, our attention was focused on an almost wholly external view of the S.R.O. world, which drew its impressions from newspaper accounts and official documents, to a close description of S.R.O.'s and their microecology. Attention was then directed towards some of the social mechanisms which contributed to the establishment and maintenance of the S.R.O. way of life. I've attempted to show how, at least in the eyes of those who ostensibly are there to serve them, S.R.O.'ers are different from the area's other residents. This chapter will take us right into day-to-day life in the S.R.O. world. The perspective employed in this chapter examines the social life of the S.R.O.'s from the vantage point of those living in them.

Following the ethnographic and naturalistic perspectives detailed in previous chapters, my analysis has employed the very categories and distinctions which the S.R.O.'ers themselves use to order and organize their social world. In a larger sense, I hope to identify those interlocking systems which the native peoples have constructed to satisfy their regularly occurring needs.

In this chapter the process underlying social differentiation and the mechanisms which contribute to the construction and maintenance of social groups will be considered first. The nature of the groups established will be described and their integration into the S.R.O. community's structure will be discussed. In addition, the social networks and other social systems which operate in the community will be explored to obtain some understanding about the interconnection of the community's parts. Lastly, interest will be directed towards the culture of the S.R.O. world. Issues such as a unique language, the mechanisms of spatial and temporal regulation, and attitudinal and belief systems will be discussed.

Social Differentiation

S.R.O's on the Upper West Side and elsewhere span the entire spectrum from those which could be considered totally "closed" to entirely "open." What is perhaps the most characteristic quality of each is the amount of social heterogeneity found within it. The closed S.R.O.'s tend to have a much more socially and demograph‧ically homogeneous population than the open buildings. Differences in gatekeeping patterns are largely responsible for these vaiations. Not only are certain kinds of people entirely excluded from living in certain buildings, but they are prohibited from even spending time in and around them.

Persons in closed S.R.O.'s tend to fall into similar age cohorts—most tend to be between their late thirties and middle sixties—essentially within those years considered to be the most economically productive. The sex distribution of these buildings can be characterized as leaning towards a preponderance of males. The overwhelming majority of those living in closed S.R.O.'s are regularly employed. Interestingly, room rents tend not to be much higher in these closed S.R.O.'s than in the open ones. It is the judgment of the gatekeepers and not any means test which established and maintains the differentiation.

The closed S.R.O.'s are reminiscent of the rooming houses that Zorbaugh wrote about in The Gold Coast and the Slum.[1] Since most of residents in them are employed in those marginal occupations having erratic or irregular working hours (janitors, porters, night-watchmen, swing-shift workers, and the like), opportunities for regular social interaction are somewhat limited. In these closed S.R.O.'s the building tends to provide little focus for interaction. This non-S.R.O. orientation helps to explain why closed S.R.O.'s exhibit little community spirit. With the individual's principle commitment directed towards individualistically defined goals (for example, social mobility), the amount of time and energy that he is willing to expend for either the construction or maintenance of community tends to be extremely limited. One thirty-seven-year-old black man, living in the Westmoreland, a hotel which the police describe as a "model S.R.O.," described this lack of interest in his building:

> What you mean community? I gotta take care of "Number 1" first. I pays my rent, I work hard, I ain't really concerned with the peoples here. . . . I working seven days a week—you know I told you, I done took that other job on top. So now I just come back to my house [his room] and sleep. . . . I ain't really concerned.

In a subsequent interview, the respondent signified a strong desire toward social mobility. Words and phrases like: "I work hard," "I want to get ahead," "I can take care of myself," were an important part of his vocabulary. He was future-oriented and would define any activity not directed towards the realization of his goals as meaningless, or at best, frivolous. Interestingly, interviews with this respondent and others like him, had a theme and flavor similar to those offered by newly arrived European immigrants.[2]

The amount and intensity of social interaction occurring in these closed S.R.O.'s, however, is still greater than what would be found in conventional apartment buildings. Ecological factors are responsible for these differences. Conventional apartments are constructed with each apartment as a self-contained module. Each unit, therefore, has living/sleeping areas as well as individual cooking and bathing facilities. Since these facilities must be shared in an S.R.O., people are forced to evolve patterns of accommodation. Interaction, in this case, is still limited since the individual's primary orientation is towards the use of the facility, rather than sociability with others.

The opposite of these patterns occurs in the case of the more open S.R.O.'s. In these buildings, employment is seldom an entrance criterion. These S.R.O.'s are characterized by their heterogeneity; persons tend to be of all ages. Also, while there is a preponderance of nonwhites throughout the S.R.O. world, on the individual unit level the open buildings are more ethnically mixed than the closed buildings. The last, and perhaps most significant factor in the observed heterogeneity is the level of behavioral diversity tolerated in these open buildings. The range of behavior acceptable in closed buildings is noticeably more narrow. Persons exhibiting behavior which is normally defined as strange or potentially threatening are either denied entrance to the building or expelled. This is definitely not the case in these open buildings, where a tremendous amount of variability in essentially every aspect of behavior is tolerated, and even accepted.

A fairly pervasive belief in the S.R.O. world is that distinction made on the basis of color or ethnicity "stops at the cage [desk] downstairs." S.R.O.'ers affirm that in the S.R.O. world, people are evaluated entirely on the basis of their own merits and not their color; this belief was confirmed by observation. Many interracial marital and sexual relationships were observed, and friendship groups were not constructed along ethnic lines. While the S.R.O. world is a racially integrated one, this de facto integration appears to have few ideological underpinnings, encouraging the speculation that it is the result of ecological factors.

Status or prestige distinctions are not automatically made along ethnic lines. However, distinctions which are important in the larger society, such as wealth or possession of a unique skill, are also meaningful within the S.R.O. world. Since these resources are much scarcer in the S.R.O. world, one's relative status position is defined by both degree of access to these resources *and* willingness to share them. The simple possession of resources is not enough to assure one's position; one must be willing to actively participate in the social life of the building to achieve and maintain a relatively high position.

The relationship between the possession of resources and the allocation of status or prestige can be seen by considering those persons who live in the S.R.O. world, yet are separated from other S.R.O.'ers by considerable social distance. An elderly woman, who would be considered wealthy by S.R.O. standards (having a moderate sized savings account and regular income from a pension) provides a good illustration. A DOSS caseworker who established a relationship with this woman, discovered that she had sufficient resources to leave the S.R.O. at any time, but refused to do so. She was a social isolate who participated little in the social life of the community. Had this woman been more willing to interact, her access to monetary resources would have placed her in a relatively high status position. Moreover, the isolation that her life-style imposed tended to leave her unprotected, and she was in constant fear for her physical safety. Others with access to considerably less resources, yet who participated more fully in communal life, were accorded a much higher status position. Since these persons were not isolated, efforts were made to protect or look after them, and consequently their position was considerably more secure.

Group Formation

In the S.R.O. world, as in other situations where work is not a major focus of social interaction, associational groups crystallize around personal need and/or similarity. When need is considered, factors like chemical dependencies (such as drug addiction and alcoholism), a special sexual orientation, or involvement in marginal or illegal activities will closely define the nature of the group. My investigation was concerned with the formulation and maintenance of these groups. Below, we will discuss the functions and operations of these groups in the social structure of the S.R.O. world.

Chemically Focused Groups

For those persons committed to the pursuit of intoxication, a way of achieving and maintaining a chemically induced high must be discovered; this implies not only assuring a steady supply of drugs, but also the satisfaction of other physical and social needs. To succeed in these areas one must mobilize a degree of social organization among different kinds of people. External, or ecological, factors have a profound effect on both the level of organization and the type of groups which emerge. Before describing the several kinds of group adaptations, it is useful to consider some of the observations I made on the nature of these groups and my speculations on the effects that external/ecological constraints have upon them.

Stable groups of alcoholics and opiate addicted persons seldom, if ever, occur. Alcoholic persons tend not to trust narcotic addicts and the addicts often are contemptuous of the "wine heads." These groups tend to be further differentiated by age. Alcoholic drinking groups are composed of older persons while the drug using groups tend to maintain a considerably younger membership. The older, more passive alcoholic persons tend to fear these younger, more aggressive drug users. Most will readily recount incidents in which they are robbed by "the junkies" or "dope heads."

The issue of trust appears to figure importantly in the limits of social solidarity found in each group. Groups composed of addicts are much more poorly integrated and less stable than comparable groups of alcoholics. At least partially responsible for this difference in group solidarity is the nature and type of the addictive situation. While both groups are committed to the pursuit of intoxication, various external factors, not the least of which is the legality of one substance and the illegality of the other, strongly influence the group integration and the interaction possible. As one of the drinking men explained during an interview:

Respondent: We'se really different than those junkies. . . . When a man really want a drink and he can't get one, well that all there is to it. . . . You ain't gonna go see some dude bustin' other peoples upside his head to get the scratch to buy up a jug. No siree! We'se ain't like them junkies at all!

Interviewer: What about your friends here—your drinking buddies, don't you get along with each other as well as the junkies seem to get along among themselves?

Respondent: [Here the respondent expressed some surprise at the apparent naiveté of the question, and then replied:] That ain't bullshit how them junkies get along. They so nice and friendly now but one of 'em begin to get sick and you see how fast he rippin' off stuff. . . . You see how fast he stealin' his friend's shit—no siree! We ain't like that!

Subsequent observations did, for the most part, substantiate this informant's account of the differences in group interaction. Group structure among those persons identified as addicts tended to be transitory. Due to the highly illicit nature of narcotic drug use, there is little opportunity for more permanent groups to form. Addicts discussing coping strategies allowed that the most important thing to do was to maintain a low profile of visibility. The community, as they saw it, had little difficulty with the fact that someone might be readily identified as an addict. What was threatening, however, was a "concentration" of such deviants; and here concentration was only vaguely defined. The presence of, say, two (known) addicts together called immediate attention to them. The presence of three or more was defined as almost intolerable, causing members of the larger S.R.O. community to see the situation as being so serious that "something must be done." The hotel security or management personnel would be summoned. This was a rare occurrence since the interactions among addicts were brief and specific. Moreover, interview data with these naroctic addicts suggested that the probability of their arrest and then at least partial passage through the legal/judicial system was relatively high. The convergence of these factors rendered the formation and maintenance of well-integrated, stable groups rather difficult.

This, however, is not the case among the alcoholic population. Even though the ecological environment in which it operates is essentially the same, the configuration of internal and external forces is strikingly different. While it is probably true that alcoholics are among the most misunderstood people we know, and that their condition (that is, their addiction to alcohol) evokes not sympathy and understanding, but contempt and derision, the alcoholic is considered more pathetic than threatening. As such, he enjoys a considerable amount of social isolation and for the most part (with the exception of certain fairly well-defined ecological areas, such as skid row), he finds that the agents and forces of social control pay little attention to him. Moreover, his chosen drug is entirely legal, readily available, and inexpensive.

Although his environment is essentially a hostile one, there is nothing in it as potentially group-disintegrating as one finds in the addict's case. If anything, the environment tends to provide the factors which encourage the emergence of a culture and the support of groups. In order for these persons to sustain their life-style, they must be (at the very least) assured of adequate shelter, alcohol, nourishment, and protection from physical harm. Some social buffer is also necessary, and its presence will permit occasional displays of bizarre behavior without disintegrating consequences resulting. In addition, the buffer provides the assurance of the availability of care or assistance in the case of illness. Collective solutions have evolved for these drinking men in the S.R.O. community.

Helping Pairs

On the most basic or simple level is the pairing-adaption to the survival problems posed by an addictive life-style. In this arrangement, two persons of opposite sexes (but not necessarily so) live together. This adaption was found to occur among both alcohol- and opiate-addicted persons. Interestingly, among alcoholics, in all of the unions known, both partners drank. Among opiate users, unions in which one member was addicted and the second was not were not at all uncommon. The nature of the social interaction in each union, however, was quite similar.

Involved drinking (that is, to the point of incapacitation) by each member tended to be cyclic. In most cases people would drink some alcohol on a daily, or close to daily, basis, with reasonably long periods of relative sobriety separating these incapacitating incidents. Typically, only one partner would incapacitate himself while the other would remain relatively sober and care for his mate. This arrangement assured that the inebriant's physical safety and supply of alcohol would be maintained.

A drinking spree characteristically lasted between a few days and two weeks. The alcoholic beverage most often consumed was an inexpensive, fortified, domestic wine. Wine is the chosen beverage for several reasons. Wine delivers the most alcohol per unit of money, and informants reported that since it supressed the appetite for food, available resources can be used entirely for alcohol. Some informants suggest that since wine delivers its alcohol in a more dilute form than spirits, it is easier to consume. This is especially important if one suffers from the complex gastrointestinal difficulties that are usually associated with chronic alcoholism. It is this anorexic property of wine that can have the most enduring effect on the individual. At the end of a two-week spree, the drinker usually finds himself in a weakened condition and in need of care. This care is provided by the other partner. At the termination of the spree, it is imperative that the drinker has ready access to a supply of alcohol. This alcohol is necessary to stave off the onset of characteristic alcoholic withdrawal symptoms which are common after a long drinking spree.

The assistance of the other partner is particularly vital at this time. One woman, who identified both her common-law husband and herself as alcoholics, described some of her feelings about the life style:

Respondent: You wanted to know why I put up with him? [referring to her man in an alcoholic stupor on the bed] Well, just let me tell you ... it's like that song on the radio now "I never promised you no rose garden". .... Life ain't easy, we just do the best we can, somebody has to take care of him, so I guess it just might as well be me. 'Sides, Jack [her man] will always do the same for me. .... He's not a bad man he don't beat me, and he don't run around with all sorts a other women.

Interviewer: Lillian, you told me a while back that once Jack got drunk and beat you which made you leave him. Would you mind talking a little more about that, please?

Respondent: Oh that, tha's even funny now. Happened, I don't know ... I guess 'bout year ago. He got himself good and juiced up—mosta the time he's OK, this time I don't know why, he got mean and he hit me pretty good. I know, I wasn't gonna stand around for that. ... I'll take care of him, I'll clean up his shit ... pardon my French, Mr. Harvey ... but I won't have him beating on me so I up and left him.

Interviewer: What happened then, did he stop drinking?

Respondent: Hell no! He just kept on drinkin'. ... Next thing I hear, they got him in Bellevue [the psychiatric ward of the hospital]. That fool—he be runnin' up and down the halls buck-naked, screamin' that cats are comin' to bite his penis off. I guess you know the rest ... signed him out, brought him home and just take care of him now.

This incident is highly representative of this alcohol-adaptive pattern. It is clear that if the member attempts an incident without the buffer provided by the protecting partner, his potential for behavior which will be labeled as problematic increased dramatically. Once this behavior achieves a degree of public recognition, the probability of the intervention of control agencies becomes much greater. This can be generalized to other aspects of S.R.O. living as well. Essentially, the issue is one of resources; these resources are measured in both material and nonmaterial (that is, social) terms. As in other extreme situations (for example, prisons, forced labor camps, disaster areas) the possession of even a very small margin can have a dramatic impact on the life situation of the members possessing them.

The helping-pair is the simplest and least specific response to the problems posed by the maintenance of an alcoholic life-style. As in any other relationship, the couples had their ups-and-downs, but most appeared to be fairly stable; although their lives together were occasionally punctuated by separations, the pairs I studied had been together for an average of four years. All reported basic satisfaction with their present arrangement and none indicated that they might wish to terminate their relationship in the foreseeable future. For others in the community though, the helping-pair adaption was not feasible. In order to sustain the alcoholic life-style, these people looked to larger groups to satisfy their needs.

Group Adaptions

The first of these group adaptions is not dissimilar to a more widespread ghetto pattern. Previous research has indicated that in the ghetto areas in New York City, groups of alcohol-addicted men live together in communal arrangements.[3] For these men, the drinking group provides almost the sole focus of their daily round of interaction. The drinking man's primary loyalty is to his drinking group and life without the group is unthinkable for him. The economic organization of the group finds one individual, often known as the "main man," responsible for providing the housing arrangements. In the case studied, and in most other cases reported, this "main man" had been able to establish himself as the superintendent of a tenement building. He then quietly moved members of his drinking group into his basement apartment with him. He "rented" the living space to his friends in return for their labor in maintaining the building.

The group's norm demanded that all resources, both financial (when available) and material, be pooled. Although the men were not always willing donors, money and goods were distributed throughout the group. An elaborate mental accounting system, however, was maintained and each man claimed that he knew "exactly" what was "owed" to him. The fact that at least some of these debits and credits were fictive mattered not at all for the group. The negotiations and renegotiations of these "accounts" figured importantly in maintaining the group's solidarity.

A similar pattern was observed in the S.R.O.'s. These drinking groups, responding to different ecological pressures, tended to be slightly smaller, containing five or six permanent members as opposed to the average of eight or nine members characteristic of the ghetto variety. Otherwise, the groups were similar in every regard. Housing was provided by a "main man" who ostensibly held the lease on the room. Even though some men in the group did have rooms in the hotel and would return to them to sleep, the major focus of their interaction was still the drinking group. The group was instrumental in fulfilling almost all of the needs of its members. Not only did it assure that the available alcohol would be distributed, but it assisted in the distribution of other resources as well.

One of the most striking characteristics of these drinking groups was their solidarity. Members clearly defined the boundaries of their own group and carefully guarded against intrusion by outsiders. The men clearly asserted just whom they would be willing to drink with and, of course, by extension interact with. As a member of one such group of men recounted:

> What you said before ... that just all wet. This here, just as surely as God made little green apples, this here ain't no skid row. Ain't gonna go catch us hangin' out on Columbus [Avenue] there lookin' for someone to pass a jug with ... I'ma just stayin' right here with my buddies and bein' sociable ... ain't that right fellows?

The groups are seen as permanent in that they endure over time, changing or replacing members, yet remaining structurally recognizable. It is through this permanence that the rudiments of a cultural tradition is possible. These drinking groups are entirely dissimilar to the skid row bottle-gang which fulfills only a limited number of ad hoc functions (such as the pooling of resources for the purchase of alcohol, a transitory focus for interaction) and then disintegrates. The continuity and stability of the group is supported by the benign hostility of the environment, the absence of diverting and/or competing institutional structures, and the internal structure and organization of the group.

The small size of the drinking group contributes positively to its cohesion by assuring nonspecialized interaction among its members. While each group may contain a single sociometric star, his presence is not so overwhelming that the group runs the risk of disintegration in the eventuality of his absence or departure.

As in the larger ghetto adaption, the most pervasive of this drinking culture's norms are the ones that govern sharing. While there may be occasional complaints about compliance in a specific situation, there is overall agreement that it really represents "the way things are." The sharing and concomitant reciprocity assures the group's solidarity since debts are measured in nonmaterial as well as material terms. If, for example, a man is wanted by the law, or anyone else with hostile intentions is searching for him, his drinking buddies will cover for him, forgetting who he is or where he might be. He will be quietly warned, which will allow him the opportunity to take whatever action is warranted. Members are very quick to recall these instances and will publicly remind the individual who they feel is indebted to them. Most importantly, though, these individual instances are projected to the entire group as a corporate body, thereby assuring a large measure of integration and internal cohesion.

Social control is effected through the imposition of both positive and negative sanctions. Since the member looks to the group to satisfy essentially all of his needs, group approval is crucial to continued support.

The negative sanction most often employed involves the threat of expulsion. For these persons, the threat of expulsion provides a double hazard. Expulsion means both subjection to a potentially hostile environment, the cessation of support in the eventuality of illness or some other emergency, and the diminution of status to the level of social isolate.

Quasi-Familial Arrangements

While the drinking group is a distillate of a larger ghetto pattern, it is likely that the matriarch and her quasi-family of alcoholic men is unique to the S.R.O. world. In this adaptation, one finds the expected group of adult male drinkers, but the focus of the interaction is a woman who has assumed a quasi-maternal role. The men are treated very much like her "children." They are cared for, fed, supplied with alcohol, nursed if ill, and protected, and directed.

While none of these women actually live (conjugally) with the men they are caring for, the largest part of the daily round of each is invested with the other. If the need does arise, as in, say, the case of illness, men will spend the night with the matriarch but the interaction tends to be limited to caretaking. While one occasionally hears a measure of bawdy talk and sexual innuendo between the matriarch and her family, no instance of sexual relations was ever reported. To the men she cares for, such would almost be un-thinkable.

Within the S.R.O. community these women occupy a high status position. Most have lived in the same hotel for several years and tend to be known and highly respected by all. They tend to be older women with a mean age of about fifty-five; the youngest in her late forties and the oldest past seventy. Most have had families and children who are already grown or have left. As one of these matriarchs, a stout, black, grandmotherly looking woman, explained during an interview:

Respondent: These here [motioning to the several men in the room] ... these here just like my babies now. They know that they got to be good boys, or out they go ... ain't no cussin' or fightin' 'lowed here—I don't mind if 'n they takes a taste or two [a drink] nows an then—but there ain't gonna be no carryin' on while I'm here.

Interviewer: Sorry, M'am, but could you tell me how you met some of the men who are here now?

Respondent: Don't know if I can rightly say. ... Some a the boys we go back a long time together ... maybe two, three years. Yazoo [referring to a man] here, this boy's only been commin' around for a bit now. I guess one day I just started helpin' folks out and before I knows it this boy here brings a friend who hungry and then another. It just kinda snuck up on me.

As one might expect, while the matriarch's primary orientation is to "her boys," she still performs a large number of caretaking, integrative, and control functions for the larger S.R.O. community. Since her position is so central, it would be useful to consider some of the things these matriarchs do within their quasi-families and how these activities affect the larger S.R.O. community.

In every way, the matriarch is the central figure in this drinking group. All of the group's interaction revolves around her; when she advances an opinion, everyone listens attentively and she is seldom contradicted. A reproving glance is often enough to silence a man or effect a change in the direction of the conversation.

Money and most material goods or resources are disbursed directly through the matriarch. Men would cash welfare, veterans', or social security checks, receive their food stamps, and surrender it all to the matriarch. She would then disburse small amounts of money during the period between checks. Food stamps were used to buy the food which would be prepared for the communal meals, or kept available if anyone was hungry.

In addition to the disbursement of money and foodstuffs, other goods would be hoarded and allocated as well. Bottles of wine were held in reserve in the eventuality of someone's need. The alcohol would never be used for anything but "medicinal" purposes, that is, to stave off the onset of tremulousness or any of the other conditions associated with alcoholic withdrawal. Several instances were observed in which women hoarded not only wine but some psychoactive drugs that are used to treat alcoholic withdrawal. These minor (Valium, Librium) and major (Thorazine, Stellazine) tranquilizers would be solicited throughout the hotel and held against future need.

A rather wide variety of drugs—analgesics, psychoactive and antibiotic—are available in the hotels. Many persons, especially those who receive their medical care from hospital clinics, find themselves with multiple or excessive supplies of medications. S.R.O.'ers are seldom encouraged to actively participate in their own treatment by the medical caretakers servicing them. As a result, medicines (of every kind) are seldom taken as professionally directed. Usually they are taken only until the symptoms diminish, or taken once and entirely discontinued if an immediate remission of symptoms does not occur. The remaining drugs quickly find their way into the community where their use is organized into patterns of self-medication and utilization by indigenous medical caretakers, such as these matriarchs.

While these matriarchs extended their caretaking activites as far as treating potentially life-threatening situations, even the most mundane considerations of their families were attended to. For example, one woman kept a wide-mouth gallon jar full of cigarette butts that she had collected from hallways and ashtrays. Anyone in need of a smoke was invited to either extract the tobacco and roll his own, or simply smoke what was left of the butt. The collection and distribution of second-hand clothing was another caretaking function assumed by these matriarchs.

The matriarchal group tends not to be as cohesive as the all-male, essentially leaderless group of drinking men. In the case of the matriarch, since the group is organized around this central figure, members persist in the group entirely at her pleasure. In addition, many of these matriarchs have favorites and this tends to have a profound impact on the amount of solidarity that the group can generate and maintain.

The matriarch is an important figure in the larger S.R.O. community. Since they offer a high level of organization, these women and their quasi-families are known throughout each S.R.O. Common sense knowledge in the community maintains that if anyone is in trouble and needs help, he can go to Missus Bertha or Missus Mae (or whomever) and receive food, medicine, or counsel. As such, the women occupy central positions within the S.R.O. community, often serving as nerve centers for communication and occasionally the distribution of goods or other resources.

Another function performed by these matriarchs has to do with the arbitration of differences within the S.R.O. community. Due to their relatively high status, they are often called into a dispute, generally involving the obligation of one member to another, and asked to give an opinion. In most instances, the disputing parties abide by her judgment. By involving the matriarch as a "judge," each party was able to save face and leave with at least a measure of equity.

Some of the more sophisticated managers have recognized the prominent place in the S.R.O. social structure that these matriarchs occupy and have sought to negotiate some sort of arrangement with them. In some cases, they have attempted to coopt the women by offering superior room accommodations, reduced rent, or similar advantages, believing that the aid and support of the matriarchs will facilitate the task of social control within their building. In cases of such successful symbiosis, things do improve. Since the woman has a greater information base than the manager, she can quickly identify an individual as a "troublemaker" and then report him to the manager, who is able to enlist the aid of the police to expel him from the building. From a somewhat different perspective, observation does suggest that the generalized interest by one of these women can have a profound effect on the incidence of bizarre behavior which occurs in a building. The extra mechanics of the process are unclear at this time, but it seems likely that the fusion of control and caretaking functions has a salutary effect. Another way the matriarch consolidated her position in the community was by acting as an advocate or ombudsman for the residents in the building. In this role the matriarch would often intercede between an S.R.O. manager and tenant and mediate the differences. If, however, the S.R.O.'er persisted in his troublesome behavior, the manager could expect at least the implicit support of the matriarch in the eviction of the offending party.

While these matriarchs perform a fairly wide variety of internal caretaking functions, occasionally the role becomes more specialized and assumes a more formal, rather than entirely informal, character. The case of an S.R.O. woman who found herself in charge of a community program illustrates this transformation.

In New York City, a neighborhood organization was established to continue the work of a community organization project. As in other such projects, it was determined that instead of a credentialed professional being placed directly in charge of the day-to-day operations, the needs of the community could best be served by having a local person in control. One S.R.O. resident, a woman whom project personnel had come to rely on, and who was well known and liked in the community by both S.R.O.'ers and managers, was invited to take over the position. As soon as she agreed to take the job, her activity shifted from informal operation in one building to a more formally structured, administrative role. Expectedly, her days were now occupied at an office: filling out forms, arranging meetings, conferencing with a small staff, distributing used clothing and household goods to the needy, listening to complaints, and all the various and sundry things done by poorly supported local administrators.

Her impact, on a directly personal level, was substantially reduced as her commitment to and involvement with the "professional" aspects of her position increased. How much social distance would ultimately come to separate her from the S.R.O.'ers she was working with could not be determined at the time of my study. The observations and impressions of several persons within the community, however, appeared to concur in the belief that in some way a community organization was valuable. However, they felt that "she was doin' more good where she was at" (before assuming her administrative role). In the long run, whether this is indeed the case remains, of course, problematic. In a social world full of persons seeking direct contact, the loss of even one leader can be deeply felt.

Structure and Cohesion Through Sexuality

In the three adaptions described above, each type encompassed different peoples who had their special needs fulfilled through the structures of the groups. Our attention will now be directed towards structures erected on the basis of sexual needs. "Normal relations" (that is, heterosex) are deemed essentially nonproblematic and will be discussed later in the chapter. Since a higher level of organization is necessary to sustain them, homosexual relationships have greater impact on the social structure of the S.R.O. community. As in cases of other behavior which carries with it the probability of being labeled as deviant, homosexual activity and the persons committed to its patterns have had to evolve collective responses to affect the satisfaction of needs.

Women involved in lesbian arrangements are rather common throughout the S.R.O. world. The relationships observed were all fairly longstanding (most had been together a year or more) and separate interviews with each of the partners suggested a reasonable degree of stability. This is not to say that the relationships appeared to be without occasional tension, but such appeared to be "normal" within the bounds of any exclusive social-sexual relationship.

Typically the organization of the relationship called for one woman to permanently play the dominant or male role; within the community she was known as a "bull-dyker." The other partner, playing the passive or female role, was referred to as the "fem." It is interesting to note that at the time of the study, homosex activity in the S.R.O. world was still organized along very traditional lines. Since this proved to be the case, the sexual roles were rather firmly established. With all of the current interest and involvement in gay women's liberation, I would expect to encounter a blurring of these role distinctions if I were to revisit the community.

Since a culture of poverty exists in the S.R.O. world, deviant behavior (at least in its nonthreatening forms) is readily and even casually accepted. One woman, during an interview, briefly recounted how she found her way into such a relationship.

> Well honey, you really want to know where I'm at ... been now, been wit' Chocho [her partner] 'bout three years. ... I guess you can say we in love. First time I ever wit' another woman was in jail. I was frightened but it was OK. Then I got out and I met up wid' Chocho here, I got scared. ... I say this jail-house shit, it ain't no good ... you ain't crazy or nothin'. But then I be wid' Cho an' she say its cool, honey, its cool, everything copesetic ... I know just how to take care of you ... you leave it to me. And man, dig it, Cho' just beautiful. ...

Within the S.R.O. community these lesbian pairs tend to fulfill several important functions. Since the relationships are characterized by a fair degree of stability, this social stability tends to transform itself into geographic stability. The geographic stability of people such as these contributes to the preservation of the "character" of the various buildings.

Stability makes possible the development of a number of important processes. Not unexpectedly, the permanence of the couple as such encourages a measure of commitment to the community, most likely as a further means of securing physical safety and expanding one's social space. In a socially disorganized situation, the alternatives available are severely limited: the individual can simply isolate her/himself and through this isolation achieve a measure of security; yet by doing so, she/he radically limits her/his freedom of movement. Some organization, no matter how minimal, provides for both adequate physical security and a large increase in the available alternatives. This, in turn, makes for greater personal freedom and autonomy.

Such was the case in one of the moderately sized open S.R.O.'s studied. Two of the pairs lived in one apartment wing and the other lived in a different wing, on the opposite side of the building; all had been in the building for well over eighteen months. In both instances, the pairs had been able to effect considerable control over their life-space. They were able to pressure the manager into repairing the locks on the general apartment door. In this way, the entire unit could be secured, therefore allowing residents to operate more freely within without fearing for their safety. (This gave the residents free access to both the lavatory and kitchen facilities and obviated the need to lock oneself in and out of one's room.) Keys were provided to all the residents in these wings, and they could come and go as desired. For regular visitors who were not residents, and for residents as well, a code was devised so that by knocking on the door in a certain way, entrance could be obtained. All of the residents agreed that unless a positive identification could be made no one would be admitted. While members of the stable pair were primarily interested in their own security and comfort, the positive neighborhood effects resulting from the creation of the secured enclosure had a profound effect on the life-style of the more than ten other S.R.O.'ers living in that wing.

In addition to a positive effect on security, these stable pairs fulfill other functions for the S.R.O. community. Many have evolved sharing arrangements with other residents who surrender their food stamps in return for prepared meals. Often this would begin casually as other S.R.O.'ers come to the stable pair and ask for food, or as one or both members of the stable pair become concerned about the welfare of a third person and offer him assistance. After a while the arrangement became routinized and mutual expectations and obligations were set.

Besides the sharing of food and often alcohol, both of which are common denominators of exchange in the S.R.O. world, these stable pairs frequently act as information centers. Since they occupy a central place in the community social structure, much of what may be happening in an S.R.O. can be quickly learned from one or both of the partners. The individuals in the pair use this centrality to both strengthen and consolidate their position in the community by serving as information brokers who exchange information about various people and events for other intelligence or material resources. The geographic permanence and social stability of the pair contribute to their success. The members of the pair often have ready access to the building's manager since they have demonstrated their desire to protect his interests by their efforts o improve the S.R.O. environment. Such access becomes particularly valuable when there is talk about selling the building, making substantial changes in policy, or the like. Under almost every circumstance (t e single exception being a strong tenant/community organization which, if it could not influence the sale, could safeguard the rights of the residents during and after the transition), the tenants are entirely uninvolved in any of the activity involved in a sale or policy change. However, they do demonstrate the expected interest and concern in things that will directly affect them.

The male homosexual arrangements observed were dissimilar to the female adaptions: almost entirely lacking was any sort of stable pair. (In the several hotels intensively studied, only one such pair was noted; these men had been together for more than two years.) Instead, what was observed was more of the expected pattern, constructed along the dimension of a "free-floating community," of men coming together for limited encounters and then separating again.[4] Due to this impermanence, any such group is necessarily more limited in impact. Interestingly, even in the S.R.O. world, there is relatively more social stigmatization attached to male homosexual behavior than to female homosexual behavior. This encourages the speculation that in addition to the relative impermanence of the groups, the individual finds it necessary to invest comparatively more of his energy in dealing with the deviance label, thereby limiting his impact in other areas.

Besides sustaining each other by providing food, shelter, and alcohol (and other drugs on occasion) the male homosexual group functioned efficiently in the exchange of information, which was not limited only to other gay people, but encompassed almost every aspect of S.R.O. living. Intelligence information was not held solely within the gay community but would quickly find its way outwards. This was one of the vectors by which people living in one S.R.O. were made aware of the fact that "somebody, maybe the man [the police], was askin' around 'bout them." This advanced warning would allow them the opportunity to take whatever action appeared indicated.

Voluntary Associations

Voluntary associations tended to be the least common type of social group. For example, groups that were as well organized as gangs (that is, associative groups having an externally recognizable structure in which a number of specialized roles could be observed) or organized athletic sport teams, were extremely rare. While several friendship groups were noted, the members were very quick to point out that "these was just dudes that hung together."

A very notable exception was found in one of the larger S.R.O. hotels studied. Several factors converged to bring forth a powerful, all male, voluntary associative group which exerted a substantial impact on the lives of the S.R.O.'ers living in that building. This group, called the "Rumblers," is important because it illustrates that even a small amount of organization can be readily transformed into strength.

A prominent figure, known to almost all at a large hotel, was a man called "Bimbo." At the hotel he officially served as the house security guard, and was distinguished by both his appearance and demeanor. Physically impressive, he stood six feet, three or four inches tall and weighed more than two hundred fifty pounds. Although he was light-complexioned, he had distinctly black features. There was very little question as to his actual strength. A heavy "sap" or blackjack was always in his pocket and no one ever doubted his willingness to use it or any other convenient weapon. He was reputed to have a very quick temper and was said to carry a grudge for a long time. In the hotel, and in other parts of the S.R.O. world, he had the reputation of being "one bad motherfucker." With an air of bravado, several informants indicated that "ain't no way [they're] afraida Bimbo." These remarks, however, were offered in private and their behavior in his presence was deferential, to the point of being obsequious.

Although Bimbo had at one time lived at the hotel, he no longer did so. The management, however, as part of his working arrangement, provided him with a suite of rooms rent free. He, himself, changed the lock on the door and installed an elaborate magnetic police lock. No one was ever admitted to the rooms without Bimbo, and only a very select few were ever admitted at all. Although his official duties as a security guard required his presence at the hotel between the hours of midnight and 8 A.M., he could usually be found at the hotel from early afternoon on.

Bimbo was accompanied by a coterie of several young to early middle-aged men who called themselves the "Rumblers." All were black and superficially they appeared to be some of the most socially and psychologically intact people at the hotel. None had any serious chemical dependency problems, although psychotropic substance use (especially alcohol and marijuana) was not uncommon in the group. The Rumblers liked to think of themselves as a social club or civic association; manifestly the club was "dedicated to improving the living conditions and social atmosphere of the hotel."

During one of the periods of municipal interest in the S.R.O. problem, Bimbo's Rumblers had received a fair amount of encouragement and support from the social service professionals active in the community. Following the social work theory underlying "community organization," the most efficacious way of assisting a community was by working through the existent community structures. To these professionals, the Rumblers seemed like an ideal place to begin. During 1970 and 1971, the Rumblers were in the process of attempting to implement some of their plans to improve the hotel's recreation facilities.

More than a half century ago, when the hotel had hosted an affluent clientele, elaborate facilities had been built into it. For example, in the hotel's basement, now very long unused, could be found the remains of an extensive gymnasium with a swimming pool and Turkish bath facility. In addition to fully restoring this area, the Rumblers had plans for several rooms, adjacent to the lobby, which would be converted into club rooms by the installation of such equipment as pool and card tables. In addition, there would be a mat room for the practice of the martial arts, and a comfortable, dimly lit lounge. Turk, one of the Rumblers, explained some of their plans during an interview:

Respondent:	Now you lookit' here ... this here gonna be a room with a couple a pool tables, 'an some card tables over there. That other room I showed you ... we gonna make that a lounge. You know, you got a fox [woman] you take 'em there and zowie! [He paused here to "give skin."] And you already seen all the stuff in the cellar ... uhm huh, it comin' right along.
Interviewer:	Turk, all you have shown me has been empty hotel rooms; most haven't even been cleaned yet. And the gymnasium in the basement looks like it hasn't been touched in years. When do you think that all of this is going to be completed?
Respondent:	When it all gonna be finished? Well, I don't rightly know. ... All I know is that Bimbo, he say, it comin' right along.
Interviewer:	Where is all the equipment and the money to fix this place up going to come from?
Respondent:	Bimbo says, it all gonna be contributed. ... When this place get together it all gonna be donated ... Bimbo say so.

While the rank and file Rumblers had an idea about what was going to happen, it differed materially from what Bimbo was actually doing. In subsequent interviews with the hotel's management and the head of the social service staff, it was revealed that Bimbo did *not* have any understanding with either of them concerning the utilization of the space. The hotel's management allowed that since there was no current need for the space, they found "nothing wrong with letting some of the boys play around with it." They were quite definite, however, in stating that if the space could be used more profitably, the Rumblers and their plans would be immediately preempted. Interviews with the social service staff suggested much of the same. Bimbo had approached them for both money and material. When he was told that he would have to submit a written proposal outlining his plans, he was unable to formulate such a proposal. The present social service coordinator, in fact, intimated that he was rather suspicious of "any plans" that

Bimbo might have. In an interview, the social service coordinator recounted some of his experiences with this local leader:

Respondent: When I first started working in this project [slightly more than two years earlier] I was introduced to Bimbo and the other Rumblers by some of the other staff. They explained to me how Bimbo and the other Rumblers were "natural community leaders," and that our work in the area would be more effective and meaningful if we might work through them. At the time it seemed like the entirely right thing to do. ... Everybody was talking about "community control" and I really believed that a community had the right to decide its own destiny. ... Shit, right out of school—what did I know?

Interviewer: I'm sorry, I think I lost your train of thought. What sort of things were you and the other workers supposed to be doing for the community?

Respondent: Well, all sorts of things. The stuff that we did ourselves, like the games group [e.g., bingo, pokeno], the current events discussions groups, and the weekly movies—all of those went well. Well, we didn't get as many people out as we had hoped, but the events ran smoothly enough and there wasn't much overt acting-out behavior. But this was only a small part of the total program; in addition to our casework, the plan called for the setting-up of a whole recreational program, a meals program, and a holiday party program. It was in these parts of the program that we thought Bimbo and the Rumblers could be used. Well, almost from the beginning I thought I began noticing some funny stuff.

Interviewer: Funny stuff? What do you mean funny stuff?

Respondent: OK, I'll give you and example. ... When the project first began, we planned a full range of recreational activities. One of them was a bus ride excursion out to a park about fifty miles from the city. Following our plan, we let Bimbo make the arrangements. He said that he needed $100 deposit for the buses and for other incidentals. We were able to take the money out of a special account and give it to him as soon as he asked for it. In any case, when the trip was over we received a bill for the buses which showed that only a ten dollar deposit had been paid. When I spoke to Bimbo about it, he was rather evasive but promised to return the money. ... Well, that was more than a year and a half ago. Since then I've asked him about it on numerous occasions, and each time I receive the same promise.

Interviewer: Is that all? Or are there other things that you might have noticed?

Respondent: OK ... that was the only thing that really affected me personally. But there's a lot more going on. You know about the free community supper we provide before the Wednesday night meetings? Well, I showed you the storeroom full of food. OK, there's only three keys to that lock. I have one, the managers have one, and Bimbo has one. Why? He's the hotel's security guard, so he was able to convince the management that he should have complete access to every area of the hotel. Well, there's just one heck-of-a-lot of loss between one delivery and another. ... I know we don't use a fraction of the food that's there and then is missing. ... I'm sure Bimbo has something to do with it.

Interviewer: Didn't you report it to Mr. Kissler [the supervisor]?

Respondent: Oh yeah—I told him about it and he said that he'd look into it. Well, nothing happened, or rather everything kept happening and the next time I spoke to him about it he just flat out told me it wasn't any of my business and I just better take care of my own duties. Since then I've learned how to just close my eyes about certain things ... I know we could probably be doing more for the people. but you've just got to keep your head above the water.

This interview highlights several facets of the S.R.O. world. Bimbo's Rumblers have been able, at least partially, to bridge the gap separating the S.R.O. world from the larger middle and working class world "outside." Since they have evolved ways to operate at this interface they are able to successfully exploit aspects of both. Having himself identified by the social service staff as a "natural community leader" made it possible for Bimbo to secure access to much of what these "missionaries from the outside world" were able to offer.[5] The fact that some of what Bimbo did was, at best, questionable mattered little to the higher echelon social service staff who clearly perceived their mandate as "working through the people." The loss of a "natural community leader," who was as readily visible as Bimbo, would be seen by them as constituting a severe setback to the project.

Bimbo and the other Rumblers enjoyed a quasi-symbiotic relationship with the hotel's management as well. The other Rumblers, living throughout the hotel, functioned as an information collecting system for Bimbo. All those people who regularly operated extralegal, or actually illegal businesses within the boundaries of the hotel did so only under an arrangement with Bimbo. For example, while the hotel's management disclaimed any knowledge of either regular drug trafficking or even any addict living in the building, both were actually in evidence. Both, if known (and ultimate discovery was a certainty), could only persevere with Bimbo's consent. Bimbo received monetary return from drug dealers for allowing them to do business in the building. Users were allowed to stay only if they provided Bimbo with information concerning other users in the building and other illegal activities. In one instance at least, a white, female addict reported that she had to have sexual relations with Bimbo as her payment for the privilege of living and operating around the hotel.

In the event of noncompliance, expulsion from the building was swift. Bimbo simply described the individual as either generally undesirable or a troublemaker and the management ordered his eviction. If the tenant accepted the verdict, he or she left with little or no difficulty. On the other hand, if the resident did not accept the verdict, Bimbo would make it impossible for him or her to enter his or her room by plugging the door. If, further, the resident still wished to maintain an intransigent position, the threat of physical force (or violence) at the hands of Bimbo and his associates was very real.

Bimbo and the spoilers have been able to develop and maintain a position in which they operate at the interface of the legitimate and illegitimate worlds. Interview data from one of the Rumblers, as well as less direct evidence, suggest that Bimbo was active in a stolen merchandise operation. While little direct trafficking in these goods occurred in the hotel, much of the material was stored in the building until it had a chance to "cool off." The respondent reported that the goods were kept in the suite of rooms that the hotel's management granted Bimbo. While the respondent, himself, had never been in the suite, he was absolutely certain that this was where Bimbo kept the stolen goods that he (the respondent) would periodically receive. Because of the obvious difficulties involved, this aspect of the Rumblers' operation was not (and probably could not be) studied.

Corroborating evidence for this operation was provided by one of the social service workers. Roughly a year earlier he mentioned that he was interested in buying a stereo phonograph set for his home. Somehow, Bimbo heard about this and suggested that a friend of his had just left for California, and that Bimbo was "trying to get rid of [sell] his things" which happened to include an almost new stereo set that worked perfectly. Naturally, since Bimbo liked the worker and "thought much" about what they were trying to do in the hotel, he offered to let the social service worker have the stereo at a tremendous saving. The worker expressed his willingness to examine the set and Bimbo promised to produce it the next day. He did produce the set, but it was not what the worker wanted. Bimbo then told him of "another friend" and advised the worker that he could produce the second set in a few minutes if the worker desired. The second set was produced and it, too, was rejected. At that point, Bimbo said that he had purchased a stereo set that he was "saving for his special girlfriend's birthday," but that since he was short of cash, he would be willing to let the worker examine it. This time the worker was satisfied and agreed to purchase the set. The worker, who claimed to be knowledgeable about currently available equipment, suggested that the set's retail value approximated seven hundred dollars, although Bimbo was only asking two hundred dollars for it.

The amount of control that the Rumblers was able to exercise in the community was striking. Bimbo was quick to perceive that since only a very low level of community organization existed, a group such as the Rumblers could have a tremendous impact. Further support was derived from the fact that the managers of the hotel, feeling as beleagured as they did, were entirely willing to surrender almost all of the control functions to Bimbo. From the managers' limited perspective, Bimbo had been quite successful: drug use and drug traffic in the hotel was almost entirely "controlled" and actual or potential "troublemakers" were quickly identified and ejected.

Other Social Groups

Up to now, attention has centered on those groups structured around a major need or central focus of the S.R.O. member's life; these need-oriented groups are found within the S.R.O. world. Other groups seem to lack the same impact and solidarity. While not as striking, these other kinds of groups still serve a number of functions in the community. Below, some of these other groups and their functions will be considered as we conclude this viewing of the forms of social differentiation found in the S.R.O. world.

The S.R.O.'s are similar to all other communities because that indefinable relationship which can only be alluded to as "friendship" does occur within them. The relationship may be as fleeting and casual as the willingness to temporarily suspend the facade of civil inattention and exchange a daily or occasional greeting; or it may be as deep as two elderly persons who, during waking hours, are virtually inseparable. In addition, it necessarily encompasses all of the possibilities between the two. As in other communities and other situations, friends tend to be somewhat similar in at least some of their attributes (such as age or sex) and are able to provide the other with something that he or she needs.

Contrived Groups

Since the S.R.O. world possesses many of the characteristics typically found in the culture of poverty, a dearth of instrumentally oriented groups exists. Groups such as political parties, civic improvement associations, and religious or church organizations are almost wholly lacking. While the focus of such voluntary associations tends to be goal directed, their social structures tend to be unspecialized enough to allow sociability and organization, and quasi-organized recreational activities.

The absence of such groups was a major concern of the social workers who were active in the area. At that time, group work and community organizations were the dominant work modalities. These professionals believed that the community could,best be served through the establishment of voluntary organizations. Since direct social action groups were not even considered, it was decided to focus on recreational activities; thus "special interest groups" were formed. For example, there was a current events discussion group, table games group, a sewing group, and others of a similar nature.

The original plans called for the social worker to serve as the social catalyst around which the group would crystallize. Then, once the group was functioning smoothly, the worker would quietly exit. It was assumed that the group would persist because its members would have developed the necessary social skills to sustain it. This, however, proved not to be the case. It was evident that both the group's integration and perseverance were entirely dependent upon the social worker who had formed it. As such, when a worker left the field, the group that he had formed and was involved with invariably disintegrated.

This was illustrated by the fate of the table games group when its founder left the field to return to school. Because the social service cadre determined that the activity was valuable, they requested that another worker be assigned to continue the group. The requirements were minimal: the group leader, a day or two in advance, had to remind residents that the games would be held as usually scheduled; often a poster announcing the event would be placed in a well-traveled, conspicuous place. Prior to the game, the leader had to purchase cigarettes which were distributed in lieu of cash prizes, and make sure that the necessary chairs and tables were set up. When the group was assembled the cards and markers were distributed and the games could begin. For the game itself, the leader would draw numbers out of a drum, call them out, check the cards of the winners, and distribute the prizes. Very shortly after the new worker took charge, attendance at the games dropped sharply; after three consecutive weeks, only four persons came at all. The group activity was subsequently discontinued. When erstwhile group members were interviewed, they reported that they had stopped attending because they were displeased with the new leader. Although their rejection of the group was emphatic, their reasons tended to be ambiguous. Some felt that the "new" worker did not read the numbers correctly; others felt that he read them too fast or too slow; and one respondent finally summed it up by stating, "it just ain't the same since Mr. B. don't do it."

Other groups were initiated by the social service staff to provide assistance in the administration of the service project. Since the project's philosophy demanded that local people be involved in *all* phases of the work, S.R.O.'ers were recruited for such low-level work as office receptionists who answered the phone and relayed messages. While the environment was one that could easily encourage the creation of a strong feeling of solidarity and, ultimately, a well-integrated colleague group, this did not occur. Social interaction only occurred around the professional workers, and when they left the scene, the interaction, for the most part, ceased. These groups, much like others having a non-S.R.O. or extra-S.R.O. focus, could be characterized as being short-lived and lacking in effect.

A Final Note On Social Differentiation

Although the question of group structure is not directly involved here, I would like to provide some additional observations on social differentiation and social morphology. This is being offered because it is one of the few areas in S.R.O. life that appears to have a racial basis.

Blacks who are newly entering the S.R.O. world appear to operate somewhat better than whites. They are able to find enough similarity to their previous experiences to assist them in first identifying, and then participating in, the existent social networks. As such, these young men and women find it possible to operate both within and outside the S.R.O. world. As a result of this ability, they are able to mobilize resources within the S.R.O. world to assist them in their other endeavors.

For those whites who have made a commitment to S.R.O. living, integration into the community's social s ructure and social networks has occurred. For the transient white, however, the situation is strikingly different. Many of these people reported that they were formerly immersed in the hippie or counterculture. Although they were still interested in certain aspects of the life-style, such as drug usage, dress and grooming, and argot, they reported losing the sense of ideological commitment that they once had. Most reported extensive travels throughout the county's metropolitan centers and expressed an unwillingness, for the present, to settle down. Almost all described themselves as "loners" and reported little interest in having anything to do with the hotel and the people living in it. One young man was asked about why he was at the hotel and not in a more popular area like New York City's Greenwich Village East. He reported that "the East Village is just too much of a hassle, too many things to get into. . . . Here I can just hang loose and split whenever I want." It is probable that perhaps at least a few of these young people will, after a while, form some attachment to the S.R.O. world.

Many of these younger transients have had extensive experience with the counterculture, and have even "dropped out" of it and into the level of the social structure which S.R.O. living represents. Very few seem actually satisfied with S.R.O. living, but they perceive few other available alternatives. An interview with one of these young transients elicited some of his perceptions of the S.R.O. world. (The interview occurred immediately after the respondent attempted to sell me some L.S.D.)

Interviewer: Why did you want to sell me the acid?

Respondent: Hey man, ain't no way I'm gonna drop any acid here, man. . . . It'd be a bummer, man.

Interviewer: What's so bad about this place?

Respondent: Don't you know, man, this place is got real bad vibes, man. . . . I ain't doin' no acid here, man.

Interviewer: Are you doing any shit [drugs] at all?

Respondent: Sure man, since I've been here, man, I've really been into downs [sedatives and hypnotics], man, it's the only way I can hack this place, man.

His experience was not atypical of others, many of whom appeared to drift in and out of the S.R.O. world, and continued to return because they did not have the resources which would allow other choices.

The S.R.O. as a Little Community

The Economic System

Because it is similar to a little community which lacks the resources necessary to support an independent economy, only a very few S.R.O.'ers can look entirely to their community for support. Money flows into the community and then quickly leaves it with very little remaining to circulate and gradually accumulate. This one-way flow assures that money cannot become a community resource which would ultimately improve the quality of life which is available. In this section the economic factors in operation within the S.R.O. community are considered along with some of the social patterns which have evolved around them. We should, of course, bear in mind that most of those presently living in the S.R.O. world are at, or are very close to, the subsistence level. Moreover, it is likely that a substantial proportion of the S.R.O. population subsists on fixed incomes of one sort or another. In addition to being particularly vulnerable to economic fluctuations such as inflation, scarcity of goods, and the like, fixed-income people find their ability to control their money severely limited. A person on welfare, for example, cannot have a bank account, be gainfully employed, or change living arrangements (i.e., marry or even cohabit with someone) lest his or her allotment be decreased or even suspended.

For most of those living on a fixed social service income, every bit of their money is accounted for. Social workers have ostensibly planned a budget with each client which allows for all of the necessities. The budgets, however, generally reflect past conditions and there is no built-in factor for cost-of-living escalation. For many of the elderly, especially those who use a variety of proprietary medicines, the budget is particularly hard to live within since costs for these drugs are not reimbursable. In order to purchase these drugs, cuts are often made in the money allocated for food; consequently, their diets consist largely of inferior foods.

As one might expect, the situation is particularly bad for those who are alcohol-dependent. As the two-check cycle progresses, the type of alcohol consumed switches from spirits or hard liquor to the cheap, fortified wines. Moreover, the individual, as his cash dwindles, is necessarily forced to choose between alcohol and food. The choice, apparently, is not a difficult one to make as the rather high association between chronic alcoholism and malnutrition demonstrates.

Since money is such a scarce commodity which leaves the S.R.O. system so quickly, other mediums of exchange were evolved. One such medium of exchange is federal food stamps. It is not uncommon for people to pool their stamps, thereby making it possible to increase both the quantity and quality of food available. Instances in which books of food stamps were resold outright, thereby allowing the seller additional money for other goods, were reported; the extent of this practice, however, was not assessed. Many of my informants intimated that they had heard about it and that they would not be adverse to participating in such a transaction.

S.R.O. Business

Like other small communities, the S.R.O.'s support varied kinds of businesses. The business patterns are necessarily in the "service" and "merchandising" areas since the community does not produce anything of its own. These indigenous enterprises could be further classified along the dimensions of their legality: illegal; questionably legal; and legitimate.

Illegal businesses seldom receive strong censure from the community. (The single pattern in which there is censure involves the trafficking in illegal, especially narcotic, drugs.) Other patterns of extralegal entrepreneurship are integrated into the S.R.O. community. These services typically involve policy, shylocking, and bootlegging, and are utilized by many of the community's members. The meaning of illegality, as it relates to business, merits some consideration. Like other culture of poverty communities, the S.R.O.'s are not willing to entirely embrace the norms and definitions of the larger world. The case of drug trafficking is illustrative because the community perceives drugs, especially opiates, as threatening. Other illegal businesses, if not receiving open endorsement, do not evoke the same radical control response that drug trafficking does. Moreover, because of the strength of the proscriptive norms surrounding the drug trafficking and the concomitant control efforts, drug dealers can have only a limited impact on the community's social structure. This is applicable to only the low level dealer. Previous research has suggested that the larger suppliers, with several illegitimate enterprises, can exert considerable influence on a community. Entrepreneurs supplying the other marginal services have the support of both the community's members and (minimally, the tacit acknowledgement) of the social control agents active in the community. This occurs for two reasons. The first suggests that while such activities as policy, shylocking, and bootlegging may be illegal, the S.R.O. community does not consider them to be immoral. The second, and perhaps the most important, reason suggests that in the purveying of these services, the marginal entrepreneurs engaged in them simultaneously fulfill a wide variety of essential functions for the community.[6]

In the S.R.O. world, playing the numbers is a well-accepted community activity. When looking at other underclass communities, researchers have observed that the daily bet, no matter how small, is one of the major mechanisms by which the truly indigent aspire to fortune and often fame as well.[7] While my investigation made no attempt to assess the prevalence of the policy operation within the S.R.O. community, I did find that almost "everyone" knew with whom and where a bet could be placed. Also, "everyone" was able to read the racing results in the daily newspaper to determine whether he or she, or a friend, might have come in lucky.

Bets tend to be rather small. A bet of one dollar was considered a large one and most informants, who were regular (often daily) players, suggested that their usual bet was seldom more (or less) than 25¢. Methods used to choose the combination of the three numbers on which the bet is placed ranged from the expected numerological conundrums and dream books, to bizarre, idiosyncratic formulations, such as inspecting the daily newspaper for the random or stray printer's marks that appear and then divining their combination through these marks.

S.R.O.'ers who regularly play the numbers were asked why they preferred this kind of activity to, say, New York's newly legalized off-track betting. Most complained that they found it inconvenient to leave their building and go to a betting parlor which was only a few blocks away. Others complained that a poorly dressed person was shunned by the other patrons, and made to feel very uncomfortable by the clerks. And lastly, but of great importance, they reported that the minimum two dollar bet was "just too rich for their blood" and that it discouraged their utilization of the service.

In direct contrast to legalized gambling was the folk (or extralegal) system in operation within the hotels. S.R.O.'ers who regularly played the numbers never dealt with anyone above the level of a numbers runner, the lowest member of the organization. The runner, however, was able to provide a personalized service for them. The runner would come directly to the player's room for both the taking of the bet, and the less likely event of the payoff. Since the service was a personalized one, elaborate accounts were maintained between the runner and his steady clients. The runner realizes the value of such an account to his business volume and readily encourages them—knowing, of course, that his tip—generally 10 percent of the winnings, will often be substantially greater if he makes the additional effort.

The interaction between runner and client that extends beyond the business transaction is of even greater importance. Since the runner moves freely throughout the larger S.R.O. community, servicing the several hotels in his allocated territory, he is able to amass a large amount of information and gossip which he willingly passes on. By being a routinely available source of information and news, he serves a vital communication function for the community. For people who are not ambulatory, the numbers runner serves as a primary source of information about what may be occurring in the community. Without his regular contact, these home-bound persons would undoubtably be even more isolated.

The runners will assist their regular clients by specially delivering messages or small packages for them. One new runner, during an interview, reported that he actively encouraged such activity, believing that it would provide him with an alibi if he ever had any difficulty with the police. It should be stressed that these extra services have been so well incorporated into the norms of the business exchange that both parties have come to accept them without question. In addition, in those instances where a runner might balk, it is likely that he will find the level of business falling off and his position in the community becoming considerably more tenuous.

While the numbers runner is just a small part of a greater enterprise, the bootlegger working an S.R.O. is almost invariably an independent. Almost all, however, operate under the aegis—even "franchise"—of someone like Bimbo, or even the S.R.O. manager himself. Like other extralegal enterprises (with the exception of illegal drugs) the level of service provided is equal in importance to the product offered. In New York, the sale of alcoholic beverages, with the exception of beer and cider, can only occur in a licensed package store, bar or restaurant. As in other such regulated businesses, both the times and situation of sale (for example, who may be served) is rigidly controlled by the state alcoholic beverage control commission. Package stores offering wine are closed by law on Sunday, and most neighborhood shops tend to close around midnight. The drinker who is without an adequate supply will not be able to purchase alcohol legally until the establishments reopen (S.R.O.'ers dislike drinking in bars for many of the same reasons New York off-track betting parlors are shunned.) Also, since S.R.O.'s are not characteristically located in skid row areas, the skid row type bar is not available to S.R.O.'ers. The answer to the dilemma of an after-hours alcohol supply comes in the adaption of the bootlegger. Interestingly, although they are usually heavy drinkers themselves, the bootleggers observed seldom demonstrated the degree of physical or psychological deterioration exhibited by many of their regular customers.

Bootleggers would stock only a single brand of wine, buying it by the case, thereby saving something over the usual retail price. Most dealt only in pint bottles, believing that it would be better business to require only a small cash outlay by the customer (who often didn't have much money) than to risk making a larger sale in the hope of realizing greater profits. Although expensive, the bootleggers were well patronized because they offered a steady supply of alcohol when no other was available. Additionally, they would also deliver the wine directly to their customer's rooms, and they would be willing to deal on a credit basis.

A similar pattern of bootlegging was observed in S.R.O.'s in a western state. Here, however, the pattern was considerably more elaborate. In this situation, many of the city's S.R.O. bootleggers had entirely exchewed buying pint bottles of wine. Instead they would collect discarded wine bottles and refill these from gallon bottles that they had purchased. Economically, this represented a substantial advance over the direct purchase method in which the cost of the wine was considerable. There is some indication, however, that customer satisfaction was more in question. Here customers reported that bootleggers were watering down the wine. These complaints were, in several instances, confirmed when I had the opportunity of assisting a local merchant in the preparation of his orders.

The bootlegging business is possible because the indigenous entrepreneur is capable of meeting the customer's conditions. Of the three conditions described, the steady availability is probably the least important. It is the willingness to deliver the product which figures most prominently into the enterprise. In New York City, although most of the area's state-licensed package stores will make deliveries, none are willing to deliver a single pint of wine. Moreover, many of these stores categorically refuse to make any deliveries within an S.R.O., claiming that the buildings are just too dangerous to go into. The bootlegger who lives in the hotel and operates under the aegis of one of the local "strongmen" has no reservations about operation in the S.R.O. Finally, since his business is essentially a small-scale one, no order is too small to be profitable.

The price of the wine would vary depending upon the day, the time of day, and the time of the month. Not unexpectedly, prices tended to be lower during the normal business hours but would climb noticeably on weekends and after hours. Prices would vary depending upon the time of month. As with fully legitimate enterprises operating in ghetto and poor areas, prices would increase in the beginning and the middle of the month, corresponding closely to the distribution cycle of welfare checks.[8] However, bootleggers working in the S.R.O. world charge more for wine at both the beginning and the end of the cycle. The raise at the beginning of the cycle is rather easy to define: people have more fluid money and are therefore more likely to spend it. Prices, however, are increased at the end of the cycle as well, when people have little money. Like the satisfaction of other chemical cravings, the possession or lack of money makes little difference in the search for the desired substance. Since the bootlegger is willing to extend credit (something that a licensed package store is prohibited from doing) to a customer who currently has no money, but who has the expectation of receiving some very soon, the customer most readily agrees to the increase in price.

The extension of credit is an essential aspect of the social organization of all marginal enterprises within the S.R.O. The bootlegger, like others engaged in extralegal enterprises, operates under the (direct or indirect) aegis of the management. Through this collusion, he finds it relatively easy to assure his debts. In some instances, the hotel's manager, while cashing a check for a tenant, will deduct, in addition to rent and other legitimate charges (for example, phone calls), the money that the hotel's bootleggers and loan sharks have "garnisheed" on the welfare or social security check. While such direct cooperation between manager and extralegal operators is rare, a less direct collusion between the two is very common. Here, the marginal entrepreneur positions himself closely to the lobby window and intercepts his debtor as he steps off the line with his cash in hand. In such circumstances, the owing member finds it difficult to either disclaim his debt or simply make himself unavailable until all of his money has been spent.

Legal/Legitimate Enterprises

Since the S.R.O.'s contain a substantial population of old and not fully ambulatory people, there are many shut-ins. In response to the needs of these shut-ins, a business enterprise constructed around running errands emerged in the S.R.O. world. The jobs performed by these errand-runners are essentially simple ones: purchasing the daily newspaper, food, alcohol, cigarettes, and medicines. The runner is rewarded with a small tip (seldom more than twenty-five cents). Each runner has a carefully developed clientele whom he services regularly. As one would assume, the volume of business is small. In a system where monetary flow is both scarce and fixed, even small differences can have a significant impact on a person's opportunity.

The relationship between runner and client should be seen more in symbiotic terms and not as a simple commercial transaction. Like other such patterns in the S.R.O. world, this relationship is characterized by its nonspecificity. From the runner's perspective, his involvement provides the extra income, but more importantly, it provides a way to help structure his time. His days now need not be wholly internally ordered; his daily round is determined, in a large way, by the set pattern of visits. In addition to this structure, many of these runners suggested that the business provides them with a feeling of worth. As one described it:

> Running errands is my business, I got my own territory here and everybody knows it.... They know I do good work and won't cheat them none. Like Mrs. McAvoy ... she needed her medicine yesterday, but I was at Roosevelt [the hospital clinic] so that poor lady hada wait all day for me to get back.... Ain't that something? She wouldn't even think about asking anybody else to do it for her. Mosta my customers are exactly the same ... if they want something they'll leave a message at the desk and they won't let them send anybody else up.

In addition to the goods that he delivers, the runner functions as an information resource. Many times it is the contact with their runner that provides these shut-ins access to information that would not otherwise be available. In some extreme cases, the runner offers the sole or major source of direct human contact. In this way, it is the runner who is instrumental in the formation and maintenance of the social network.

On a more personal level, the prestige and satisfaction of knowing that several people are actually dependent upon him can be achieved with only a minimal investment. Like others in the S.R.O. world, these runners attach great importance to finding and maintaining a fulfilling role in a social structure that has few universally recognized distinctions.

Other business ventures aimed at the S.R.O. community attempt a kind of short-sighted, but conventional, merchandising: these endeavors have been called "big-hustles and little stakes." In the S.R.O. community, as in others, those people forever involved in "get-rich-quick" schemes can be found. These endeavors generally offer inexpensive, inferior merchandise for sale at a considerable profit. In the course of just a few months, one of these entrepreneurs had offered cheap transistor radios, costume jewelry, and chicken and soul food dinners for sale to the community. In each case, the project was begun with a considerable amount of fanfare on his part—and a corresponding lack of enthusiasm on the part of the public he was attempting to interest. The projects, however, were quickly discontinued when a few sales had been made. After each episode, the less-than-successful promoter would cast aspersions on the intelligence of his public, but within a short time he would have yet another fool-proof scheme ready for promotion.

A major exception to the inability to make money from the S.R.O. community was the social functions offered by Bimbo and the Rumblers. On holiday occasions (Christmas, Thanksgiving, and Easter) the Rumblers organized a holiday dinner and dance. Calling these events their "Annual Benefit to the Community," the parties were given with the full support of the social service projects. The social service personnel provided much of the food, with the exception of meat, from the DOSS stores. Money was advanced to the Rumblers to cover other costs. Tickets to the function were printed several weeks in advance and sold by the Rumblers. Social service personnel also sold tickets; if a person didn't have the money, the worker would invariably advance him the ticket and collect from the client's next welfare check. All money collected was turned over to the Rumblers with the understanding that they would repay whatever loans were incurred. Although I was never able to directly audit the expenses, social service staff informants suggested that the parties resulted in net profits of not less than two hundred dollars for the Rumblers.

In preparation for the parties, a few faded decorations were placed in the hotel's grubby ballroom, and white incandescent light bulbs were painted over with pale watercolors. The only rules imposed by the social service staff stated that no alcoholic beverages were to be allowed in the ballroom; a Rumbler was posted at the door to assure that no one entered with any. The Rumblers, however, were particularly pleased with the no drinking rule. Spirits and wine, by the cup, were covertly being sold by the Rumblers at considerable profits.

For the S.R.O.'ers, the parties delivered less than the invitations promised. Many complained that there was not really enough food; that they found the portions to be too meager, and that the Rumblers denied requests for seconds. Many S.R.O.'ers reported that they were pressured into hurrying through their meal so that more people might be accommodated.

The events during the party itself revealed much about the S.R.O. population. Some of the young black men came wearing elaborate outfits and would periodically retire to their rooms to change. Most people did not dress especially for the party; women often wore faded housedresses and the men wore everyday street clothes.

Among the guests, the interaction was characterized by a flatness of affect and a standoffishness that suggested a basic uncertainty about the situation and what one's obligations were. For one S.R.O.'er, the party was like others he had attended in a rather different setting:

> You wanta know what I think 'bout this party? It just like bein' back in the joint. [He had just returned from a stay in a state hospital.] She-it—just lookit' the peoples.... Them womens dancin' wid womens, them dudes just settin' like they ain't really there.... An lookit the social workers ... they dancin' wid everybody jus' like they always do. I guess mosta these people used to it anyway.

For most S.R.O.'ers, the parties simply pass with little effect remaining. The social service staff exhibits more enthusiasm than the residents. Few residents reported actually looking forward to parties and even fewer talked about them afterwards. S.R.O.'ers have come to view these functions as something that is imposed upon them, with which they, as individuals can have little real involvement.

S.R.O. Business and Outside Influence

As one would expect, business within the S.R.O. community was not usually viewed by the "legitimate" businesses in the area as constituting any sort of competitive threat. In the case of illegitimate or illegal dealings, they were either conducted on such a small scale, operated so covertly, or protected so well that the operation was secure. If, however, an S.R.O. business achieves any degree of visibility, it finds itself in danger. The fate of a little establishment in one of the hotels illustrates this. The account reveals how difficult it really is for S.R.O.'ers to move beyond the confines of traditional roles and life-styles. The story began when two elderly female residents approached the social service staff and suggested that they were interested in establishing a little restaurant in the hotel's ballroom. They argued that they were already feeding a number of people and the ballroom was only being utilized once a week for community meetings. As a final argument, they stated that a restaurant in the hotel itself, serving wholesome meals at low cost, would be valuable to the community. After several meetings, the social service staff approved the project, and "Mom's and Miz Mable's Restaurant" was born.

The little restaurant was almost immediately successful. Because the women were well respected in the community, there was widespread acceptance of their enterprise. The serving, eating, and cooking areas of their operation were kept immaculately clean. Mom and Miz Mable had been able to find some colorful tablecloths which added much to the normally drab and dreary ballroom. The food was well cooked, plentiful, and very cheap. The menus leaned towards soul food. A typical meal would consist of vegetable or chicken and rice soup, meat (often ribs, hamhocks or chicken), vegetables (heaps of collard, mustard, or turnip greens), bread, canned fruit, and coffee. The total meal would cost approximately seventy-five cents. Within a short while, Mom's and Miz Mable's little restaurant was prospering. Besides the walk-in trade, many of the shut-ins would have their runners purchase and deliver meals to them. The operation was soon so successful that persons living in nearby S.R.O.'s began coming for meals.

By all accounts, there should have been universal approval and support for the enterprise. Wholesome meals were now available to a population that needed them. Mom's and Miz Mable's soon became a gathering place and many lonely people were able to meet friends, or at least have an alternative to the isolation of a small room or park bench. As the business grew, the proprieters discovered that they needed additional help, so a few S.R.O.'ers were employed. The social service staff were very pleased with the results, and saw the project as a prototype of one which might have a great potential for rehabilitation. All things considered, Mom's and Miz Mable's represented the best of the American system of free enterprise.

Outside influences, however, were soon to make themselves felt. A nearby luncheonette/coffee shop quickly came to define the little restaurant as a threat. The issue was further complicated by the fact that the premises, on which the luncheonette was located, were owned by the same holding company that owned the hotel. The luncheonette was totally dissimilar to the little restaurant in the hotel. The proprietors were recent Greek immigrants. Although their business was regularly inspected by the New York Health Department, one still had questions about the level of hygiene. The food was neither as appetizing nor as plentiful as the food that Mom's and Miz Mable's prepared, and was considerably more expensive. S.R.O.'ers complained that the proprietor hurried them out of the luncheonette and discouraged any sociability in their establishment.

Since the luncheonette received a considerable part of its business from those S.R.O.'ers who had been granted a "restaurant allowance" from the DOSS (granted to clients who lack cooking facilities or for medical reasons cannot cook), the steadily increasing popularity of Mom's and Miz Mable's little restaurant was looked upon as a real threat by the luncheonette's proprietors.

The proprietors complained to the hotel's management who initially referred them to the social service staff. Since the social service staff was now in support of the little restaurant, the proprietors were able to get little satisfaction from them. As the loss of business began to be more keenly felt, additional pressure was applied. The luncheonette's proprietors lodged a formal complaint with the health department, alleging that a restaurant was illegally operating in the hotel. The possibility of any official action, however, proved a sufficient threat to the hotel's management and they forced the DOSS staff to close the little restaurant. As with so many other things, the S.R.O.'ers accepted their loss quietly; any other outcome would have been improbable.

Observations on Social Organization

It is this quality of extreme marginality that renders any collective action in the S.R.O. community so tenuous. Within such a social environment, all collective efforts directed at effecting some kind of change, almost regardless of who initiates them, can easily be neutralized. The failure seems to have two complementary roots. The first relates to the observation that the social-cultural systems operating in a culture of poverty situation make it difficult for viable interest groups, capable of mobilizing any general support, to emerge. The second focuses on the quality of marginality of any such groups that do emerge, which renders them particularly defenseless. The convergence of these factors makes the defense of any indigenous S.R.O. organization problematic, at best.

Further Observations on Social Organization

When the ethnographic method is applied to the study of more complex societies, it is sometimes difficult to provide meaningful divisions. I had little difficulty describing need-structured groups because it was possible to identify a major need of the individual's life and then to trace the organizational response to its satisfaction.

Now we wish to turn our attention to the arrangement of people in more general relationships such as coupling, friendship and parenthood.

Kinship

Male-female relationships within the S.R.O. world are similar to those found in other economically and socially depressed areas. Little real distinction is made in the community between legal or "preacher" marriages and common-law arrangements. Informants report that various pension and welfare laws actually make it economically undesirable to legalize a union. Many interracial unions were noted, and the organization of these were in no observable way different from ethnically similar unions. Such relationships were seldom, if ever, accorded any special notice by other S.R.O.'ers in the community. However, some members of the social service staff and the hotel's managers were often uncomfortable with interracial unions.

The pattern of "serial monogamy" observed in other economically depressed black areas was observed in the S.R.O. world as well.[9] Within the S.R.O. community, its organization and impact was found to be not dissimilar from earlier reports.

In regard to children, again the S.R.O. community is not unlike other depressed areas. While children m y present an economic and social hardship, they are not unwelcome. Although the ratio of children-to-adults residing in the hotels was never quite as great as one would expect to find in a tenement or other such setting, at the heart of New York City's "Welfare hotel crisis," the presence of children in certain hotels was noticeable. Not unlike children in other depressed ecological settings, much of their time is spent in groups outside of their households. It was not uncommon to see groups of young children playing in the hallways of the hotels well into the early hours of the morning. The children would stay until they got tired and then they would retire to one of their group's "houses" (rooms) and sleep for several hours. In some instances, one might even find a number of children sleeping in the hallways.

Children, from about six years of age up, were granted a maximum amount of autonomy and older children (from eight or nine years and up) were accorded a very large amount of responsibility in caring for their younger siblings. Mothers would often leave for an entire day, giving a nine year old child responsibility for others. While most of these occasions passed without incident, there occurred during my study at least several instances of tragedy when unsupervised children lit fires or fell from windows.

Family structures supported this autonomy for mothers and their children. For varying periods of time, mothers would care for their own as well as other women's children. No stated arrangement was made for the sharing of child-rearing duties; instead, the youngsters would come and go at will. Those mothers who were interviewed seemed to express little anxiety about the whereabouts of their children, reporting that "they around somewhere . . . they just probably hangin' 'round." These children eat when hungry and sleep when tired.

Symbiotic Patterns

A major factor in understanding relationships found in the S.R.O. world looks to the scarcity of available institutional resources. Due to this scarcity, S.R.O.'ers are forced to rely almost entirely on themselves and each other for assistance and support. This is d fficult enough for a person who is physically sound and psychologically intact; the person who is ill or infirm in any way finds the task of just getting by to be considerably more difficult. S.R.O.'ers are well aware of the effect of these limitations. Given the very high incidence of any kind of infirmity in the S.R.O. world, accommodative patterns capable of neutralizing problems have to be evolved. A way of maximizing one's opportunities by combining his own strength with that of another has to occur. One rather common social pattern could be seen as the synthesis of the best "parts" of two less-than-intact people into a fully operational unit. In this adaption a person, usually bedridden, would unite with another person who was fully ambulatory, yet who might be either feeble-minded or noticeably mentally impaired. The relationship was sustained by having the physically infirm (yet mentally intact) person provide the direction for the ambulatory (yet feeble-minded or mentally ill) member, who would then execute the decisions. For example, the bed-ridden member would manage the money and affairs of the pair, leaving the ambulatory member to do all of the necessary physical work (such as shopping, cooking, and providing protection.)

Communications Networks

One of the organizational problems which is confronted by many communities involves the development of ways in which to keep members informed of what is happening. This problem is compounded by the diversity of the individual S.R.O. buildings and their geographic diffusion. Above, we alluded to a number of these communication patterns in our consideration of the gay community; we also examined the role of different kinds of runners in maintaining the flow of information. This section will conclude by examining the work of other persons involved in the transmission of information in the community. Since the S.R.O.'s present unique ecological problems to their inhabitants, we will consider some of the forms of interaction that have arisen in response to these problems.

Much information passes from S.R.O. building to S.R.O. building by means of hotel managers and DOSS personnel. Managers exchange information during their daily lunches and then some of this information is released to selected residents. Here, intelligence concerning possible changes in ownership, increased police surveillance, projected or imminent changes in building policy, increases in drug activities and the like, would be exchanged and then quickly disseminated throughout the building.

The action of the DOSS personnel was very similar. Workers who had caseloads that encompassed several buildings would disseminate information from client to client, who in turn would channel it into one of the communication networks to be found within the building.

Information entering a S.R.O. building via the manager is received by the building's employees first. Desk personnel, who have primary access to the information, then pass it to security and custodial workers. These, in turn (depending upon which social network they are involved in) then convey it to one of the key individuals (often one of the matriarchs), at which point the dissemination proceeds outward from there. In this manner a bit of information is known throughout the building within several hours of the time it enters.

These informational social networks have a key member who serves as a major node for news. Key or nodular persons generally tend to spend all of their time within their S.R.O. building; in many cases, seldom leaving their rooms or the immediate vicinity. The physical layout of the S.R.O. building is instrumental in the formation and maintenance of these informational nodes. Nodes were to be found at the end of the hall-wing from which it is possible for the key person to observe his entire hall-wing without having to leave his room. Their doors were kept open during all their waking hours, thereby making interaction with any passerby likely; runners would often stop to visit with them for a short while as they made their appointed rounds. Information was carefully collected by key people and, perhaps even more carefully, disbursed by them. The system appeared to operate remarkably well and information traveled very freely within any given S.R.O.[10]

The Community Comes Together

The structured information system is an important vehicle for the transmission of news. In addition, S.R.O.'ers find themselves gathering together on a regular basis. The most important of these is "check" or "mothers' day" (so named because of the disbursement of Aid to Families with Dependent Children—AFDC—money) which occurs regularly on the first and sixteenth of each month; other disbursements, such as pension and social security payments, are received then as well.

The event is so important in the community that special provisions are made for it. On the morning of check day, hotel managers draw an adequate sum of cash from bank accounts to be able to cover all of the checks. Hotel security personnel naturally accompany them to the bank, and are always on hand. The post office receives checks—which are all ostensibly mailed directly to the clients—the day before and has the mail presorted by building.

Word spreads quickly throughout the building "that the checks are here" and residents begin queuing up outside the cage. Within a very short time, numerous residents are standing in the lobby waiting for their checks. An almost festive air prevails. S.R.O.'ers who had little or no money during the final part of the previous two-week cycle expectantly look forward to receiving the money. Numbers runners, shylocks, and their heavies, bootleggers, and other S.R.O. "credit merchants" scan the rapidly gathering crowd, noting their debtors and anticipating settling their accounts.

There is usually a measure of good natured bantering between those standing on the line and the creditors awaiting payment: "Hey, man, you ain't lookin' for me this week, man!" or "Ain't got nothin' for you, babe!" were typical of remarks passed back and forth. In some cases, more boisterous residents, to the delight of others in line, would play "the dozens" (verbal derogations gradually increasing in severity) with the creditors and a lively repartee ensues. Occasionally, an argument between creditor and client ensues and the spectators are treated to a heated exchange. The scene might be viewed as reminiscent of market day in a small village. People coming together, exchanging information, gossip, and often a bottle disguised in a paper sack. Most S.R.O.'ers appear delighted by this break in the usual routine of their lives and report eagerly looking forward to the invariable performances and displays, as well as the change in their daily routine that the money would once again bring.

Note on the Culture of the S.R.O. World

In an earlier chapter I discussed the distinction between "culture" and "social structure." The distinction, of course, is purely analytic: group structure and the information about its operation are intrinsically interwoven, separable only through the working of the sociological imagination. To the present, this study has focused (as much as possible) on the social organization and social structures found in the S.R.O. world. Other observations, however, might best be considered within the category commonly designated as "culture." In this concluding section our attention will be directed towards some of the patterns that the S.R.O.'ers themselves have evolved to "make sense" of their everyday world; this implies, as well, a set of attitudes and beliefs about the shape of the (social) world in which these people live. Below, some of the major components of the S.R.O. culture have been selected for consideration in an attempt to see even more deeply into the lives of S.R.O. residents, these outposts of the forgotten.

Regulation of Time

From a middle class perspective, perhaps the most disturbing cultural element of the S.R.O. world is its seeming timelessness. Time, as measured by hours and minutes (perhaps even days) has little meaning within the S.R.O. world. People sleep when tired, waken when refreshed, eat when hungry, and drink when thirsty. Time is not demarcated by machine, but by event and occurrence. For many S.R.O. residents, the change from day personnel to evening and night personnel within their building signified the division of the day. Larger units of time, such as seasons, were marked by the holidays and the changes in daily routine brought about through them.

"Death's Season" was the period of time occurring between the months of January and March. The period was particularly dreaded by many of the older residents who believe that this was the time when most natural deaths occurred in the community. Moreover, this period was universally viewed as a particularly depressing one.

Most S.R.O.'ers report feeling a psychological let-down at the close of the holiday season. The months from January to March generally bring a prolonged spell of bad weather during which heating equipment in the buildings is wont to fail, making life uncomfortable at best. Moreover, the bad weather tends to restrict S.R.O.'ers to the building, encouraging boredom and inactivity among those who would normally seek stimulation outside. Not unexpectedly, the evidence of violence, to both self and others, is high during Death's Season. Rather typical of the S.R.O. residents' feelings are comments such as:

> ... if only, if only Mama [the respondent] can get through this time ...

And then afterwards:

> Thank goodness—it's March and we'er mostly still here ... it'll be OK now, I can feel it.

The most significant of external factors instrumental in the regulation of time is the arbitrary two-week cycle imposed by the disbursement of welfare and other monies. Recall that since such a large proportion of the community looks to these payments as their major source of income, the entrance of this resource into the community has a profound effect upon it. Not only does the semimonthly disbursement provide the occasion for an almost festive gathering, but it also means an instantaneous change in the consumption patterns and life-style of the recipients.

The beginning of the two-week cycle dominating the lives of many S.R.O.'ers sees a qualitative, as well as a quantitative, change in the patterns of consumption. Drinkers will switch to spirits and hard liquor. Ot ers in the community, however, are quick to point out that although these people are now boasting of their consumption of spirits, this will only last as long as their money, and then they will readily return to a less prestigious beverage such as "pluck" (S.R.O. argot for cheap wine). In the community this turnabout is known as the move from "whiskey and gin days ... then's pluck."

As the end of the fiscal cycle approaches, the community is characterized by a gradually settling depression—people have no money and they realize that it will be almost impossible to obtain any. Many do not even have the money necessary to buy food. With the arrival of the checks it changes radically. The level and intensity of social interaction in the building increases noticeably as many more residents begin once again freely visiting others.

There is indication that the level of deviant behavior increases as well. Many S.R.O.'ers report that the incidence of violence and overtly bizarre behavior increases during the first days of the fiscal cycle. One explanation which is occasionally heard suggests that the cycles correspond with the full moon, and the advent of the full moon causes marked changes in human behavior. The hypothesis that I work with is, regrettably, a good deal more prosaic. It looks to a number of factors beginning with the entrance of more alcohol into the community, the change in the intensity of social interaction, and the leap in aspirations fostered by the entrance of even the small amount of fluid money into the system, which causes this notable change in behavior. Not unexpectedly, both building security personnel and law-enforcement officers warily look forward to this period for the increase in trouble. One hotel security guard, for example, explained that he has to spend "the whole goddamn night of every check day, puttin' peoples to bed." A law enforcement officer, in another interview, reported that his work gets increasingly more difficult during this period because so many of the older people are vulnerable to the muggers who become particularly active in the area right after the welfare and social security checks are distributed.

Culture and Community

We have come to see each S.R.O. building as being reminiscent of a small village community. Then, in aggregate, all of the S.R.O. buildings in a city can be seen as a larger community, having its own boundaries, culture, and organization. Up to now, the study has emphasized the organizational aspects of the S.R.O. world. The remaining portion of this chapter will focus on those components of S.R.O. living which can be seen as cultural. The culture of the S.R.O.'s will be presented in the context, process, and artifact of community.

The existence of a viable collective conscience within the individual S.R.O.'s quickly focuses attention on the presence of "community." Extreme violence, involving an assault or death, is reacted to with shock by all of the community's members. For example, the murder of the pregnant woman in the Hotel Enfer so deeply troubled the community that everyone demanded that the killer be brought to justice. The death of a child who fell twelve stories down an elevator shaft similarly provoked the wrath of the community, and all of the building's residents, no matter how different, demanded that "something be done."

Any death, however, evokes some sort of collective response. Even the passing of an older woman who spent most of her time secluded in her room, was not unnoticed by the hotel's other residents. The strength of these collective sentiments can be realized by contrasting this to a similar incident in a more conventional, middle class building, where often the only indication of a death is a funeral wreath placed on a door. S.R.O.'ers often attend funerals of other residents whom they knew sometimes only slightly. Interestingly, it was the death of an old man that provided me entrance into building that I was having trouble gaining access to. I was able to gain the confidence of residents in the building after I made funeral arrangements for an elderly man, saving him from burial in an unmarked pauper's grave in Potters Field. Word of the undertaking spread quickly through the community and I found interaction in the building greatly facilitated.

Births were greeted with a similar show of interest. Although they did not evoke the same intensity of response, S.R.O.'ers did know when a birth occurred and most would freely offer the parent(s) congratulations.

A World of People, Not Personnel

The S.R.O. world has an intense personal orientation. While status distinctions indigenous to the community are recognized and do effect interaction, many S.R.O.'ers refuse to deal with the outside world in a less than personal way. This property was made clear when it became necessary for me to assemble an alcoholics' treatment group.

The group was longstanding and fairly popular at the hotel. There were approximately eleven regulars who made up the core of the group, and another dozen persons attended periodically. The group was led by a professional "alcoholism counselor" (himself a recovered alcoholic) provided by a local hospital. To encourage attendance, the meetings were held at a regular time and place each week. Although the meetings were held regularly, the social service staff would still hang posters announcing them. Yet the single most important factor influencing attendance was a very popular DOSS worker who, an hour before each meeting, visited each member and *personally invited* him to the meeting.

One week, however, the worker was unable to be at the hotel for the meeting. He called me several hours before to dictate the list of the regular members, and requested that I personally visit each one to remind him about the group and invite him to attend. His instructions were followed and some fifteen people were contacted. Out of this number, only three did actually attend the meeting. This becomes more understandable when we consider that S.R.O.'ers defined attendance at the meeting as a favor to and/or recognition of this well-liked social worker. The fact that this group might actually be able to provide some real benefit or help with a drinking problem was seen as being entirely secondary.

S.R.O.'ers did have a clear recognition of what the boundaries of their world were. Geographical boundaries were defined socially so that S.R.O.'ers perceived that they would be rejected, or worse, if they left the S.R.O. world. For example, when asked why they would not patronize certain business establishments, these responses were offered: "I wouldn't go in there—they don't make our kind feel welcome;" or, We got no place in there." The same process kept S.R.O.'ers out of public facilities. The experience of a recreational program designed to "broaden the horizons" of S.R.O. people exemplified how restricted the S.R.O. world can be.

The project was conceived with the intention of using the large number of historical and cultural monuments located on the Upper West Side of Manhattan to enlarge the recreational options available to S.R.O.'ers. One of the first locales chosen for the program was the American Museum of Natural History. The museum is perhaps one of the finest natural history museums in the world, offering exhibits on almost every conceivable subject. While most of the informants knew of the physical presence of the museum, considerably fewer of them knew that it was a museum and what one might expect to find inside. Even fewer had ever gone into the museum, believing that they would either be barred from entrance or in some way harassed once inside.

The project was predicated on the belief that a positive experience might neutralize these negative attitudes. I was involved with members of the social service staff who organized the first "field trip" to the museum for a group of the hotel's residents. Although the proposed trip was initially greeted with much enthusiasm, as the appointed day approached the interest seemed to wane. On the day of the trip it even proved somewhat difficult to locate all of the people who had signed up for the trip. Finally, the group was assembled and everyone (there were nine in the group) made their way to the museum. Once inside, the group was accorded no special interest by the museum's guards. After a while most of the group appeared relaxed and began to take an active interest in the exhibits. Some lively conversation, for example, was generated by the animal exhibits, where a few of the men vociferously debated the relative fighting abilities of a lion and a water buffalo; a similar heated discussion developed over the relative worths of star sapphires and rubies.

By the time we returned to the hotel, much of the enthusiasm had dimmed. Members of the party, while reporting that they had had a good time at the museum, expressed doubt about whether they "saw all they were going to see"; one woman even expressed some doubt about her ability to locate the museum again. The most common response indicating ambivalence about a return visit, however, suggested that they (the S.R.O.'ers) did not feel as though they belonged there. "It's just not our kinda place," one said.

Names Within the S.R.O. Culture

A community is, of course, made up of people, people who come to see and treat one another as individuals. One problem for the community to solve is how best to provide some recognition of this individuality. within the S.R.O. community, names, to a large degree, satisfy this need. If a person has been socialized into the S.R.O. culture, one can readily assess another's place in the community by the moniker that he or she has. In this way names are useful in designating prestige or social distance.

Two types of nicknames are commonly employed. The first were nondesignative names and demonstrated integration and positive acceptance in the community. Names such as Chip, Monk, Priest, Wagonback, Tiny, K.O., Turk, Bimbo provide just a few examples. The name itself tells something about the person carrying it; but more importantly, it is held and called with affection. Often the moniker extends beyond the individual building into the larger S.R.O. community; more people are likely to know a "monikered" than a "nonmonikered" person.

Other monikers, however, reveal something about the person, and in doing so signify a degree of social distance or isolation from the community. For example, names such as "The Cat Lady" or "Cat Woman" refer to an elderly woman who maintains an indeterminate number of cats in her room. The "White Princess" is a black woman who wore unusual garb, consisting of layers of plastic which she painted white, along with herself and all of her posessions. The "Squirrel Man" is an elderly man who spends his days feeding animals in the park. In each of these cases the community recognizes that the person's individual interest superceded even minimal social participation. As such, the designative moniker is used to identify his special interest and signify his social distance or isolation.

If a woman is called by her surname prefixed by "Miss" it signifies a similar degree of distance or the recognition of some special eccentricity. When a person is designated by his given name, it generally signifies a friendly or neutral acceptance. Surnames prefixed by the formal address of Mr. or Mrs. signify a measure of social distance. Older residents, that is, those who have been living in the building for many years and have seen the population change around them, were almost always addressed in this way. Similarly, members of the community-at-large invariably address the S.R.O. matriarchs by formally prefixed surnames.

In addition to the information about the community and its members that is conveyed by personal names, the ways in which larger objects are designated can be equally as revealing. The population divides itself into two identifiable groups on the semantic designation of the S.R.O. building itself. The first of the two groups encompasses the older, permanent residents. Generally, they are the whites who have been living in the building for more than a decade. They have witnessed the change in both the building and surrounding neighborhood. The second group represents the more numerous of the S.R.O. population: the immigrants to the city, the minority group members, the alienated, and the chronically ill. The idea of "community" is implicit in the language of each.

For the older residents, the building is more than a place to live. For many it has assumed an almost anthropomorphic quality and is seen as a "friend" against whom they measure their own decline. For them the hotel is always referred to as "The House." The following quote illustrates this:

> The House has certainly come down . . . I can remember when the highest and the best used to live here . . . and now just look around . . .

For these older residents, it seems as though the final act of a drama is in the process of unfolding and following this performance both the stage and the theatre are to be emptied for the last time.

For the more recent residents, "house" has a different meaning. "House" denotes one's room. One person will tell another: "I'm going to my house now" or "Them's [referring to some young men] no good . . . they always breaking into people's houses!" The reference to one's room as his house, the usually free social interaction, and the presence of children playing in hallways very much gives the social life of an S.R.O. the flavor of a small village community.

Notes on Mobility and Commitment

While everyday life is necessarily oriented towards living with one's fellows, S.R.O.'ers (as all people, everywhere) still have some sense of their place in the world. It is through this knowledge that people come to judge the worth of their life-style. Whether a person will be able to effect any changes in this life-style, however, is contingent upon the resources that he is able to mobilize. How the resources he actually does possess, or has access to, will be allocated is strongly influenced by his orientaton to the world.

Using such a conceptualization, the S.R.O. population can be divided into four major groups: S.R.O.-oriented, security strivers, downwardly mobile, and upward mobility-oriented.[11]

S.R.O.-oriented persons have accepted the range of life-styles available in the S.R.O. world. The level of tolerance for questionable behavior, the minimal responsibility, the available forms of support, and the intense social interaction available are all perceived as positive rewards. Whether the acceptance has occurred through deliberate choice, though, is at this time problematic. In other words, whether repeated failures in other areas and endeavors have convinced the person that the S.R.O. world is one, and perhaps the best, of the remaining options; or, whether the life-style was freely chosen was not systematically investigated.

S.R.O.-oriented persons report no desire to leave with the larger S.R.O. world or the building in which they are currently ensconced. Most have established a firm position within their small community, and through it all of their needs are adequately satisfied.

Security strivers are people who are committed to the S.R.O. way of life yet are somewhat unhappy about their present location. The complaints are most often registered in terms of security: "The building and the other residents are OK," they report, "but it's those outsiders who make all of the trouble." These people are seeking an S.R.O. environment which is more secure. They canvass the buildings in their area, hoping that a vacancy has finally occurred in one of the preferred S.R.O.'s.

The downwardly mobile people are those who are finding that social interaction is becoming increasingly more difficult. Many of these drift in and out of society's correctional or control institutions. While their behavior would be labeled as unacceptable in the larger middle- or working-class society, the S.R.O. world, with its greater tolerance, offers a secure social niche for them. While most of them probably aspire to stasis, if their behavior becomes increasingly more troublesome it is almost certain that they will find their way into the downward mobility spiral (described in an earlier chapter). As such, they discover that as soon as their behavior falls below the minimal standards set by one unit, they are ejected and forced to seek another that permits more latitude in behavior. Each step down forces them into more "open" and less prestigious S.R.O.'s

The upward mobility-oriented person aspires to eschew S.R.O. life altogether. Statistically, this population is less numerous than the S.R.O.-oriented one; within it two rather well-defined groups can be identified.

The first of these, who have been designated as working class mobiles, typify conventional patterns of upward mobility. These are people who believe that hard work and a life-style stressing temperance and moderation will ultimately assure them social and material security. Members of this group regard the S.R.O. as only a temporary place to live until they are able to accumulate the resources necessary to move into a more conventional dwelling. Since there is such a strong commitment to work, their participation and involvement in the social life of the S.R.O. community is minimal.

The second group, which is the least numerous of all, is composed of younger men who are waiting for their "big score." While these younger men are actively involved in the social life of the S. R. O. community, their orientation is to the outside world which can reward their "hustle" with material wealth. The hustle may involve either the get-rich-quick schemes or some kind of illegal or questionable business. In each case, the hustler looks forward to the end of his problems and a fantasy world of riches, which can be achieved if he can just muster enough *flash* for the really "big score." For most, the really big one is never landed and life adapts itself to the small scale rewards and satisfactions offered by life in the S.R.O. community.

The Social Life of an S.R.O.: A Summary

This long and rather invo ved chapter brought us right into the heart of an S.R.O. building. From our sociological or anthropological perspective, we examined its social structure, culture, and social organization. Hopefully, through it we were able to transcend some of the conceptual constraints and get some sense for what S.R.O. life is about. Although much of the descriptive material used in the chapter was drawn from the experiences that I had while living in New York City's welfare hotels and S.R.O. tenements, the organization, patterns, and culture of S.R.O.'s in other cities across the nation is not dramatically different. The challenges and problems of living without money in a money-oriented society present a unifying thread for all S.R.O. lives, independent of geographic locale.

The S.R.O. world presents an ecological alternative to marginal life in either middle or working-class society, the ghetto or the slum. While the S.R.O. world produces little or no wealth of its own, it does possess a well integrated, fairly stable economic system. This system combines elements of both the straight and the deviant worlds. In a larger sense, it is this combination of elements that best characterizes the S.R.O. world. The S.R.O. world extracts elements of ghetto culture and either changes or combines them with others to produce something unique.

On a more personal level, the chapter considered many of the accommodations that made collective life in a difficult environment possible. Human relationships arose to meet the challenges posed by a hostile environment, or to satisfy some special needs or problems presented by a person. We saw the ripple effect that even a minimal amount of social organization brought about as larger social patterns evolved. For example, the stability enjoyed by the pair of lesbians had a positive effect on others living in the S.R.O.; or, the matriarchs, who in providing for their families, offered both care and guidance to others in the S.R.O. community

A community, having its own culture, does exist in the S.R.O.'s. The community is bound by a unifying collective conscience. A cultural tradition, complete with its own language and meanings, is available. This culture, having both normative and informational components, transcends any given S.R.O. unit and unites the changing generations of S.R.O. dwellers.

The most important question that *Outposts of the Forgotten* addresses was contained in this chapter. It is the question of order. How is it possible for so many people, especially those as deeply troubled as many in the S.R.O. world appear to be, to live together without the war-of all-against-all occurring? By seeing the S.R.O. world as a differentiated, integrated, and stable social system, some understanding of the question was reached. The community cares for the weak, the sick and the troubled because structures and information exist. Adequate cultural information exists to manage those situations that could be disorganizing or disastrous in another context. Since the S.R.O. world has several strata, persons unsuccessful in one place are able to make their way to another, in which, presumably, they can find a niche. Underlying all survival however, is the fabric of accommodative relationships which both sustain and control the individual.

NOTES

1. Harvey Zorbaugh, *The Gold Coast and The Slum* (Chicago: University of Chicago, 1929).

2. Israel Zangwill, *The Melting Pot* (New York: Macmillan, 1909).

3. Harvey A. Siegal, "The Drinking Man: Notes on The Life Style of the Ghetto Alcoholic," *Yale Sociology Journal* 1 (1971).

4. Maurice Leznoff and William A. Westley, "The Homosexual Community," *Social Problems* 63 (1956): 257–63.

5. Herbert Gans, *The Urban Villagers* (New York: Free Press, 1962), chap. 7.

6. While the following discussion will focus on activity in the S.R.O. community itself, it is not unusual for S.R.O. residents to work in illegal or deviant enterprises. Many of those S.R.O.'ers who are engaged in some types of illegal activities will do little of their actual business in the S.R.O.'s. All of the women actively engaged in prostitution, for example, reported that although they were occasionally sexually active in the S.R.O. community, all of their "Johns were off the street." Most reported that the issue was entirely an economic one—if one wanted to make money, it was necessary to leave the community where sex was relatively easy to come by, and focus one's efforts on a different population.

7. Oscar Lewis, *La Vida* (New York: Random House, 1965).

8. David Caplovitz, *The Poor Pay More* (New York: Free Press, 1962).

9. William McCord, et al., *Life Styles in the Black Ghetto* (New York: W. W. Norton, 1969).

10. No attempt was made to assess the amount of distortion that would occur from the time information entered a building to its final dissemination. It is my impression, however, that certain kinds of information (for example, that concerning police, illegal activities, specific individuals etc.) was less likely to be distorted than others (such as the sale of the building or new management policies).

11. The existence of a third, significantly smaller group—*Transients*—is recognized. Persons like the drop-out from the counter culture would fall into this category.

Chapter 6

Summary and Conclusions: The S.R.O. World and Beyond

Introduction

Outposts of the Forgotten began with a largely external descriptive portrait of the S.R.O. scene, the setting, and its people, finally progressing to a closer look at the mechanism and processes which maintain the S.R.O. world's distinctive character. The social life of this world was examined from the perspective of an active, participating member, bringing into focus such things as their daily rounds and usual patterns of social interaction, their management of time and space, and the range of available alternative life-styles. This concluding chapter will once again establish a measure of distance from the S.R.O. world.

Two separate but related themes will be presented. The first concerns the S.R.O.'ers themselves. Given the nature of the community and the culture of the S.R.O. world, can we identify any special adaptions and skills which equip S.R.O. residents for full participation in this social world? The second considers the S.R.O. world as a whole. Although a community in its own right, the S.R.O.'ers are still attached to the larger society. While some of these interconnecting points have already been considered, our interest will now shift from a behavioral to an institutional perspective so that we can consider what function(s) the S.R.O. world fulfills. How is it equipped to satisfy these functions? These are questions to be addressed.

This concluding chapter will consider some of the natural history of the S.R.O. world. The basic questions about the treatment of socially terminal and troublesome people, posed in the beginning of the book, will be considered here. My research has asked questions about survival. Given the underlying conditions, how is social life possible? What special adaptions arise to meet the challenges posed by a hostile environment?

Life with Few Material Assets: The S.R.O.'er and S.R.O. Culture

For an upper, middle or working class person, moving is usually an uncomfortable experience. People report a feeling of disassociation while all of their belongings are packed away or otherwise unavailable. While some of the anxiety experienced may reflect a concern about the security of one's possessions, other more significant factors are in operation. Factors such as the relationship between material possessions and social identity are important in understanding some of the differences which separate the S.R.O.er from others.

In *The Presentation of Self in Everyday Life,* Erving Goffman suggests that people, in the course of everyday life, manipulate a number of significant symbols.[1] The process of social interaction involves the "management of impressions"; this can be described as the fostering and reinforcing of a definition of situations sympathetic or beneficial to the individual.[2] To effect this end, a person has several resources at his disposal. He has his physical self; the way he holds his body, his expressions and demeanor. He has, as well, the ability to communicate, to "team-up" with others so as to have them work along with him in his attempt to control or influence the flow and direction of interaction.

Since each interactional episode is seen as being "staged" for a specific audience, the idea of a "stage" and "performance" is brought to mind. Persons directing the performance have at their disposal, besides the actors and their actions, "props" which are used to make the performance more convincing. So too, in the "real" world; one uses his possessions to lend credence to his performance. The upwardly mobile person, for example, surrounds himself with furniture and possessions that attest to success, or the academic often invests his home with books and objects d' art, all demonstrating his good taste and involvement with a life of the mind. Social interaction occurs in "front stage regions," the physical place where the performance is actually staged, while the actors prepare themselves for their performance in a "back stage region" from which the audience is, for the most part, excluded.[3]

In everyday life this process is almost wholly nonproblematic: performances are routinely planned, organized, and staged using all of the individual's available resources. The interesting sociological question is: What happens if a performance has to occur without access to the usual resources? Stated more specifically, what special conditions does the S.R.O. world place on successful social interaction?   What are some of the constraints involved in S.R.O. living that must be overcome to render performances there nonproblematic?

One of the most striking things about the S.R.O.'s is the lack of space. Higher status persons have considerably more access to back stage regions for the organization and preparation of their performances. The spacial constraints imposed by S.R.O. living severely limit the amount of available nonpublic areas. Since the area in which most performances are staged is "public" rather than "private," the S.R.O. resident has little control over the arrangement of props to bolster the credibility of his performance, and must learn how to maximize the impact of those symbols which can be invested on his or her person. In other words, because of constraints imposed on the use of material props, the S.R.O.'er has come to rely on his ability to demonstrate credibility through the vehicle of his or her self and person, complemented by only a few easily portable, symbolic props. It is for this reason that the absence of material possessions is *not* experienced by the S.R.O.'er as the same kind of hardship that a higher status person feels.

The manager's order to "get-your-shit-together-and-move-on-out" is not greeted with the same dismay by most S.R.O.'ers that it would evoke in other populations. Since the member looks almost entirely to himself, the several possessions hastily thrown into shopping bags are not seen as the stuff from which an identity can be forged.

For these S.R.O.'ers, eviction is but a minor crisis involving hardship yet apparently causing little disorganization.

The use of this dramaturgical perspective aids in understanding other kinds of behavior observed among some S.R.O.'ers. The overly flashy dress or the occasional elaborate, large automobile, for example, is a way of influencing interaction in an entirely public place. Such symbolic props are seen as the equivalent of the higher class set-up. While the area is defined as wholly public, the presence of any markers can, in some way, add to the credibility of the performances being staged. The strength of the scheme, of course, rests upon the fact that while the props are outstanding in their audacity, they actually fall within the bounds defined as (at the minimum, legally) acceptable for the situation. As such, it becomes difficult for social control agents to evoke any but the mildest, and in this context, almost encouraging sanctions.

The implication of these findings suggests that in a life that offers little in the way of material comforts, success is defined in other terms. Learning the skills necessary to present one's credibility and to operate freely, easily, and effectively in different locales makes for successful S.R.O. living. For those who have mastered these skills, a larger part of the S.R.O. world is opened. This unfolding brings new freedoms and even greater satisfaction.

Commitment to the S.R.O. World

We began the study with a consideration of some of the work done on unattached people living in metropolitan centers. Although published several decades earlier, *The Gold Coast and the Slum* by Harvey Zorbaugh described life in an area of the city reminiscent of much of what I found in the S.R.O. world. [4] Let us briefly return to this earlier work so that by comparison we can highlight some of the uniqueness of the presentday S.R.O. world.

The earlier work portrays an older section of the city; buildings that have been changed and modified from their original form to accommodate single, perhaps rootless individuals. In this work Zorbaugh carefully notes that this is a region in which few children are to be found and conventional families are not plentiful. More specifically, it is a world holding many of the misfits of society; eccentrics, loners, people with blasted hopes and ambitions who are living from day-to-day. In the "World of Furnished Rooms" personal comfort and even human life are held rather lightly; suicides are not uncommon and people show little concern or interest in their neighbors. The world of furnished rooms is definitely distinguished from that of a boardinghouse life. Boarders were more than nameless residents and the house offered, at the very least, a semblance of family life. The proprietors of furnished rooming-houses, on the other hand, were interested only in receiving the rent a week in advance.

From the roomer's perspective, this social world provided little in the way of comfort and support. In this description of this "half-world" Zorbaugh characterizes both the social world and its life-styles as tenuous:

> The conditions of life in the world of furnished rooms are the direct antithesis of all we are accustomed to think of as normal in society. . . . Where no one knows anyone else in his own house, to say nothing of his own block; where there are no groups of any sort—where [all] these things are true it is obvious that there can be no community tradition or common definition of situations, no public opinion, no informal social control. As a result, the rooming-house world is a world of political indifference, of laxity of conventional standards, of personal and social disorganization.

> The rooming-house world is in no sense a social world, a set of group relationships through which the person's wishes are realized. In this situation of mobility and anonymity, rather, social distances are set up, and the person is isolated. His social contacts are more or less completely cut off. His wishes are thwarted; he finds in the rooming-house neither security, response, nor recognition. His physical impulses are curbed. He is restless, and he is lonely.[5]

The social world that Zorbaugh depicts appears to be particularly bleak and lonely; both socially disorganized and somehow frustrating all personal needs. In contrast I found the S.R.O. world to be rich in social relationships and able to satisfy the many and often exotic needs of its denizens. There appeared to be little "social disorganization" in that we were able to observe many informally defined social structures, groups, and a recognized system of folkways. While ecological conditions, and to a lesser degree, the social morphologies of the population were somewhat similar, the S.R.O. world had the essential attitudes, feelings and organization, or what social scientists call the *Gemeinshaft* necessary to characterize it as a community; the world of furnished-rooms had frustrated, lonely, atomistic people living lives of quiet desperation.

The identification of these differences suggests an interesting sociological question: Given the apparent similarities in ecology and morphology, what factors could account for the radical differences in social organization that have been observed between the two worlds? To answer the question, two complementary perspectives could be employed: one that looks to the difference in methodology; and one that introduces additional sociodemographic and social factors into the analysis.

The methodological tack is a very simple one. Recall that previous chapters suggested that many of the early researchers such as Zorbaugh did not have access to the store of methodological knowledge that presentday researchers draw upon. This implies that the more subtle forms of social organization, such as would be found in an area characterized by high mobility and seemingly secretive lives, might go unnoticed. One might even hypothesize that while never as rich in social organization as the S.R.O. world, the world of furnished rooms did have some rules and organization, but that they were so subtle that the earlier researchers were unable to perceive them.

Not entirely discounting the methodological weakness, differences in both ecological and morphological factors appear to be weightier. These differences are manifested both social-psychologically and behaviorally.

Although he was never really explicit about the social characteristics of the population he was examining, Zorbaugh's writing suggests that it was somewhat different than what was found in the S.R.O. world. On the morphological side, one receives the impression that the denizens of the "World of Furnished Rooms" were overwhelmingly white in ethnicity, that most were in the productive years of life, that is, between the ages of twenty and forty-five, and most had migrated to the city (Chicago) to realize some career or personal ambition.[6] In contrast, what sociodemographic information we do have about the S.R.O. world suggests a population that is older, predominately nonwhite, and so frequently demonstrating severe health and social problems as to make regular, gainful employment problematic. The population seems to show little commitment to recognizable career or personal ambitions.[7]

It is the convergence and interaction of these factors which distinguish the S.R.O. world. The sensitizing concept which aids in the explanation of these differences is psychological and social commitment to a social world.[8] In Zorbaugh's "World of Furnished Rooms" essentially no commitment could be discerned. Its roomers were fully preoccupied with realizing their larger goals and social participation in the locale in which they lived was defined as worthless; their needs were satisfied in other areas. Most were strongly future-oriented and accepted the privations of furnished-room living as an unpleasant yet necessary step to the realization of their goals. Another impediment to sociability relates to the background of these people which has inculcated into them such strong norms of personal conduct that interaction in all but the most structured settings (for example, a church social) was rendered extremely difficult.

The population of the S.R.O. is strikingly different in each of these respects. Few S.R.O.'ers hold strong aspirations to high career goals. Most have made a commitment, albeit a passive one, to S.R.O. living and because of it, look primarily to this small social world to fulfill their needs. Through this commitment people necessarily share a similar *Weltanschauung*. In turn, these shared definitions and meanings become the basis for a community. Finally, commitment to S.R.O. living entails socialization into the culture of this community and full placement and active participation within its social structures.

Those persons located in the S.R.O.'s and not committed to the S.R.O. way of life—such as the counterculture drop-outs and transients—demonstrate a social-psychological orientation and life-style remarkably similar to the social isolates described by Zorbaugh. This can be generalized to suggest that an individual will experience feelings of marginality, rootlessness, and anomie unless he is able to make some commitment to a distinct social world. Without such a commitment, and thereby deprived of meaningful interaction and satisfying social participation, the situation of such an alienated person is, at best, tenuous.

The S.R.O. World As a Sociocultural Phenomenon

Ethnographic and community studies have clearly demonstrated the importance of considering their findings in a larger contextual sense. William F. Whyte in *Streetcorner Society*, for example, found it important to trace the connection between the gangs he was studying and the organized rackets and political groups of Cornerville. Others found it necessary to document the interconnection of the industrial plant they were studying to both the local community and the geographically removed and yet bureaucratically related centers of policymaking. A final example can be drawn from Herbert Gans's study, the *Urban Villagers*, which related both acculturation and urban redevelopment to changes in a traditionally oriented culture.[9]

Data and impressions of the S.R.O. world will be combi ed using the natural history approach. In this light an inclusive, wholistic view of the social world under study becomes possible. This natural history perspective facilitates seeing the relationship that the phenomenon has to the needs and organization of the larger society. Moreover, this perspective helps us to understand both persistence and change in the phenomenon.

The Making of the S.R.O.'s: A Brief Review

In most places S.R.O.'s emerged in response to the need for inexpensive housing capable of accommodating an unattached population in the metropolitan area. S.R.O.-type accommodations were created by the division and then subdivision of conventional apartment structures into a series of single rooms which shared sanitary and domestic facilities. As shifts in employment and residential patterns occur, the most intact of the S.R.O. population leave. What remains is a human residue of aged, physically or psychologically impaired people, or persons wishing the anonymity that such an urban life-style might provide. Units are taken as well by recent immigrants to the city: poor blacks from the South and Spanish-speaking people, many of whom enter the United States illegally. Social service professionals who are charged with relocating or placing problem cases (for example, releasees from state mental hospitals, parolees, etc.) find that S.R.O. accommodations are the only type available. And, most recently, in places like New York City (which experienced a crisis in the availability of low-income housing), S.R.O. hotels and tenements have become a ready resource for the "temporary" housing of indigents until more suitable accommodations can be located. In this almost round-about way the S.R.O. world has come to be a repository for many of the misfits, castoffs, and casualties of society.

Once again we have come full circle. The book began by examining some of the many problems posed by socially terminal people in modern day society. The focus of this final section will be away from the people and on the S.R.O.'s themselves. S.R.O.'s will become increasingly more important as the more traditional ways of handling our socially terminal people gradually vanish or are radically changed.

The problems of extreme poverty, and the troubles and ills regularly associated with it, have always existed. A distinction has been made betwen the "deserving" and the "undeserving" poor.[10] The "reputable poor" were much like the rest of society but fate had willed them to destitution. Although economically similar, the "disreputable poor" were not only impoverished but were seen as morally deficient as well. These are our social casualties: the drifters and vagabonds; the chronic drunkards or drug users; the ones who refuse to "work honestly" for a living choosing instead an "easier" path; and those who no longer have any utility for society and have neither provision nor kin to support and care for them. Each society has had its measure of these social casualties. Formal structures were established for the containment of such people and an official control process evolved to assure that the more troublesome would be quickly dealt with. The end result saw many of these disreputable poor contained in the almshouses, mental hospitals, prisons, nursing homes and other such total institutions established for the care of the social casualty. The laissez faire value system in the United States has encouraged an informal as well as institutional response to these social casualties. In American cities from the late 1860s on, many of the homeless, rootless, and in all ways troubled persons came to be associated with an area known as "skid row." The person not able to fully care for himself, addicted to alcohol or no longer committed to maintaining a persona of social competence, can and will have his minimal needs satisfied within this area. Since the skid row enjoys a measure of social isolation from the other parts of the city, it has been able to evolve a culture of its own. This specialized culture, in conjunction with the complex of external and indigenous caretaking institutions operating in the area, makes life possible for these social casualties.

The S.R.O. world should unquestionably be considered in a similar context. As a viable, specialized, fully integrated, naturally occurring social phenomenon, it relieves the state of the responsibility of caring for these kinds of social casualties. What distinguishes it from skid row, however, is the existence of a cultural orientation that emphasizes the relative autonomy of each individual unit. As a social alternative, the skid row hotel or flophouse lacks the capacity to satisfy either the same number or range of individual needs as a lone S.R.O. building. This quality of autonomy makes the S.R.O. a more adaptable phenomenon than the skid row. For a skid row to be operable it necessarily requires more space and personnel. Consequently, it is significantly more visible and therefore more liable to external regulation or even destruction. The low profile maintained by many S.R.O. units enhances their ability to function with only minimal outside interference.

In this larger perspective, then, the S.R.O.'s are alternatives to either custodial oriented total institutions or open society. They provide indigenous care for those who are either incapable of caring for themselves, or those who find social participation in an open setting problematic. Institutionally, this suggests designating the S.R.O.'s as half-way areas located between the "open" and the "closed" (in the sense of intensively regulated) parts of society. Within such a setting, the person exhibiting behavior that would call for his confinement in a closed or total institution can find comfort, support, assistance, and the necessary measure of social control. The S.R.O.'s as half-way areas should not be synonymous with the therapeutic half-way house which is manifestly used to reintegrate deviant (most often chemically dependent or mentally ill) people back into society, because it is a viable, permanent alternative to either of society's poles.

Without the support and control provided by the S.R.O. community, many would find social participation in a more open setting impossible. An example illustrating this is provided by the case of a young woman who was a participant in an experiment in New York City which intended to convert S.R.O.'s into more conventional apartment buildings. According to the plan, an S.R.O. building would be condemned, thoroughly gutted, and then rebuilt so that it would contain a smaller number of fully self contained studio apartments.[11]

From some perspectives the experiment was a success, and from others a failure. Renovation, as one might suspect, decreased the total number of units available. People who were already living in the building were given the first option of moving back in. Many, however, simply drifted off and presumably found S.R.O.-type housing elsewhere. Others who were temporarily relocated moved back into the newly renovated facilities. Some of these people (to date no satisfactory statistical assessments could be obtained) apparently made a successful adjustment to the new living arrangements. Others, however, did not and either voluntarily left or were evicted from the building.

One such person was a young woman who was living in one of the hotels that I studied. Much to the disappointment of the social services professionals who had conceived the renovation project, the girl never "adjusted" to the changeover to conventional type units and was asked to leave the renovated building. The professionals had been particularly interested in her case because of her youth (she was twenty-six at the time of the experiment) and the fact that she had attended some college. After her eviction from the building, she reported that she had been unhappy with all of the "official rules and regulations" that had been imposed, and that all of the other tenants there were "just too damn snooty and uptight." From the perspective of other tenants, her life-style was having a detrimental effect on the general ambiance of of their building. They objected to both her desire to invite other young people into the building and her large collection of discarded objects. Now, however, she was happy about the S.R.O. hotel that she was currently living in and the other residents found little about her that they could complain about.

Although this is a single case, in a larger sense it does suggest that without the support and tolerance found in the S.R.O. world, many people would have difficulty sustaining themselves. Without the ongoing intervention of the official and informal caretakers and structures active in the S.R.O. world, life outside of an institution, for many of these people, would be at best problematic. The openness of the S.R.O. world in its degree of toleration towards deviant behavior, combined with an indigenous social control system, reduces the probability that S.R.O. people will come in contact with official control agencies. Without such a system, repeated involvement with these official agencies would be a certainty for many members. Lastly, the size and extent of the S.R.O. world permits a measure of mobility. This factor makes it possible to settle into an appropriate and comfortable social niche.

Social scientists have concluded that each society will produce its "quota" of casualities (or deviants).[12] The S.R.O. world is rightfully seen as one of the ways in which the disposition of these troublesome members is expeditiously and quietly accomplished in the modern urbanized society. Every sizeable city in the nation today has "natural areas" where these outposts of the forgotten can be found.[13]

A Look Towards the Future

The S.R.O.'s and the social world which they contain makes possible a half-way area—in terms of caretaking and control— etween "straight" open society and the total institution. As such, it provides for the care, support and protection of a portion of the social casualties which society produces. In terms of the future of the S.R.O. phenomenon, some important changes in the ecology of the cities, medical technology, and cultural styles will possibly increase the size of this population. To conclude, a brief look at these trends and their impact on the S.R.O. world is valuable.

Skid row is seen as being institutionally similar in function to the S.R.O. world. Some recent data, however, are beginning to suggest that skid row, as a distinct ecological phenomenon, is disappearing and possibly will entirely cease to exist within the next two decades.[14] The question that naturally arises is: What is going to happen to this skid row population once their usual area of operation is renovated out of existence. It is, of course, highly unlikely that they will simply vanish. As skid row shrinks, its population necessarily searches for other alternatives.

The treatment of the mentally ill is another area which has been, and presently is, undergoing significant change. Beginning some two decades ago, with the revolution in care made possible by the introduction of tranquilizing drugs, there has been a move away from long term, custodial-type care. The extensive use of these tranquilizing drugs and the more recent interest in community psychiatry suggest that many persons, who previously would have been contained in hospitals, will find themselves back in the community. For many of these, the combination of drugs and supportive services will be adequate and they will remain functional in a conventional setting. Others, however, will neither operate adequately enough to fully integrate back into society, nor so poorly that institutional confinement is inevitable. Instead, they will need some support and acceptance, at least episodically, for their troublesome behavior.

The implication is that given the maintenance of the status quo, the S.R.O.'s in the nation's urban centers will continue to expand in response to increasing demographic pressure. It is likely that in addition to the concentration of S.R.O.'s in the older sections of the city, a *diffusion* of S.R.O.'s throughout an urban area will occur. Diffused and socially isolated, the S.R.O. population can be expected to increase while attracting little attention.

Once again we confront the question of what to do with our socially terminal population. The social indicators are clear in their implication that this population will continue to grow. Traditional modes of containment, such as skid row and institutional confinement, are vanishing. The S.R.O. world provides a viable, real community which cares for and satisfies the needs of people who are actually or potentially troublesome. Resources should be allocated to assure that this community may go on caring for people whom many would rather forget. As it is, much of the S.R.O. world is ugly because of our neglect and indifference. It is our responsibility to provide the fiscal means to correct these abuses while not overtly destroying the positive aspects of S.R.O. living. Planning efforts must reflect the shape of the S.R.O. world itself. It is unreasonable to assume that we will solve the problem by creating only a single type of residential unit with the intention of concomitantly offering a small number of supportive social services. While both of these are unquestionably needed, the long-term plan must include a range of alternatives progressing from conventional type apartment housing on one pole, to something similar to the most open S.R.O. on the other pole.

Housing plans, however, are relatively simple to formulate and equally simple to effect if resources are available. The more difficult question has to do with the people themselves. We are coming increasingly closer to the time when it will be necessary to examine our feelings and expectations about this socially terminal population. As a nation we will be forced to determine whether what we want for them is at all reasonable, given the place they have been allocated in our world.

NOTES

1. Erving Goffman, *The Presentation of Self in Everyday Life* (New York: Doubleday 1959, pp. 208–38.
2. Ibid.
3. Ibid., pp. 106–41.
4. Harvey W. Zorbaugh, *The Gold Coast and the Slum* (Chicago: University of Chicago Press, 1929), pp. 69–87.
5. Ibid., p. 82.
6. Moreover, at the time of his research Chicago could be characterized as experiencing incredible increases in population. The population of the city grew at the rate of about one-half million per decade for three decades beginning in 1900. Neighborhoods grew and changed hands so rapidly that sometimes the only constant feature appeared to be mobility. Since most of these were either foreigners arriving in the large waves of migration or recent immigrants from rural areas, totally unaccustomed to big city ways, it is relatively easy to see the connection between "high mobility" and "disorganization" [M. Stein, *The Eclipse of Community* (New York: Harper and Row, 1960), p. 16].

7. This is, of course, a large generalization. Many of those living in the "closed" S.R.O.'s exhibited a strong commitment to upward social mobility.

8. Severyn T. Bruyn, *The Human Perspective* (Englewood Cliffs, N.J.: Prentice Hall, 1966).

9. Herbert Gans, *The Urban Villagers* (New York: Free Press, 1962).

10. David Matza, "Poverty and Disrepute" in *Contemporary Social Problems,* eds. Robert K. Merton and Robert A. Nisbet (New York: Harcourt, Brace and World, 1966).

11. City of New York, Housing and Development Administration, Office of Problem Housing, "A Rehousing Program for S.R.O. Tenants Using a Municipal Loan and Providing Tenant Services," mimeographed (New York, 1970).

12. Emile Durkheim, *The Rules of Sociological Method,* trans., Sarah A. Solovay and John H. Mueller, 8th ed. (New York: Free Press, 1938).

13. Robert E. Park, *Human Communities* (Glencoe, Ill.: Free Press, 1952).

14. Howard M. Bahr, *Skid Row* (New York: Oxford University Press, 1973).

Bibliography

Abrahamsson, B. "Homans on Exchange: Hedonism Revisited." *American Journal of Sociology* 76 (1970): 273–86.

Andelman, David. "Boy, 8, Falls 15 Floors to Death at Welfare Hotel." *New York Times,* 22 February 1971, p. 33.

Anderson, Nels. *The Hobo.* Chicago: University of Chicago Press, 1923.

———. *The Urban Community: A World Perspective.* New York: Henry Holt, 1959.

Arensberg, Conrad. "The Community Study Method." *American Journal of Sociology* 60 (1954): 109–24.

Bahr, Howard M. *Skid Row.* New York: Oxford University Press, 1973.

Ball, Donald. "Ethnography of an Abortion Clinic." *Social Problems* 14 (1967): 293–301.

Bates, Alan P. and Cloyd, Jerry S. "Toward the Development of Operations for Defining Group Norms and Member Roles." *Sociometry* 19 (1956): 26–39.

Becker, Howard S. "Problems of Inference and Proof in Participant Observation." *American Sociological Review* 23 (1958): 652–60.

———. *Outsiders.* New York: Free Press, 1963.

———., ed. *The Other Side.* New York: Free Press, 1964.

Bernard, Jessie. *American Community Behavior.* New York: Holt Rinehart, 1962.

Biddle, Bruce J., and Thomas, Edwin, ed. *Role Theory.* New York: John Wiley, 1966.

Black, Donald J., and Reiss, Albert J., "Police Control of Juveniles." *American Sociological Review* 35 (1970): 63–77.

Bott, Elizabeth. *Family and Social Networks.* London: Tavistock Publication, 1957.

Bruyn, Severy T. *The Human Perspective.* Englewood Cliffs: Prentice Hall, 1966.

Burns, Eveline M. *Health Services for Tomorrow.* New York: Dunellen, 1973.

Center for New York City Affairs, New School For Social Research. *A Program for Tenants in Single Room Occupancy and for their New York City Neighbors.* New York, 1969.

City of New York, Housing and Development Administration. "Fact Sheet on Single Room Accommodations." Mimeographed. New York, 1970.

Clark, Alexander and Gibbs, Jack P. "Social Control: A Reformulation." *Social Problems* 12 (1965): 398–414.

Clinard, Marshall B, ed. *Anomie and Deviant Behavior.* New York: Free Press, 1964.

Clines, Francis X. "Welfare Family of 7 Still Looks for Permanent Home in the City." *New York Times,* 7 March 1969, p. 29.

———. "Hotel in 'Village' Step to Nowhere." *New York Times,* 16 July 1970, p. 36.

Coser, Lewis. "The Sociology of Poverty." *Social Problems* 13 (1965): 140–48.

Cressy, Paul. *The Taxi Dance Hall.* Chicago: University of Chicago Press, 1929.

Cressey, Donald, ed. *The Prison.* New York: Holt, Rinehart and Winston, 1961.

Denzin, Norman. "The Logic of Naturalistic Inquiry." *Social Forces* 50 (1971): 166–82.

Durkheim, Emile. *The Rules of Sociological Method.* Translated by S. A. Solovay and J. H. Mueller. 8th ed. New York: Free Press, 1938.

DuWars, Richard E. "The Definition of the Situation as a Community Distinguishing Characteristic." *International Journal of Comparative Sociology* 3 (1962): 262–76.

Eggan, Fred. "Social Anthropology and the Method of Controlled Comparison." *American Anthropologist* 56 (1954): 743–60.

Feldman, Arnold S. and Tilly, Charles. "The Interaction of Social and Physical Space." *American Sociological Review* 25 (1960): 877–84.

Freilich, Morris. "Toward an Operational Definition of Community." *Rural Sociology* 28 (1963): 117–27.

Gans, Herbert J. *The Urban Villagers.* New York: Free Press, 1962.

Gillin, John. "Methodological Problems in the Anthropological Study of Modern Cultures." *American Anthropologist* 51 (1949): 392–99.

Goffman, Erving. *The Presentation of Self in Everyday Life.* Garden City, N.Y.: Anchor Books, 1959.

———. *Asylums.* Garden City, N.Y.: Anchor Books, 1961.

Gold, Raymond L. "Roles in Sociological Field Observations." *Social Forces* 36 (1958): 217–23.

Gouldner, Alvin. "The Norm of Reciprocity: A Preliminary Statement." *American Sociological Review* 25 (1960): 161–78.

Gray, Allison. "How the Hotel Clerk Sizes You Up." *American Magazine*, 1922, pp. 54–55.

Greenfield, Margaret. *Social Dependency.* Berkeley: University of California Press, 1963.

Gross, E. "Symbiosis and Consensus as Integrative Factors in Small Groups." *American Sociological Review* 21 (1956): 174–80.

Harrington, Michael. *The Other America.* New York: Macmillan, 1962.

Hatt, Paul. "The Concept of Natural Area." *American Sociological Review* 11 (1946): 424–27.

Hayner, Norman S. *Hotel Life.* Chapel Hill: University of North Carolina Press, 1936.

———, and Ash, E. "The Prison as a Community." *American Sociological Review* 5 (1940): 577–83.

Hiller, E. T. "The Community as a Social Group." *American Sociological Review* 6 (1941): 189–202.

Hillery, George A. "Definitions of Community: Areas of Agreement." *Rural Sociology* 20 (1959): 111–24.

———. "A Critique of Selected Community Concepts." *Social Forces* 37 (1959): 236–42.

———. "Villages, Cities and Total Institutions." *American Sociological Review* 28 (1963): 779–91.

Hirschi, Travis. "The Professional Prostitute." *Berkeley Journal of Sociology* 7 (1962): 33–39.

Hoffberg, Barbara, and Shapiro, Joan. "S.R.O. Service-Research Project." Mimeographed. New York: Columbia University Urban

Center and St. Luke's Hospital Center's Division of Community Psychiatry, 1969.

Hoggart, Richard. *The Uses of Literacy.* London: Chatto and Windum, 1957.

Hollingshead, A. B. "The Concept of Social Control." *American Sociological Review* 6 (1944): 217–24.

———. "Community Research: Development and Present Condition," *American Sociological Review* (1948): 136–46.

Hollingshead, A. B. and Redlich, Frederick C., *Social Class and Mental Illness.* New York: John Wiley and Sons, 1958.

Homans, George C. "Social Behavior as Exchange." *American Journal of Sociology* 62: (1952) 597–606.

Horwitz, Julius. *The City.* Cleveland: World Publishing, 1953.

———. *The Inhabitants.* New York: Signet Books, 1961.

———. *The W.A.S.P.* New York: Atheneum, 1967.

———. *The Diary of A.N.* New York: Dell, 1971.

"Hotels Without Hope," *Time* 4 January 1971.

Hunter, David R. *The Slums.* New York: Free Press, 1964.

Irelan, Lola M., ed. *Low Income Life Styles.* U.S., Department of Health, Education, and Welfare. Welfare Administration (undated).

Junker, Buford. *Field Work.* Chicago: University of Chicago Press, 1960.

Kaufman, Harold F. "An Approach to the Study of Urban Stratification." *American Sociological Review* 17 (1952): 430–37.

———. "Toward an Interactional Conception of Community." *Social Forces* 38 (1959): 8–17.

Kelly, Fred C. "Human Nature in the Lobby." *Hotel Management,* May 1922.

Kimball, Solon. "Problems of Studying American Culture," *American Anthropologist* 57 (1955): 131–42.

Knight, Michael. "Squalor is a Way of Life at a Welfare Hotel Here." *New York Times,* 28 January 1971, p. 39.

Lewis, Oscar. *La Vida.* New York: Vintage Books, 1965.

Leznoff, Maurice, and Westley, William. "The Homosexual Community." *Social Problems* 4 (1956): 257–63.

Liebow, Elliot. *Tally's Corner.* Boston: Little Brown, 1966.

Lyford, Joseph. *The Airtight Cage.* New York: Harper and Row, 1966.

Lynd, Robert, and Lynd, Helen. *Middletown.* New York: Harcourt, Brace and World, 1929.

Mann, Peter H. "The Concept of Neighborliness." *American Journal of Sociology,* 60 (1954): 168.

McCord, William, Howard, John, Friedberg, Bernard, and Harwood, Edwin. *Life Styles in the Black Ghetto.* New York: W. W. Norton, 1969.

Merton, Robert K., and Nisbert, Robert, ed. *Contemporary Social Programs.* New York: Harcourt, Brace, and World, 1966.

Meyer, Julie. "The Stranger and The City." *American Journal of Sociology* 56 (1951): 476-83.

Miller, S. M., and Riesman, F. "The Working Class Subculture: A New View." *Social Problems* 9 (1961): 86-97.

Montgomery, Paul L. "Success Reported in Relocating Welfare Families Out of Hotels," *New York Times,* 16 April 1971, p. 41.

Nadel, S. F. "Social Control and Self Regulation." *Social Forces* 31 (1953): 265-73.

Padilla, Elena. *Up From Puerto Rico.* New York: Columbia University Press, 1958.

Park, Robert E. "The City: Suggestions for the Investigation of Human Behavior in the City Environment." *American Journal of Sociology* 20 (1915): 577-612.

————. *Human Communities.* Glencoe, Ill. Free Press, 1952.

Park, Robert E. and Burgess, E. W. *The City.* Chicago: University of Chicago Press, 1925.

Pharr, Robert D. *S.R.O.* New York: Doubleday and Co., 1971.

Polsky, Ned. "The Hustler." *Social Problems* 12 (1964): 3-15.

————. *Hustlers, Beats and Others.* New York: Doubleday, 1965.

Rainwater, Lee. *Behind Ghetto Walls.* Chicago: Aldine, 1970.

Redfield, Robert. *The Little Community.* Chicago: University of Chicago Press, 1953.

Reiss, Albert J. Jr. "The Sociological Study of Communities." *Rural Sociology* 24 (1959): 118-30.

————. "The Social Integration of Queers and Peers," *Social Problems* 9 (1961): 101-20.

————. *The Police and the Public.* New Haven: Yale University Press, 1971.

Roberts, Steven. "Ginsberg Assails Welfare Housing," *New York Times,* 4 February 1967, p. 24.

Rose, Arnold. "Interest in the Living Arrangements of the Urban Unattached," *American Journal of Sociology* 33 (1947-48): 483-93.

————. "Voluntary Associations Under Conditions of Competition and Conflict," *Social Forces* 34 (1955): 159-63.

————, ed. *Human Behavior and Social Process*. Boston: Houghton Mifflin Co., 1962.

Ross, H. Lawrence. "The Local Community: A Survey Approach." *American Sociological Review* 27 (1962): 75–84.

Roucek, J. S., ed. *Social Control*. Princeton: D. Von Nostrand Co., 1947.

Schumach, Murray, "New Crime Drive Focuses on Hotels." *New York Times*, 3 December 1967, p. 1.

————. "Welfare Cases in Hotels Called a Modern Horror." *New York Times*, 23 November 1970, p. 1.

————. "City Plans to End Welfare Abuses Involving Hotels." *New York Times*, 24 November 1970, p. 1.

————. "City is Assailed on Agreement to Pay $10,000 a Year to a Welfare Hotel to Hire Private Guards." *New York Times*, 21 January 1971, p. 35.

Seeman, Melvin. "On the Meaning of Alienation." *American Sociological Review* 24 (1959): 783–91.

Shapiro, Joan. "Dominant Leaders Among Slum Hotel Residents." *American Journal of Orthopsychiatry* 39 (1969): 644–50.

————. "Reciprocal Dependence Between Single Room Occupancy Managers and Tenants." *Social Work* 15 (1970): 66–73.

————. *Communities of the Alone*. New York: Association Press, 1971.

Shaw, Clifford R. *The Jack Roller*. Chicago: University of Chicago Press, 1930.

Simmel, Georg. *The Sociology of Georg Simmel*. Translated by Kurt H. Wolff. New York: Free Press, 1950.

Simpson, Richard L. "Sociology of the Community: Current Status and Prospects." *Rural Sociology*, 30 (1965), 127–49.

Srole, Leo, and Kischer, Anita K. *Mental Health in the Metropolis*. New York: McGraw Hill, 1962.

Stein, Maurice R. *The Eclipse of Community*. New York: Harper and Row, 1960.

Stokes, Charles. "A Theory of Slums." *Land Economics* 48 (1962): 187–97.

Sutherland, Edwin H. *The Professional Thief by a Professional Thief*. Chicago: University of Chicago Press, 1937.

Suttles, Gerald. *The Social Order of the Slum*. Chicago: University of Chicago Press, 1969.

Sutton, Willis A., et al. "The Concept of Community." *Rural Sociology* 25 (1960): 197–203.

Sykes, Gresham. *The Society of Captives*. Princeton: Princeton University Press, 1958.

Van Gelder, Lawrence. "Welfare Family Has $54,080 Rent." *New York Times,* 29 January 1971.

Vidich, Arthur, Bensman, Joseph, and Stein, Maurice. *Reflections on Community Studies.* New York: John Wiley, 1964.

Wallace, Samuel E. *Skid Row as a Way of Life.* Totowa: Bedminister Press, 1965.

Wallant, Edward L. *The Pawnbroker.* New York: Signet Books.

Warner, W. Lloyd. "Social Anthropology and the Modern Community." *American Journal of Sociology* 46 (1941): 785-96.

Weisemann, Steven. "Welfare Hotel Residents to Get Housing Priority." *New York Times,* 10 March 1971, p. 25.

West, James. *Plainville, U.S.A.* New York: Columbia University Press, 1945.

Whyte, William F. *Street Corner Society.* Chicago: University of Chicago Press, 1943.

———. "The Social Structure of the Restaurant." *American Journal of Sociology* 54 (1949): 302-3.

Willmott, Peter. *The Evolution of a Community.* London: Routledge and Kegan Paul, 1963.

Zelditch, Morris. "Some Methodological Problems of Field Studies." *American Journal of Sociology* 67 (1962): 566-76.

Zorbaugh, Harvey W. *The Gold Coast and the Slum.* Chicago: University of Chicago Press, 1928.

Index

NAMES

Alderman, David, 31n.

Bahr, Howard M., 198n.
Ball, Donald, 35, 53n.
Becker, Howard, 54n.
Biddle, Bruce, 126n.
Blumer, Herbert, 54n.
Bott, Elizabeth, 54n.
Bruyn, Severynt T., 198n.
Burns, Evelin M., 126n.

Caplovitz, David, 184n.
Clines, Francis X., 11, 30n.
Coser, Lewis, 126n.

Denzin, Norman, 45, 54n.
Durkheim, Emil, 35, 198n.
DuWars, Richard E., 54n.

Erickson, Kai, 35, 54n.

Farr, Robert Dean, 18, 31n.
Frelich, Morris, 54n.

Gans, Herbert, 54n., 78, 126n., 184n., 192, 198n.
Goffman, Erving, 126n., 127n., 186, 197n.

Golar, Simeon, 31
Gouldner, Alvin, 127n.

Harrington, Michael, 37, 53n.
Harwood, Alan, 54n.
Hayner, Norman S., 6, 30n.
Hillery, George A., 53n.
Hirshi, Travis, 53n.
Hoffberg, Barbara, 76n.
Hollingshead, A. B., 53n.
Homans, George C., 127n.
Horowitz, Julius, 17, 31n.

Junker, Buford H., 31n.

Knight, Michael, 31n.

Leibow, Elliot, 46, 54n.
Lemert, Edwin, 36, 53n.
Lewis, Oscar, 38, 53n., 184n.
Leznoff, Maurice, 54n., 184n.
Lynford, Joseph, 30n.

Martin, Arnold, 31n.
Matza, David, 37, 53n., 198n.
McCord, William, 184n.
Montgomery, Paul L., 31n.

Padilla, Elena, 54n.
Park, Robert, 42, 53n., 54n., 198n.
Polsky, Ned, 35, 53n.

Rainwater, Lee, 54n.
Redfield, Robert, 51, 55n.
Reiss, Albert J., 54n., 126n.
Roberts, Steven, 30n.
Rose, Arnold, 30n.
Ross, Lawrence, 55n.

Schumach, Murray, 11, 12, 30n., 31n.
Schwartz, Ruth, 30n.
Seeman, Melvin, 126n.
Shapiro, Joan, 18, 76n., 126n.
Shuttles, Gerald, 54n.
Siegal, Harvey A., 184n.
Simmel, Georg, 78, 126n.
Simpson, Richard L., 53n.

Stein, Maurice, 53n., 54n., 197n.
Sugarman, Jule, 16, 30n.
Sutherland, Edwin, 35, 53n.
Sutton, Willis A., 53n.

Thomas, Edwin J., 126n.

Van Gelder, Lawrence, 31

Wallant, Edward Lewis, 126n.
Weismann, Steven, 31n.
Westley, William A., 54n., 184n.
Whyte, William F., 6, 30n., 54n.
Willmoth, Peter, 54n.

Zangwill, Israel, 184n.
Zorbaugh, Harvey, 5, 30n., 184n.,
    197n.

SUBJECTS

Aim of study, see Methods of study

Airmail, 59

Alienation, 39, 81

Analysis of data, see Methods of study

Anomia, 85

Area, 2

Bowery, see Skid Row

Broadway Central Hotel Affair, 16

Brownstones: definition, 3

Caretakers: bureaucrats as, 80; clinics as, 103-4; as containment agents, 79; definition, 19, 78-79; demographic characteristics, 105-10; doctors as, 98-103, 115-17; external, 78, 80; internal, 79; matriarchs as, 142-44; medical, 94; owners and managers as, 104; pharmacies as, 104; police as, 8-9, 86-94; psychiatric social workers as, 22, 95; psychiatrists as, 22; psychologists as, 94; role conflict of, 103; role defined, 104-5; role strain of, 79, 80; social characteristics of, 105-10; social service project of, 95-96;

SRO's view of doctors as, 101-2; SRO's view of service-oriented, 96-98; visiting nurses as, 22, 94, 97; welfare as, 80

Caseworker turnover, 23

Checks, 27, 173, 176

Chicago School of Sociologists, 42

Children, 170-71

Communication: check day, 173; network of dissemination, 171-73; within SRO community, 147

Community: as a theoretical concept, 33, 39-44; closed stations of, 68, 114, 130; collective conscience of, 184; open stations of, 68, 130; outside influences on SRO business in, 167-69; stations of, 57-74

Cop: a bag, 27; drugs, 53

Culture of poverty: as a theoretical concept, 33; definition, 37-39

Deviant behavior, see Social deviance

DOSS: definition, 9

Economics: annual community benefit, 166; bootlegging, 162-64;

business patterns, 158-60; errand running, 164-65; gambling, 160-62; get-rich-quick schemes, 165; outside influences on SRO business, 167

Firearms, 92-93
Functions of SRO world: halfway areas, 194; tolerance and support, 195

Ghetto dwellers: compared to SRO dwellers, 4
Greenwich Hotel: conditions, 11; description, 7-8
Greystones: definition, 3
Group formation: chemically focused, 133; drinking, 138; helping pairs in, 135; homosexual activities in, 145-48; illegal activities in, 153-54; kinship relationships in, 170; main man in, 138; managers attempt to co-opt matriarchs in, 143; matriarch and family in, 140-44; norms in, 136, 138-40, 143; sanctions in, 140; sexually focused, 144; special interest groups in, 155-57; voluntary associations in, 148-55

Hainsworth case, 13
Hanging out, 27
Hotel Cherbourg, 22
Hotel Enfer: impressions of a caseworker of, 61; doctor affair at, 115-17; as a study site, 22-25
Hotel Kimberly, see Welfare hotels
Hotel Nazir, 27

Institutional resources: lack of, 171

Laissez faire value system, 193
Lock out: definition, 124; plugging, 153

Marginality: as characteristic of poverty, 39; definition, 4; in litigation, 82; quality of, 169; SRO world as alternative to, 183
Media: New York Times, 10-12; Time. 14

Methods of study: aim of study, 46; boundary definition, 50-53; difficulties encountered, 41; ecological time, 52-53; focus of study, 174; methodology defined, 44-48, 190; problem of entrance, 21; research instrument, 24-25; research role, 26-29; setting of the study, 1-2; study problem identified, 18-20, 183, 185-86; summary and conclusions, 185-97; unit of analysis, 49
Mid-Manhattan Health Services Project, 22

Nonreferral list: definition, 16

Patterns of control: with DOSS personnel, 113; with police, 110-12; with residents, 121-26
Planetarium Council: composition of, 9-10
Police, see Caretakers

Raw jaw, 92
Rikers: definition, 11
Rooming house: conditions of life in, 5
Skid Row: description of typical, 59, 193; disappearing of, 196; institutional supports of, 7; social isolation of, 4
Slum: social rules, 6
Social control: dimensions, 42; operationalized, 43; social worker as agent of, 156-57; voluntary groups as agents of, 144-45
Social deviance: definition, 35; focus, 37
Social differentiation: definition, 44; among blacks, 157-58
Social heterogeneity: in New York, 1
Social interaction: among tenants, 131; in kinship, 170; possession of resources and, 132; status allocation and, 132
Social network, 42
Social sanctions, 43
Socially terminal: changes in methods of handling, 192-93; definition, 74

SRO: as alternatives, 194; an answer for the mentally ill, 196; anonymity in, 5-6; created by housing demand, 3; demographic characteristics of, 74-76; description, 58-61; entrance into world of, 22-24, 29; future of, 193-94; as gatekeepers, 71-74; journalistic accounts of, 77; living facilities in, 63-77; nature of accommodations, 57-61; outpost of the poor, 7; physical environment of, 61-63; population of, 3-4; reason for emergence of, 192; as setting for observation, 7; social adaptations of, 61-63; social casualties of, 74; social service project aimed at population of, 10-11, 34, 38-39; social world of, 19, 44, 48, 50-52, 57-58; socialization into, 27
SRO culture: boundary definition, 178-79; collective conscience of, 176; lack of space in, 187; lifestyle of, 181-82; nonverbal language of, 27; personal orientations of, 177; recognition of individuality in, 179-81; sociodemographics of, 190; timelessness in, 174
SRO landlords: description, 66; lack of discrimination in, 132; security measures of, 90-93

St. Luke's Project: description, 16-18; focus, 10

Taxpayers: definition, 1
The Man, 29
Tyrone Howard case, 15

United West Side Community, 26
Up, 27
Upper West Side: heroin distribution point, 70; location, 1; changing population of, 2; first residents, 2-4; as a social problem, 7-8
Urban population: social disorganization, 5-6

VISTA: definition, 22; impression of workers, 57

Waldorf Astoria: as emergency housing, 13-15
Welfare children, 17
Welfare hotel: conditions of, 8; crisis, 10-24; definition, 11; first attained notoriety, 7; as a new phenomenon, 4; outpost of the poor, 7; public reaction, 17; residents organize to shut down, 8; security in, 14
Welfare money, 114-15
Welfare rent, 12-15